T0126249

TEA LEAVES

by

Janet Mason

Bella
BOOKS

2012

Bella Books, Inc.
P.O. Box 10543
Tallahassee, FL 32302

Printed in the United States of America on acid-free paper
First published 2012

Editor: Katherine V. Forrest
Cover Designer: Judy Fellows

ISBN 13: 978-1-59493-278-6

"Soliloquy"published as "Somewhere Between Hell and Eternity"); Sinister Wisdom 68/69 -- Death, Grief and Surviving, Fall 2006.

"Chapter 3 Somebody"(published as "Somebody") in Dutiful Daughters: Caring for Our Parents as They Grow Old, Seal Press, 1999.

"Chapter 6 Violin Lessons" (published as "Violin Lessons") in Telling Moments: Autobiographical Lesbian Short Stories, University of Wisconsin Press, 2003.

"Chapter 12 Charcoal Sketches" (published as "Charcoal Sketches") in Mom: Candid memoirs by lesbians about the first woman in their life, Alyson Books, 1998.

"Charcoal Sketches" from Mom excerpted in The Advocate, 1998.

Dedication

This book is dedicated to Barbara, my partner in time;
and to my father, Albert Mason, and to the memory of my mother S. Jane Mason

About the Author

Janet Mason is an award winning writer of fiction, creative nonfiction and poetry whose LGBT literary commentary is regularly featured on *This Way Out*, an international radio syndicate based in Los Angeles and aired on more than 400 radio stations in the U.S. and also in Australia, New Zealand and throughout Europe. She is the author of three chapbooks of poetry, including *When I Was Straight* (Insight To Riot Press) and *a woman alone* (Cycladic Press). She is currently working on a novel. You can visit her at www.amusejanetmason.com.

CHAPTER 1

Tea Leaves

"Your grandmother read tea leaves."

Startled, I looked up at my mother, sitting in her gold velour chair next to the end table scattered with a few library books. From my mother's lips, this statement was a bad omen. My atheist, Bible-burning, skeptical-of-anything-less-than-scientific mother had long been a woman who believed in nothing.

Superstition—even applied to a previous generation—was not admissible.

"What did she see?"

"Her own face, probably." My mother shrugged. "I made fun of her and told her she was old-fashioned and superstitious. Eventually, she stopped talking about it."

I stopped to ponder this sliver passed to me about my grandmother, my mother's mother, who died when I was twelve. I was thirty-four years old, and this was the first time my mother told me that my grandmother had read tea leaves.

"Did she read them often?"

"I don't know. Often enough, I guess. She used to read cards, too—ordinary playing cards. She would take them from the deck and lay them out on the wooden table we had in the kitchen. An ace of hearts good luck, an ace of spades death."

My mother's shudder punctuated the end of her sentence.

She was seventy-four, the same age as my grandmother when she died.

My mother's matter-of-fact tone and my diversion into my grandmother's tea leaf reading traditions did nothing to alleviate the direness of my visit. It was a Sunday afternoon in early June. Earlier in the day, my partner, Barbara, and I had been clearing out cobwebs in the corners of the ceiling of the house that we had just bought and moved into, when I had the sudden urge to call my mother. My instincts were right. My mother told me in an uncharacteristically faint voice that she had woken up a few days ago with a crushing pain in her sternum.

"I felt like I was having a massive coronary," she told me.

My mother—who never believed in doctors—went to one immediately. He ordered some X-rays, told her it was arthritis, and sent her home with some extra strength Tylenol. When she told me this, my mind reeled. This was my mother—someone who walked four miles every day.

"Why didn't you call?" I had asked her on the phone.

"I just did," she replied.

I didn't argue, but the fact was that I had called her.

Barbara was listening to me and could tell that something was wrong. "You better go," she said. "I'll stay here and take care of things."

Barbara has always hated change. I often joked that that was the reason we were together for so long. We got together ten years ago when I was twenty-four, the same age my mother was when she met and married my father, and Barbara was thirty-two. Barbara was close to her own mother, who lived in Pittsburgh, six hours away from our home in Philadelphia, and often helped her out financially.

My mother always told me when I was growing up that "You can't criticize a man for being good to his mother." When she and my father were first married, he would come home late from work and wouldn't be hungry for dinner. "I found out," my mother would say, "that he was stopping at his mother's house after work and having a piece of cake with her."

In many little ways Barbara was a lot like my father. Just the other day, she'd left her window down in the car when I had put the air on, stubbornly insisting that she was letting the hot air out. (My father always did the same exact thing.) And shortly after we moved into our first apartment together, she went into her toolbox, took out her ratchet wrench and very sincerely told me what it was and how to use it. I found the way that she was telling me about the ratchet wrench—"You really should know about this"—to be endearing, not patronizing. I waited for her to finish. Then I reminded her of my summers of swing shift at the same industrial plant where my father worked, where I wore a hardhat and learned to drive a ten-speed flatbed truck. But it was Barbara who described herself as a "femmy butch." I would sometimes jokingly refer to her as my "lesbian husband." That she was so close to her own mother meant that she understood my concerns about my own parents and in telling me that I should go visit my mother, she was right again.

On the forty-five-minute drive over, through the tree-lined streets of my neighborhood and onto the Pennsylvania turnpike, I was in a panic about the conversation with my mother. There was something in her voice I had never heard before. A dead-end tone. A giving up. Fatalism. Illness or not, I couldn't conceive of her coming to a standstill. My mind raced.

The bottom of my world began to drop away.

"You should have stayed home with Barbara," she told me after I arrived, "and worked on the house."

"You know Barbara," I said, trying to joke. "She probably got on the phone as soon as I left and is over at a friend's house drumming by now."

"Barbara *is* a good drummer and she does know how to enjoy herself," said my mother, nodding and then wincing from the pain of moving her neck.

"Everything is fine," she said, noticing my concern. "The extra-strength Tylenol isn't working yet but it will."

She shifted in her chair and winced.

"I can make us some lunch," I said.

"I can do it," she replied and struggled to stand up.

"Sit down," I said, as I got up and went to the kitchen where I made a simple meal of miso soup and warmed up brown rice. She joined me at the dining room table.

"The soup is good. You did a good job, Janet."

"Thank you."

We ate in silence for several minutes.

"What did the doctor say," I asked finally.

Her lips pressed into an obstinate straight line.

When I asked again, she told me the HMO primary physician she went to, a man whose office was in a house on the corner of the section where my parents' lived, refused to give her a referral. The rheumatologist, who my mother wanted to see, was a woman doctor who she saw once before and liked. "I wrote a letter to her," said my mother, "but I didn't hear from her."

"Maybe we can call her," I replied. "A letter is easy to overlook."

The stony look on my mother's face told me that what was going on with her body was her business, and I simply could not drop in on her life and interfere. It had been several months since I had been to visit. Barbara and I had been busy moving from the apartment that we shared for ten years to the house that we were buying, an old farmhouse with a big backyard in the city.

My mother and my father—who was out at his monthly retiree luncheon at a nearby diner—were happy for us. In my parents' eyes, my decision to purchase a home was the second practical thing I had done as an adult. The first had been to fall in love with Barbara and settle down with her.

Good-natured, likeable Barbara had definitely passed the parent test. That Barbara is a woman—my mother would later refer to her as "my unexpected daughter-in-law"—was superseded by her working-class credentials, a stable government job with the post office and membership in a union. Even my father—who at the time could not wrap his mind around the concept of a women-only dance (where Barbara and I had one of our early dates)—was won over by her genuineness.

When we first got together, my mother hoped that Barbara would be a good influence on me with her stable government job. After finishing college, I took a relatively low-paying job in a nonprofit editorial position and several years later left this stressful situation only to strike out on my own as a freelance writer.

"Why don't you get a good government job like Barbara?" my mother would ask. "Then you can write on the side." When I resisted this suggestion, my mother simply shrugged and said, "It looks to me like she wants to be rich and you want to be famous."

When all was said and done my parents sent me a card with a parachute on it, congratulating me on starting my own business. Before signing the card, my father had had little to say except that it wasn't a good idea for me to quit my job. His advice didn't stop me from giving notice and lining up new clients. I understood where my parents were coming from. They had grown up poor and, as adults, made it into the working class. To them, a job was more than a job.

It was survival.

When I'd arrived at my parents' house and was folding up the paper grocery bags from the health food store and putting them away in the garage, I noticed that the garage was almost sparkling. When I asked my mother who cleaned it, she said, "Your father." She told me he had been cleaning it nonstop for the past few days—ever since she woke up with the crushing pain in her sternum. This was my father's way of handling what he could not control. I could see him with his broom and dustpan resolutely sweeping the concrete floor, obsessively dusting and wiping down the cans of paint and his tools with an old rag—as if by the effort of his hard work he could make my mother better.

As my mother and I sat in the living room, the only sound was the ticking of my father's retirement clock on a high shelf, his reward for thirty-five years of working swing shift at the plant. There was more to my mother's silence than the privacy she wrapped around herself like a woolen shawl. By not telling me about her problems, she was protecting me. She was the kind of mother who didn't want her problems to become her daughter's problems. Through the years, my mother's auburn hair had faded to reddish beige. Now, as if it had happened overnight, her hair had turned white. She stared at me with her green yellow eyes, cocking her head at me in an owlish curiosity.

I, in turn, searched *her* face for clues.

Was she reading her own tea leaves?

My mother was forty years old when she gave birth to me. When I was a child, a certain tension hung in the air. "Did you tell her my age?" my mother hissed to me when my best friend made an off-the-cuff remark in front of her about old people. I shook my head with astonishment and growing apprehension.I thought my best friend's comment was innocent. I hadn't said anything to her about my parents' age. But she might have been repeating something that her mother said. My parents were close to twenty years older than the parents of all of my childhood friends. They were always the oldest parents at school functions.

Two disparate generations collided in me. Even as my parents' stories about WWII—my mother dancing in the streets on V-Day and my father picking coconuts in New Guinea—swirled around me, the Vietnam War raged on the television set. Born in 1959, I was a product of the sixties. In elementary school I wore a peace sign around my neck and refused to salute the flag. This incensed my father, almost to the point of yanking me out of my seat at a Flag Day celebration when I refused to stand up. But my mother held out her hand and said, "Let her do what she wants."

In my twenties, having older parents meant that I began to worry about their well-being. Even when I didn't say anything, my mother would read my thoughts. "It's hard watching your parents get old," she once told me gently.

When we went for a walk at the shopping mall, she'd comment on the older couples she saw. "One's in worse shape than the other," she said, "and they're holding each other up. What happens when one of them falls over?"

There was no answer to her question. How could I reassure my mother about a future of which I also lived in mortal fear?

My mother had always been active—walking, eating healthy foods, reading widely, taking an interest in life. But over the past several years there were signs that she was withdrawing—what the medical professionals call "shutting down" which can happen before the final stage of life. The first to go were her women's liberation marches. There weren't as many of them as in the early seventies when I was a pre-teen and my mother took me with her and, later, in the early 1980s, when I encouraged my mother to come with me. But when smaller demonstrations did turn up, here and there, my mother refused to go.

"Oh, Janet," she would say, "you know I hate crowds." The flat, almost sullen tone that crept into my mother's voice told me that she couldn't possibly even stand the *thought* of marching around with a placard, gleefully chanting *hey, ho, patriarchy's gotta go*.

Then one year she decided not to plant her garden.

"It's too much work," she said, that same tone of resignation pressing down her voice.

For as long as I could remember, after every meal we sorted the garbage from the trash, the mulch-able from the non mulch-able, to make topsoil for next year's organic garden from the steaming pile of compost in the backyard. My parents liked to joke that they were going to be buried in the compost pile when the time came. Each summer and fall we ate the greens, the tomatoes, the endless dishes of orange squash. The garden was my mother's all consuming passion, providing her with the company of other gardeners in the organic gardening club.

Several times my mother canceled her plans at the last minute to come and see me. All she said was that she decided she didn't feel like coming—and then hung up. The thought of her not being able to endure anymore—of her simply laying down and not getting up—was inconceivable.

"After I croak," my mother once said to me, "you may want to have a baby. Your old high chair is in the attic. It's in good condition." When I protested, both to the fact that she would die and that I would someday want to have a baby, she simply shrugged. "Sometimes it's easier to raise a child without the grandparents around interfering," she said. "I'm not telling you to have a baby. You have to make up your own mind about things like that. But if you do have one, there's no reason to go out and buy a new high chair."

As it turned out, I did need the high chair for a lesbian friend who had adopted a baby. When Barbara and I first got together we had discussed the possibility of adopting a daughter. It was the early 1980s, a few years before lesbians were starting to take trips to the sperm banks. Most of the lesbians we knew with children had them in previous marriages—to men—and more than a few women we knew had been through painful custody battles. Barbara had been briefly married to a man before we met, but had no children. On one of our early dates, Barbara looked at me with her deep-set blue eyes and told me that she'd like to settle down and adopt a child.

Sitting across the table from her in the now long gone Mid-Town Diner in Center City Philadelphia, I remember being so nervous over such an idea that I wanted to run for the door.

We moved in together six months later, and our life together was so full that we put the idea of adopting a child on hold indefinitely. It had been years since Barbara and I had thought about adopting a child and viewing the empty seat of my old high chair that once held my round baby bottom was not going to change it. Still, the empty high chair brought back an old feeling that it would be nice to have a daughter. When my mother referred to the inevitable—"When I croak"—she was telling me, in no uncertain terms, that her life would end one day and mine would go on. My inability to comprehend this, and the immense sadness that I felt underneath, was more than knowing I would miss her: picking up the phone to call her with my latest success or crisis; taking pride in cooking her a special dinner that she praised; or discussing some new insight about the latest novel we both read.

This was all true, of course. I would miss her. Terribly.

My mother's death was unimaginable because she was more than my mother. She was the earth that I sprang from. She was my genesis. My creation story. Like everyone else who had not yet lost a parent, I had no idea what was in store for me as I looked at her sitting in her gold velour chair, her face drawn in on itself, at once contemplative and indifferent. Occasionally, she was still likened to Katherine Hepburn: the inquisitive eyes, high cheekbones, candid manner. But, with age, she looked less like a glamorous young woman and more like the tomboy that she had been as a child, in the pictures I stared into growing up: bowl-cut hair, watchful eyes, stubborn chin. Her features in the photo reflected my own, yet I studied them like the pieces of a puzzle.

Increasingly, as my mother aged, I heard the wavering strains of my grandmother's voice in hers. As we talked, I recognized that under our conversation was another conversation and under that, yet another. The cadences went back at least three generations. My understanding of my mother and myself had begun with my grandmother. It had taken the better part of a century for their lives to fuse into mine—often in the form of pent-up rage gusting through me.

My grandmother died when I was twelve. She was a spinner in the textile mills of Philadelphia, in the Kensington section where the old warehouses were now old hulls, broken down, abandoned. My mother grew up in this neighborhood of bustling industry—lace factories, Brussels rugs, textile mills, the Stetson hat factory, slaughterhouses full of bloody entrails and squealing animals. Devastating scenes of poverty replaced it—abandoned and crumbling houses, a tent city, homelessness, a child prostitution strip that was one of the largest in the nation. When my mother spoke of this place of her childhood, tears came to her eyes.

My grandmother, Ethel, a devout Episcopalian, life-long Republican, and wearer of white gloves, gave birth to my mother, Jane (Plain Jane, her childhood nickname), who became an equally devout atheist (burning her Bibles in the backyard) and a Democrat. My mother identified with the "silent majority," but was a feminist ahead of her time, and when the women's liberation movement caught up with her, she joined it. When I was old enough, she sometimes took me with her, the two of us marching and attending rallies, waving our matching mother/daughter coat hangers at pro-choice events. I was the less adventurous one—hanging back and watching with something bordering on amazement as my mother heckled the hecklers and squeezed the balloon testicles of a Ronald Reagan cardboard cutout.

My mother tossed away conventions with every year that she aged. Heels were replaced with comfortable walking shoes; skirts were exchanged for trousers. Eventually she discarded her bras for the skinny-strapped men's undershirts that she wore under her cotton blouses and short-sleeved shirts that looked tailored on her slender frame. When referring to her mother's insistence that she be more of a lady, my mother always said, "Who the hell did she want me to be? Jackie Onassis?"

My mother married my father when she was twenty-five years old—the story was that they met on a blind date outside the "Nut House"—and then they lived in the city for nearly another twenty years. Then, when my mother was forty-four and I was four, we moved to Levittown, a suburban tract house community built in the 1950s, one part industrial village, the other part American Dream. With a hundred-dollar down payment, the houses were affordable enough, and my father worked nearby at the chemical plant, one of the two major employers in the area along with the steel mill.

We lived on Quiet Road in Quincy Hollow (the street names in Levittown all began with the first letter of the section name) where my mother took her daily four-mile walk. "Every day I go around and around these streets like a hamster on a treadmill," my mother would say. As an adolescent, I fanned my mother's frustrations into the flames of my own self-destruction. I was drinking and drugging at fourteen. Driving at sixteen. The streets looped around my neck like a noose tightening. For me, drinking and drugging was a form of running away. When I was five I had stored pilfered Cheerios (food for the road) in the bottom drawer of my bureau until a parade of ants sabotaged my plans.

During the blurred years of my adolescence, when I was still in high school, I took the Greyhound bus to New York City. I was seventeen. It was 1976. I had not yet come out. But as if my dormant lesbianism were a homing device, I found a subway train that took me straight to Greenwich Village. When I was back above ground, I found a newspaper stand and bought a *Village Voice* so that I could read the apartment listings. I was looking for Bleecker Street which I had read about in novels and heard about in songs, but found myself on Christopher Street, hungry, and looking for a place to sit. I spotted a restaurant with tall glass windows that jutted out onto the sidewalk. It looked like a large greenhouse with clear windows. It was early in the afternoon on a Saturday. Through the windows I could see patrons sitting across from each other at small tables. Plants hung down from the ceiling between the tables. The maitre d' took one look at me and firmly told me that he could only seat two people together. I looked over his shoulder into the room full of, it suddenly dawned on me, men, it was all men, gay men, enjoying their Saturday brunch. I mumbled something and headed back out onto the street. Around the corner I found a restaurant where I sat down at a table by myself, ordered something to eat and opened the pages of the *Voice*. The apartments were all more expensive than I thought they would be and at the age of seventeen—other than mowing lawns or working the register at a fast-food joint—I had no marketable skills. So I used my return ticket back.

I was always intending to be on my way to somewhere else. But the drinking and drugging just dug me in deeper. Eventually my mother gave me a few not-so-gentle shoves and I ended up being the first in my family and the only one in my peer group to go to college. I lived at home and attended Temple University, in Philadelphia, an hour's commute away. After graduation, I moved back to the city my parents had fled from but, as a college graduate in a community of intellectuals and artists, I was worlds removed from my origins.

Despite my need to escape, I kept going back. Along with the practical reason of visiting my aging parents—the landscape where I grew up was embedded in me. There are many things that invade the lives of working-class people—chief among them poverty, or in my case, the constant threat of it. There is resignation and frustration, a foreboding sense that things will never change. Then there is the internalized self-hatred, the futility of it all.

The air I grew up breathing in Levittown was chemical-laden. On clear days the fumes were invisible. Overcast days, the air was a dirty glove clasped around our nostrils. When we drove past the marsh-lined road alongside the plant, where the stench was the worst, my mother and I would hold our noses, and my father would call it "the smell of money."

It was my father's union job, and my mother's skill at managing money, that pulled my parents out of the poverty they had grown up in. Perhaps it was because of this belief in the American Dream, be it reality or myth, that I was visited with a vague shimmering presence that eventually I came to call hope.

Economic security can be a breeding ground for denial. My mother, feisty enough to have become mythic in the minds of my father and me, had always lived in mortal fear of losing my father. Her own father had abandoned her family when she was seven, and this no doubt foreshadowed her fear. But her concerns were practical ones. My father worked swing shift in the plant's boiler room. Accidents happened. Growing up in the industrial northeast, I watched the plant explosions on the nightly news. Then there were the killers that were slow to strike. More than a few of my father's co-workers were felled by cancer of all types and early heart attacks. The summer I worked at the plant when I was in college, a man fell over dead in the guardhouse before punching out his timecard for the day—at the time, it all seemed so unfair and futile to me.

A spot of asbestos showed up on my father's lung X-ray. When my mother got the news, her face paled. My mother had always been the strong one. She was traditional in her role of housewife—revolving her schedule around my father's shiftwork hours, washing his work clothes for the thirty-five years he worked at the plant—but this didn't stop her from being the one who called the shots.

We never expected that the hand that fed us would come out of the sky to strike her down.

Today, my mother and I sat in her living room. It was cool in the house. My mother's feet rested on an ottoman covered with a thread-worn tapestry. It was a mosaic of earth-toned flowers: rust red, silvery green, dusty blue. Thin black lines outlined heart-shaped petals against a faded ocher background. As my eyes traveled along the lines, I saw my grandmother standing with the other women in the long straight aisles between machines in the textile mill, on tiptoe as she dropped the spindles on their spikes, crouching to check the weave, the warp, the weft. Close to half a century later my mother had taken the discards her mother was allowed to take home from the mill and carefully stitched them into a square cover for the iron-legged ottoman.

All it took was a nod toward the tapestry, a certain look, or a question—*Grandmom made that didn't she?*—and my mother would recite the stories, the same ones she had always told, sometimes with a new insight, a different twist. I always listened, transfixed, as she spoke.

"How many hours a day did Grandmom work in the textile mill?"

My mother looked at me, slightly confused. "I don't remember. Eight, I guess. Isn't that how long the work day is?"

I told her I was reading about the labor movement and in the early 1900s, when my grandmother started working, men and women were still striking for the ten-hour day.

"People are always bad-mouthing unions, but without them, we wouldn't have gotten the eight-hour day," said my father, who had come home from his plant luncheon and was settling into his favorite chair in the living room.

My mother looked at him and then back at me. "When I worked for the Navy Department, they told us we were better than people in unions. We were *white collar.*"

My father was silent. He looked at his watch and then at the turned off television. The game would be on in another hour.

I sighed, shoulders sagging in resignation.

Ever since I graduated from college, my mother had told me about her life like I was a stranger, her reminders sounding like admonishments: "Working people don't have a choice about what they do for a living. They just work." When my mother told me this, part of me wondered who she thought I was. Being the first in my family to go straight through high school, much less to graduate from college, did not change the fact of how I was raised. Even so, I was ashamed that my mother thought she had to remind me of the conditions of her life.

My mother felt diminished by her lack of a college education. As far back as I could remember, she always told me, "It's what's inside your head that matters," followed by, "No one can ever take an education away from you." In graduating from college, I fulfilled my mother's ambitions. But at the same time, in achieving what she could not, I betrayed her.

She wanted me to have a better life than hers. But the opportunities in my life had been underscored with my mother's resentments. To gain a better understanding of my life, I went back to research the labor movement, to read its history, its literature. Now my mother was telling me she was white collar, that she felt herself to be "better" than people in unions.

I took a deep breath. My mother was just trying to lend a dignity to her life. She was brainwashed into thinking of herself as white collar and, therefore, better than people in unions. Divide and conquer is how the powers that be have kept people in their places. But our conversation was not about white collar or blue collar. It was not about work even—or the fact that I went to college and my mother did not. We were pressed up against opposite sides of the glass divide in our mother-daughter relationship.

My mother and I were close. We saw eye to eye on most things that mattered. We read the same books, lending them to each other, sometimes even going to the bookstore together and deciding jointly what we wanted to read. There were moments between us when she seemed more like my friend than my mother.

At the same time, there was almost always an unspoken tension between us. The things that cut through us most deeply were also the things that divided us. There was—at least temporarily—my sexuality. When I came out to my parents in my early twenties, I was telling my mother, in particular, that my life would be vastly different than hers. At the same time, my lesbianism was a natural outgrowth of my mother's feminism that most definitely shaped my early sense of self.

I have always been most comfortable living in the present. Still, the past is always there, threatening to rise up at any moment, especially when my mother—who tended to listen to too much talk radio— insisted that she wanted us to discuss our feelings.

"We never talk about how we *feel* about things. I don't mean about books or politics or things like that. I mean how we *feel* about the things we say to each other," she once said to me. My mother who had sat on her anger all of her life, except for outbursts of breaking dishes and screaming, suddenly wanted me to discuss my feelings. She wouldn't drop the subject and I found myself fuming.

"Okay," I said finally. "I'll tell you how I feel. When you get on me about my weight I want to kick you in the head."

I was shocked at the force of the words that came out of my mouth. Then I felt guilty for speaking this way to my mother. But she *asked* how I felt.

My mother was silent. She didn't ask me about my feelings for a long time after that, but she also stopped bugging me about my weight.

My life was too entangled with my mother's for comfort. An only child, I absorbed her like a sponge, losing a sense of where she left off and I began.

The irony, perhaps, inherent in the tensions and difficulties between us, was that we were both so much alike. Despite her increasing resignation, I wanted her to talk about her life, including her hopes and dreams that didn't come true. She refused and in the face of her obstinacy, I became more insistent. Deep down, I felt my mother slipping away from me. My reaction to this was despair and, beyond despair, desperation. I wanted, *needed*, to know about the missing pieces of my mother's life—the puzzle that created me. The catch was that my mother wanted the same thing from me and I, too, could not deliver.

Each of us had, what my mother called selective memory. We only remembered what we wanted to, and fought like hell to forget the rest.

In my teens and twenties I often reacted to my mother's mixed messages with knee-jerk defensiveness, sometimes outrage. In my thirties, I found it easier to join her than to fight. Since my mother didn't want to talk about her health during my visit, I turned to inquiring about my grandmother's life.

"Didn't Grandmom work in a shop?"

"A shop?" My mother looked at me like I was someone else's daughter.

"Yeah," I said, "I thought she worked in a store when she was a teenager."

"No. That was a *white*-collar job. My mother was not educated. She didn't qualify for a white-collar job—even to be a *clerk* in the store. She only went to the sixth grade. That put up a wall right there. Though, she probably learned more in six years than they do today in twelve. In those days, they focused on the basics, the three Rs they called them—reading, writing and arithmetic. None of the extras they have today, like the psychology of your navel.

"When your grandmother was a girl she worked in a candy factory," my mother said, slowly and carefully.

I remembered that this was not the first time she had told me this.

"What did she *want* to do?"

My mother looked at me as if I were insane.

"No one asked her what she wanted to do," she said. "She just went out and *worked*."

She stared out the rectangular living room window into the late afternoon light. One foot rested on the ottoman's rich autumn hues. She used to swing her foot up without thinking about it. Now, as she shifted in her chair, the pain that had invaded her body compressed her face. She squinted into the distance, beyond the tract houses across the street and the identical roofs behind them. She was searching the past, looking for something she lost there. She looked like a wistful child and at the same time an old, old woman, as old as she would ever be, looking back on a lifetime that spanned centuries.

Slowly, very slowly, she came back to the present. She stared at the ottoman. The far-away expression left her face. Lines of resignation weighed down the corners of her mouth. She stared at the ottoman for another moment and then spoke. "Your grandmother didn't design that. They were all men, designers and artists, the ones who did the *important* work."

My mother's words registered on me with the sting of her own disappointments and thwarted dreams. Her abandoned portfolio was in the back of her closet, dusty and forgotten. The watercolors dried up into hard little squares long ago. The bristles on her paintbrushes had fallen off. The caps hardened onto the tubes of her oil paints. The pastels had lain there so long their colors rubbed off on each other, the orange laced with gray and blue, the pink with burnt sienna.

My mother was a woman who rejected the traditions that bound her mother's life. Before I was born, she burned her Bibles in the backyard, disgusted with the hypocrisies, the contradictions, and, most of all, the misogyny inherent in the pages that curled into ash. My mother was a woman who tried to invent her own religion and failed. A Transcendental Meditation dropout ("I tried and tried to levitate—to bounce myself off the floor by flexing my butt muscles"), she joined the American Atheists for a few years only to leave in disillusionment ("They served coffee and doughnuts and passed the plate just like all the other idiots!"). She was a woman whose ambitions had been thwarted by circumstance, gender and class. She was a woman who absorbed her mother's pain, made it her own, and passed it along to her daughter. When I tried to tell my mother that my grandmother's life was worthwhile, *important*, I was trying to convince myself that my life, too, was important.

"Without Grandmom, the spinners, the weavers, the dyers, without the *workers*, the patterns the designers thought up could never have been made into anything," I said. But my words were weak, unconvincing.

How could they be anything else, when I was not sure of myself?

My mother couldn't give me what she herself never received. "Whatever I did was never good enough," she said to me as we sat in the living room. "I never wore the right kind of hat, and even if I did I couldn't keep it on my head."

I laughed and went into the kitchen to fix myself a cup of chamomile tea. As I poured the water into the cup, I noticed a tear in the corner of the bag. A few tea leaves, crushed yellow flowers, seeped into the water and swirled around. I stared into the white porcelain tea-cup, wondering. What kind of life would I have if knowledge and wisdom were passed uninterrupted and uncensored, from my great-grandmothers down to my grandmother, mother and then to me? This world shimmered up at me for a fleeting moment. Then I saw the reflection of my mother's face in mine. The lines of resignation, her disappointments and her fears stared up at me.

I shuddered, then skimmed the floating leaves away with a spoon and went back into the living room. Like my mother, I was a hopeless realist and at the same time I was deep in denial. I didn't want to get the stray tea leaves on my tongue. Even if I could have divined the future by reading the tea leaf shapes of dark clouds and crosses, I would not have wanted to. I was wary of astrologists and fortune-tellers. It was more than a healthy dose of skepticism. It was superstition. I was afraid that if someone told me my future, I would have no choice other than to create that destiny for myself.

The only omens I could read were the memories of my past. When I was a child I brought home report cards saying I was an underachiever. In elementary school I came home with bit parts in plays in which my mother thought I should star. In junior high, my grades didn't measure up to study the foreign languages in which she expected fluency.

When I reminded her of this, she denied it.

She accused me of wanting *her* to be better.

I, in turn, denied that I wanted my mother to be anyone except who she was.

Neither of us were as sure in our denials as we would have liked to be.

Only one thing was certain: whichever way we turned the mirror, the reflection came up wanting. My mother was more stubborn than me. Her mind was made up. Their lives, her mother's and her own, were wasted, good for nothing but survival. No amount of arguing or cajoling could have changed that. But she nodded her head to appease me, and by so doing acknowledged that her life was linked with mine.

CHAPTER 2

The Almighty Dollar

Something was terribly wrong. I felt it in my bones, forged from the heat of my mother's body. Nearly two months had passed since the doctor had diagnosed her with arthritis. My mother was vanishing in front of my eyes.

Pain was searing through her body, moving from her sternum to shoulders, from her ribs to her hips. Her mental attitude, too, was waning. "Your father keeps talking about the things we are going to do when I get better," my mother told me, her voice trailing away. "I try to tell him that I don't think that's going to happen, but he won't listen."

It was a cool day for August, and we were sitting behind my parents' house on the patio under the trumpet hummingbird vine. The patio roof had started to wear thin, so my parents removed it a few years ago, leaving only the wooden beams. The result was a canopy of deep orange flowers, trumpet throated, petals long and fluted, weaving in and out of the stark white beams of the patio framing a brilliant blue sky.

A quiet sadness pressed down on us. If it weren't for the interruptions of nearby lawn mowers and weed whackers, we might have been startled by the ruby-winged whir of a hummingbird.

My mother had started using a wooden cane to help her get around. Its upside down U-shaped crook was hooked over the end of the metal arm of her chair. Just last summer, she stood on tiptoe and reached up, nimbly clamping together the mouth of a trumpet flower between her thumb and forefinger, trapping a bee inside, saying "gotcha" before letting go and jumping backward.

"I'm so mad at myself." My mother clenched her right hand around the metal armrest of her folding rocking chair. Her left hand was open in her lap, frail, vulnerable. "I should have been fighting this. I should have gone to a chiropractor, another doctor. I know it seems like I'm not doing anything."

Barbara, who has an opinion on everything, had been telling me that I should take my mother to a specialist. I tried to talk to my mother. "Oh Janet," she would say, "please mind your own business and leave me alone." When I told her that Barbara thought it was a good idea, my mother rolled her eyes and then with her eyes widening into a sympathetic expression, she said, "Barbara just feels bad because she can't spend more time with her own mother." Then with her eyes narrowing into keen perception she added, "But be careful, I wouldn't get too co-dependent with her mother if I were you."

I looked back at my mother and nodded. My mother, who called herself an "armchair psychologist," had keen insight into people and their behavior.

A few weeks after my mother was diagnosed with arthritis, a battery of blood tests came back with glowing results, and she seemed to be rallying. Her blood pressure was perfect, her cholesterol in range, her thyroid was functioning perfectly. She was most happy about testing negative on her diabetes test, the disease that led to the heart failure that killed her mother.

My mother even managed to make the drive over with my father to visit Barbara and me in our new home. I made lunch, a piece of flounder seasoned with fresh sage, brown rice, and collard greens from my garden. I stood at the stove and my mother stood in the kitchen talking to me. She casually opened the silverware drawer on the sink and began sorting the stainless steel utensils. "Like with like," she said, and in a matter of minutes the forks were with the forks, the knives with the knives and so on.

Later in the afternoon, my father was helping us put a new lock on the front door of our house. He had already taken the existing lock off the door, and we needed to go back to the hardware store. When we came back my mother was sitting in the middle of the futon, her face drawn, as she reached around with her left hand and held her right shoulder. She had always been thin, but now she looked like she had dropped a quarter of her weight. I had noticed that she was losing weight but had told myself it must be the way she was sitting. But the afternoon light, filtering through the blinds, illuminated everything I had not been able to see before.

How could I not have noticed that my mother was disappearing?

In the weeks and months that followed, I visited often. One night I dreamed that my body was filled with tumors. The image of my misshapen body slipped back into the recesses of memory. But a hint of terror remained, trapping me further in my frustration with the medical system. Its red tape, requiring my mother to fill out paperwork to see another doctor, seemed to be hurting more than it was helping. My mother lived with silence and a drawn look of resignation. I could not change a society that rendered old women as invisible, useless, past their prime.

I arranged for my mother to have a consultation with a macrobiotic counselor.

My mother who always claimed not to believe in anything, did believe in the practicalities in life—food being chief among them. She agreed to meet with him.

Barbara liked some of the macrobiotic food that I had already begun to cook, for my own issues with stiffness, colds and earaches, but she was not going to give up eating meat. The day before I had arranged for the macrobiotic counselor to come to my parents' house, we went to a barbecue at the home of one of her post office co-workers. We were sitting on the deck behind Carol's row home. Carol was a fine-looking black woman in her late forties with short-short hair who had just married a sharp looking black man with a gleaming bald head. While her husband was stoking up the grill and flipping the burgers, Carol was coolly downing more than a few cold ones. I was sitting in a wooden chair on the deck when Barbara reached over and took my hand. Carol, looking glamorous (despite the August heat and the smoke from the grill) in a gold silk tank top, was standing next to us talking to her relatives. She glanced over at us and Barbara quickly withdrew her hand. But it was too late. Carol leaned over to retrieve the gold lighter that was on the table behind us. She winked and said, "I always have a woman on the side." Barbara and I looked at each other and raised our eyebrows. Carol had confirmed what we already suspected. Her good "friend" Brenda, another one of Barbara's co-workers, sat on the other side of the deck, quietly drinking from her can of beer.

Barbara's co-workers all knew me. I often dropped her off and picked her up at work and sometimes called her during the day. She had told me that her co-workers described me as "sweet" but a label was never attached to our relationship. The post office was a relatively conventional place to work. In addition to being the only lesbian at her small post office in our neighborhood, she was the only Caucasian. Barbara's co-workers were all African American. Barbara was well aware that there were some major cultural differences. One of her co-workers, on figuring out that Barbara was "that way," told Barbara that she was praying for her. This woman invited Barbara and me to come to her church on "Men's Day." We went anyway, enjoying the music and the food afterward, and this woman ended up inviting Barbara and me to the apartment she shared with her husband and toddler son. Barbara told me that afterward she heard through another co-worker that the woman liked me so much she'd stopped praying for Barbara.

Barbara had been working at the post office since the early eighties—before that she had been a case-worker for the welfare office and before that she was a substitute teacher after she graduated with a teaching degree from a college in Pittsburgh. But it was Barbara's association with her co-workers in the post office that became an education for us.

The macrobiotic counselor had told me it was important for the whole family to participate. Barbara agreed to come. She thought, however, that there might not be anything she liked to eat—so she brought a hamburger that was left over from the barbeque and ate it in the car on the way to my parents' house.

"Uuuugh," I said, rolling down the window. "That thing stinks!"

Barbara looked at me calmly, took another bite of her hamburger and said, "Smells good to me."

At my parents' house, the macrobiotic counselor—a Japanese American man about my age—sat at the dining room table and explained the basic macrobiotic philosophy. Using charts and graphs, he illustrated how the basic American diet was making people ill, even in other countries, and how the rising impotence and infertility rates were related to the intake of animal products. Then he talked about arthritis, heart disease and cancer and how these conditions could be improved with diet. As I looked across the round dining room table where we sat, I could see my father's look of skepticism turning to keen interest.

My father had always pretended to be reluctant to try anything new—from drinking herbal tea to sampling something unusual that my mother cooked up. But my mother's insistence on a healthy diet kept my father going. His own parents—grandparents I had never met—died in their early forties from heart conditions as had one of his brothers, my uncle.

Just underneath his reluctance, his short answers when asked if he liked his dinner—"I'm eating it, aren't I?"—were a kind of gratitude. He leaned forward as he listened to the counselor, his hands trembling slightly as they rested on the edge of the table, conveying the kind of desperation that love produces. He would do anything that might possibly help my mother get better. I could see that Barbara was won over also for her own reasons. She was looking intently at the counselor's sinewy forearms. As the counselor wooed us with charts and graphs suddenly something magical began to take place. Skepticism was overcome with logic and a tentative feeling of hope filled the room.

He made us a light lunch—brown rice and miso soup in small bowls. Afterward, my mother changed into a lightweight T-shirt and sweats so that he could give her a shiatsu massage. When she came out of her bedroom and into the living room, I could see her shoulder bones jutting out like wire coat hangers under the taut ridges of her neck. Seeing her body this intimately, I could no longer deny that she was seriously ill. She looked emaciated. As I stared at her, the room tilted and I felt a thud in the bottom of my stomach as if my heart had fallen down a long hollow tube.

How could this have happened?

My mother lay on her stomach, remarking that she was turning into a skeleton with a potbelly.

"Maybe you are growing wings and becoming an angel," said the counselor, as he lightly touched her jutting shoulder blades. After he was finished with her back, he helped her roll over. He gently pressed his fingers into her pressure points along her shoulders, her pale inner arms, and then down the front of her legs. At one point, he sat back on his heels and asked her if the doctor had given her a bone density test. With her eyes shut tight and her face drawn in on itself, my mother shook her head.

When the massage was over, she could not stand up. Her arms flailed and she raised her neck with a grimace. She gave up, resting her head back on the carpeted floor, telling the counselor that my father had to lift her out of bed each morning. This was news to me. As I watched my father and the counselor lift my mother to a standing position, my own body went rigid. A buzzing started in my mind, a swarm of locusts, dark clouds, omens.

Nothing would ever be the same.

Afterward, sitting silently with my mother on the back patio under the hummingbird vine, I remembered how the counselor bowed to me before he left. I walked him out to his car, and handed him his check, and he bowed. I bowed back, but before I finished, he bowed lower. This was more than an honoring of his culture. He was acknowledging that I cared for my elders, just as he cared for his. He had left my mother with some dried daikon root, grown by his father in his tiny village in Japan.

This small man, a full head and a half shorter than me, would become indispensable as I continued to care for my mother, always returning my calls promptly, night and day. Several times he called me, out of the blue, just when I needed him most, saying, "You have very strong thoughts."

My mother was touched that the counselor had spent so much time with her—from noon until six in the evening. By contrast, her doctor had spent about ten minutes with her. As much as the counselor did, making lunch and dinner, explaining the holistic theory of macrobiotics, making dietary recommendations (and other simple things such as keeping plants in the house to create fresh air), he brought much more with him. He restored my mother's faith in human kindness and caring.

Before my mother consented to see the counselor she said, "The problem with these things is that you have to believe in them to work. You have to believe in the chiropractor, you have to believe in macrobiotics, and I don't believe in anything."

I, on the other hand, had believed in everything—at least for a little while. In my early twenties I believed in karate, bathing myself in the sweat of baptismal until the punches and kicks left me bruised and tender. Later, I had a brief dalliance with Zen meditation until my knees got sore, and then a bout with Wicca until the recitation of Goddess lore and paleolithic periods began to take the magic out of everything. My last spiritual distraction had been a form of Hindu meditation which I abandoned after finding out that women have to wear dresses or skirts in the presence of the (female) Guru.

Now, after I came in from the patio with my mother to make lunch, I found myself chanting my mantra as I washed the broad flat leaves of the collards, the curly ends of the pale green Napa cabbage. *Om Namah Shivaya.* I honor the divine presence inside myself. *Ommm Nammmaaahh Shi-va-a-a-a-ya.* I sang to myself as I steamed the greens, cooking them last to preserve the nutrients, calcium for my mother's bones.

"What's this? It looks like a big green dick with a condom on it!" My mother poked her food disgustedly with her fork.

My father—who rarely swore even when arguing with my mother—scrupulously studied the food on his plate.

I turned out far more like my mother in the swearing department, but for some reason was a little shocked. "Mom! I rolled up the greens, the way you asked."

"You're supposed to cut it up—like sushi."

I whisked her plate away, taking it to the kitchen sink and attempted to run a serrated blade through the rolled up greens—the collards in the middle and the lighter and thinner Napa cabbage leaves on the outside. Last year, when we went to visit my aunt, my mother's sister, she prepared her greens this way. My mother had remarked that the greens were too fancy to eat. Now she wanted her greens to look like sushi. When I was finished with the serrated knife, the greens on the plate looked like a jumble of two-tone curly green locks recently cut off the head of a wet and bedraggled clown.

My mother uninterestedly chewed a mouthful of greens and then looked at the scoop of brown rice on her plate. "You know why your aunt likes rice? It's because our father was a Southerner. Rice is a Southern dish, and our mother used to make it for him. White rice, not brown. White rice with butter on it. I remember this, but she was too young."

There was no evidence in my mother's voice of the seven-year-old she had been with her life gutted when her father abandoned his family. These were simply the facts. Her father had left. Unlike her little sister, she had been old enough to remember what he ate.

After lunch, my father went out for his daily walk. My mother and I sat next to each other in the living room. She had decided to change doctors. Leafing through her small phone-book size directory of HMO providers, she turned to me and said, "You're my support group." Her smile merged into mine. The silence that surrounded us was a conductor of empathy. I felt her burden of isolation, her aloneness in the world, her frustration at being trapped in her body. As her support group of one—the only child of a strong-willed mother who had always insisted on doing things her own way—an immense responsibility weighed down on me.

I took a deep breath and looked down at the directory as my mother ran her index finger along the margin of physicians. "Here's one," I said. "A solo practitioner, a woman internist with her own practice. You might have a harder time getting an appointment, but at least you won't be shuffled around between doctors like you were before."

My mother circled the listing and folded the corner of the page. She promised to call the new physician in the morning. The silence that surrounded us returned, with it a sense of lightness. Relief.

Despite my more frequent visits, I was frustrated with the gulf between us. No family traditions bound us to each other. That my parents became atheists when I was a child had worked in my favor—I learned to think for myself. I didn't have to unlearn the small-mindedness that too often comes with religion. At the same time, my parents' atheism sometimes left me searching.

Tradition is something to hold onto.

Maybe the lack of tradition is a tradition in itself? I stopped to reconsider that I may have overlooked some family traditions: screaming and breaking dishes. When my mother was a child, her mother had hurled a cast-iron skillet at her head. "I ducked," my mother told me years later, "and it went right through the window. Mama was mad at me for years. She said the broken window was my fault." My mother had altered the pattern a little bit. She vented her pent-up rage by smashing dishes in the kitchen, while I sat terrified in the other room. I remember her doing this several times, once after my grandmother died when I was twelve. The dish breaking was accompanied with the slamming of the kitchen cabinets and my mother screaming "FUCK! FUCK! FUCK!"

Nothing was hurled at my head.

I don't remember smashing any dishes when I was a child. I was probably terrified of making my mother angry. But my own suppressed rage prompted me to take the toenail clippers and cut small slits in my mother's terry cloth bath towels. I did it once, twice, and then my mother banished me from her bathroom. It wasn't till I was an adult that I took up the tradition of breaking dishes and screaming. Barbara and I were living in an apartment, which had increasingly become too cramped. Frustration had followed frustration and I stood in the kitchen, screaming while I grabbed the dishes I could live without and slammed them into the kitchen trash can.

With growing satisfaction, I hurled each plate, cup, saucer and glass bottle onto the one beneath it. When I was done, I calmly took the trash outside, past my mortified neighbor, a gay man who was smoking on the fire escape, and dropped it three stories down into the Dumpster in the apartment parking lot. Barbara was game enough to enjoy throwing the trash bags down into the Dumpster—until the apartment management moved the Dumpster across the parking lot.

For the most part, Barbara avoided conflict. She had grown up with a father who had a chemical disorder that manifested in a Dr. Jekyll/Dr. Hyde personality—abusive and congenial.

For some years Barbara had been seeing a therapist, whom she spoke highly of, and was now at the end of her treatment. She had also, from time to time, suggested that I might benefit from therapy. It was the early 1990s and almost everyone we knew was in therapy.

One day, she came home from work and I said to her, "Guess who I have an appointment with next week?" Barbara was a little taken aback at first—since I hadn't told her I was thinking of going to her therapist. I knew plenty of lesbian therapists. But the lesbian community in those days was small and insular and I wasn't comfortable seeing a therapist who might be dating one of my friends or whom I would run into at a women's music concert or the food co-op. I may have crossed some lines by making an appointment to see Barbara's former therapist without telling her first, but as it turned out, the experience of entering therapy with the same person as Barbara was helpful. The therapist, Fiora Raggi, understood Barbara and her issues with her family and, as a result, she helped both of us. Raggi was an older Italian American woman who had come to this country when she was nineteen and then went to college and medical school and eventually became a Reichian therapist. Reichian therapy was developed by Wilhelm Reich, the Austrian American psychiatrist and psychoanalyst, who developed theories and practices to dissolve repressed tensions that he called "armoring." With my therapist's guidance, I lay on her couch and kicked and screamed myself to a place of peace. And for this privilege I paid her sixty dollars an hour—a relative bargain.

That's when the family tradition of breaking dishes ended.

I poured two cups of tea, the cups sitting on the end table between my mother and me in the living room. A plywood board peeked out from underneath the seat cushion of her armchair. My father had cut the board and put it under the cushion so that my mother would be more comfortable. My mother's teacup matched the rest of her dishes— white CorningWare trimmed with gold flowers. My cup was pale green, slightly indented lines running up the sides. It was part of a set of four teacups that my grandmother picked up at a church rummage sale and passed along to my mother. It was the last one of the set. The others were broken—either by accident or on purpose.

"Remember when you used to break the dishes?"

My mother gave me a shrewd look, shaking her head. "I may have dropped a few, but not very often."

"Hmmm...." Next, my mother will be saying that she never swore. "Remember what you used to call yourself? Poor Fucking Housewife."

She nodded. "That's right. I thought that up in my consciousness raising group one night with Mrs. Bates, who used to live down the street. We called ourselves the PFHs."

Then her eyes narrowed. "But I NEVER broke any dishes on purpose. Those are good dishes. CorningWare."

My mother was doing more than denying her past. She was attempting to erase mine. If Barbara or my father were there—to cast discouraging looks at me—I might have been able to leave the past alone. But the echoes of my mother's temper that shaped my childhood hung in the air.

"You did too. Remember that time after Grandmom died? You were smashing dishes and slamming the cabinets."

"Did not." My mother shook her head resolutely.

It was impossible to get my mother to admit what she did not want to. I had better luck getting her to smoke a joint with me when I was a teenager. One night when I was out late, getting stoned and drunk and doing God knows what, I left a half-filled pipe in the ashtray of her car. She found it the next morning and came storming upstairs and thrust her hand inside my bedroom door. "Here," she said. "I think you lost something."

I thought she was going to kill me. Or at the very least I would be faced with a stony silence. A few minutes later she tapped on my door. "What?" I said, peering out suspiciously. "I want to try it," she said. "Try what?" I countered. "You know," she answered, and went back downstairs. I rolled a big fat joint and went down to join her. The first time we smoked she turned on the rock station on the radio and—to the tune of "Everybody Must Get Stoned"—she danced around the living room. The second time, she fell asleep on the couch. I think she inhaled the second time.

I was looking out the front window, watching the children across the street scamper up a wooden ladder they had nailed to the sycamore tree outside their house. I remembered the sycamore tree of my own childhood, the one that used to stand outside our house, near the sidewalk, until it was cut down. In the summer I would swing from its sturdy limbs, pulling myself up and hiding in the leaves. Autumn would find me on the ground, playing with the pompoms and pushing together the piles of leaves my father had raked until there was enough for me to take a flying leap and land on my back, looking up at my world through the crisp lacy edges of brown and gold.

One night as I lay in my room sleeping, a drunk driver plowed into the tree, leaving it standing there aslant like the leaning Tower of Pisa. He kept going, driving over the next-door neighbor's front lawn and then down a hill, where he plowed into the side of the next house.

When I was a child, this seemed like a mystery. The slender tree partially uprooted—tearing up the sidewalk—by an out-of-control car that careened from out of nowhere onto our street. Now it just seemed like good fortune that the people two houses down were away on vacation and not sleeping in their bedroom when the car plowed into it.

As I sat in the living room, lost in remembering, a feeling of being scrutinized brought me back into the present. My mother was staring at me, studying my face.

"You always asked about my life, I'd like to know about yours too."

Now it was my turn to deny the past. I pulled into myself, shrugging my shoulders in the exact motion that my mother so often made. If I brought up the time we smoked a joint together, she would most likely deny that it ever happened. And if I mentioned that the pot smoking was only the tip of the iceberg, I'd be venturing into unknown and dangerous territory. I knew she only said that she wanted to know about the things I've never spoken about. I knew she would only end up blaming herself.

When I was in my late twenties, my Reichian therapist suggested I confront my parents about my adolescent drugging and drinking. When I told her that in junior high I had bleached my hair until it was almost white—I was going through a David Bowie phase—and my mother hadn't even mentioned it, she was livid. "They were ignoring you," she charged. "How could they not see what was going on? How could they let you do that to yourself?"

I tried to explain that my behavior wasn't the fault of my parents. The problem might have had something to do with the fact that there were two generations between my parents and me, not one. Their adolescent world had been so different from mine that they simply didn't have a clue as to what to do with me. My mother probably just shrugged off my hair color as something that teenagers do—and she was right. I was the one who betrayed their trust.

I saw Raggi—for some reason she went by her last name—for several years and then she died. Her office was in the living room of an old stone house, a twin, in the slightly run-down, tree-lined section of Philadelphia called Germantown, which was not far from where we lived. Everything in Raggi's office was a shade of blue: cornflower blue walls; two cobalt ceramic bowls sitting on matching indigo end tables on the opposite sides of the room; indigo wall-to-wall carpeting and two Persian blue chairs in the center of the room and, off to the side, a sapphire blue sofa where her patients lay down and kicked and screamed themselves into a better life. In this blue room, as I had come to think of it, even the large leafed rubber plant took on a bluish cast, looking like an underwater wavy blue green stalk of seaweed. In the 1980s lesbian community I had come out in, seeing a therapist was more the norm than the exception. But in the working-class landscape that had shaped me, therapists were for the idle rich who had the time and money to dwell on their personal problems. The other scenario was that the person who saw a therapist—or a "shrink" in my father's vernacular—was severely emotionally disturbed.

Walking into my therapist's office was like entering another dimension, a magical world where she would weave together mythology and my life story, where my body and mind were connected. I left each session feeling the blood tingling in my veins in an entirely different way.

The first time I came to see this gnome-like Italian woman—who had earned her medical degree after she emigrated to the U.S.—I sat down in the chair facing her and must have been visibly nervous. "So," she said, "you have come to see the shrink."

My parents were uncomfortable with the fact that I was seeing a therapist. Once when my mother asked me why, I glibly responded that it was no big deal. "Lots of people do," I said. "They need to go back and figure out their childhoods." I couldn't have offered a worse answer. After that, every time the word "therapist" would come up—even in a context that didn't involve me—the conversation would grind to a crippling halt.

I was twenty-nine when I saw Raggi—and struggling with career issues. I had recently accepted a communications consultant position working several days a week for a large company. They had offered me a full-time job. I knew it would take over my life if I accepted it. Raggi helped me put this in perspective, "I had a patient who was always concerned about impressing his father," she told me. "He always wanted to buy a bigger house. But he didn't need a bigger house to be happy. You can always make a small house better by putting a cat in it." She pointed to her own cat who was perched on the blue rug next to the rubber plant and then smiled at me with her bright eyes.

It was Raggi who encouraged me to pursue my creative writing. "You can always get a job," she said. "You can go sell hot dogs on the street. But you are the only one who can write the story of your life."

Sitting in the living room with my mother, I looked down into my cup of tea and asked, "Don't you ever wonder what your mother's life was like?"

"I know what her life was like," my mother said. "She was my mother."

"But you don't know everything," I answered.

"That's true," she said and shrugged.

I noticed that some stray tea leaves had settled at the bottom of my cup. I passed it to my mother and asked her what she saw. "Tea," she said, barely looking into the cup.

"Look closer," I said.

My mother looked back at me and then down into her cup. She decided to play along with my game.

"What do you see?"

She ignored me and continued to peer into the cup.

"It looks like a car," she said finally. "Like the pink Plymouth Fury your father and I bought a few years after we were married. When we first started dating I asked him what he wanted out of life and he said,

'A car.' If you had a car in the neighborhood where he grew up it meant you were a big deal."

She paused and looked down into the cup again. "A car," she said, shaking her head as she handed the cup back to me.

"At least he got what he wanted," I said quietly. "What did you want?"

My mother eyed me skeptically. "No one ever asked us what we wanted." She pushed her lips into a firm stubborn line.

I knew what she wanted. I saw it in her eyes every time I mentioned a friend who had gone to art school. "Mama always said that art doesn't put food on the table," my mother would tell me. Now, during our visit, she was still silent, withdrawn and resigned. I had a sneaking suspicion that she had thrown away the sketches and charcoal drawings that she'd done infrequently over the years. But once or twice when I was growing up, I'd crept up behind my mother, looked over her shoulder, and saw her charcoal sketches. The heavy dark lines, the shaded gradations were embedded in my memory.

I grew up seeing the world, in part, through my mother's eyes. And through those eyes, I could see not only my mother's life, but her mother's, too.

It all started with my question to her: "What was Grandmom like when she was a girl?"

My grandmother—a Republican and an Episcopalian who wore white gloves and a black mesh veil to church every Sunday—had taught my mother to be a feminist. Even though my grandmother, an uneducated woman, was too busy keeping a roof over her head and being a single mother to her two daughters to be involved in any kind of social change movement. She was born in 1898. Her father, my great-grandfather, died when she was three. My maternal great-grandmother died before my mother was born, but she was able to sum up her existence in a sentence or two: "She worked for the railroads and did what women did in those days—dusting and scrubbing, cleaning up the messes that the passengers made in the train cars. And in the evening she took in mending to make ends meet."

My mother always told me that women with sons don't always "get it" about feminism. And in this sweeping generalization, she was talking about her grandmother, her mother's mother who favored her son to a fault. As a result, my grandmother grew up to hate her brother.

She was taken out of school at the end of sixth grade to go to work in the candy factory so that her brother—who her mother called "my little man"—could go to school to the eighth grade. He wore new clothes while my grandmother wore seconds from the church rummage. After their mother died, when they were grown, my grandmother and her brother never spoke to each other again. The story that was passed down to me was that the brother took their mother's insurance money and refused to pay for the funeral.

I grew up in a working-class culture of "no complaints." No matter how bad things got there was no use in feeling sorry for yourself. Besides, who had the right to complain when others were worse off? This survival tactic of staying strong by not admitting defeat and pulling yourself up by your bootstraps was passed down to me from my mother and to her from her mother. When she was thirteen, my grandmother, Ethel, went to work in the candy factory. It was 1911. My grandmother as a girl would have seen the newspaper reports that I read about nearly a century later.

TRIANGLE FIRE: 146 DEAD shouted the headlines. The fire started in the loft; the doors were locked; the workers, mostly girls. There was no escape. The fire ladders were not high enough. Everyone died in twenty minutes. They burned to death or jumped to their deaths, through the windows of the ninth floor, plunging straight through the firemen's nets, thudding against the pavement where their bodies lay in heaps.

I knew what my grandmother's life was like. After high school graduation, I'd gone to work in a factory where I inhaled the dust of paper boxes that I scooped from the assembly line, stacking the flat pieces, the larger the handful the better, to keep up with the speed of the assembly line operator. Hours of my young life faded into the endless march of die cut paper boxes down the assembly line.

When my grandmother went to work at the candy factory, she would have breathed in particles of chocolate and caramel and her thoughts would have been drowned out by the metallic clatter from the forming machines and the roaring of the ovens. Her best friend Lillian might have complained about the working conditions—the low wages, the long hours—and about the owner strutting about in his fine clothes and driving a new motorcar. When my grandmother responded, she would have most likely echoed her mother: "At least we aren't corralled with the screaming livestock in the yards on Delaware Avenue or going blind from straining our eyes on the fine work at the lace factory. At least we get paid. Things are worse elsewhere."

This echoed down the generations—from my great-grandmother

to the grandmother, to my mother and to me—the words eventually coming out of my own mouth: "Things could always be worse." When my mother spoke of her grandmother, my great-grandmother, she sketched in a life of disappointments with a few strokes. I could imagine my great-grandmother holding needle and thread in hand above her mending, telling her daughter that the agitators were dangerous. She may have reminded her daughter that twenty-nine people had been killed by the police during the Philadelphia transit strike the previous year. My great-grandmother would have held the same view as the other "respectable citizens" of the time—the trade unionists are immoral. They hold their meetings in saloons—no place for young ladies or respectable grown women."

When all else failed, my great-grandmother would have resorted to the lies and stereotypes fed to those on the bottom rungs of society to keep them divided from each other.

My grandmother insisted she was related to English royalty, an illusion my mother thoroughly rejected. The only remnant to come down to me was the fact that my ancestors came from England. The germ of royal relations was most likely planted in my grandmother's mind by my great-grandmother: the biases of the times, the working class pecking order based on ethnic backgrounds and nationality. "Those girls in New York are nothing like you," she would have said in response to the Triangle Fire. "They're foreigners, for one thing. Everyone knows that New York is full of Italians and Jews. There's hardly a native-born girl to be found there. That's what you are—a native-born girl of English descent. Things like this do not happen to American girls. Remember that, Ethelind Elizabeth. Our ancestors are royalty, kings and queens, lords and ladies."

That was what my great-grandmother would have said. But her face and her body language would have belied her words.

If my grandmother, as a girl, learned to parrot what her mother said, she also would have seen the fear written on her mother's face. And what terrified her mother terrified her.

Sitting in the living room with my mother, I stared into her face and saw my grandmother, not as I knew her, but as a girl whose life lay before her. My grandmother, Ethel, a girl who dreamed.

I stared down into my cup, swirling the water. The tea leaves separated and came together again, inviting me in.

I joined my grandmother in her dreams. She dreamed of the destiny that her mother had read in the tea leaves: a ship would come with a handsome man in a white uniform who would take her away. A man in a perfectly pressed white suit came toward her, not bothering to tip his hat. Flying above him was the queen, a diamond tiara sparkling on her head as she floated on the gossamer wings of her long white dress. Ethel was herself and not herself, picked up in the queen's filmy folds and swept off her feet. She was flying, flying.

Then she was dashed to the ground under a mountain of caramels, sticky dust sealing the cracks of her eyes. When she pried her eyes open with her fingers, she saw nothing but white, a wall of white heat, flames licking at her feet, singeing the hem of her dress. She ran between the forming machines, hurling vats of caramel behind her.

Ropes of smoke choked her. Flames whispered her name. *Ethelind Elizabeth, Ethelind Elizabeth, Ethelind...* They reached toward her with searing talon fingers. She ran by the machines, forming and casting, dipping and cooling, clackety clackety clack, and hurled herself to the open window at the end of the room. She stood on the edge, breathing hot-shimmering air.

When she looked down, she was high above the square. Police scurried like ants, holding gigantic circus hoops, the inside netting consumed by burning bodies that plunged straight through, in twisted gray skirted heaps. The wall of flames leapt to her back. She writhed, sweated, screamed.

The man in the white suit appeared out of nowhere, and turned to her with a thin-lipped smile. Taking her hand, he placed a scalding kiss on her cheek as he slipped his hand to the small of her back and pushed. She fell, back arcing, legs over her head. Tumbling backward, she was spinning, falling, flailing, her hands grasping at thin air. She fell.

My mother always told me that her generation was the silent majority. Not only her generation, but her gender and her class were also silenced. While my grandmother kept a stiff upper lip, my mother punctuated her silences with occasional bouts of screaming in the house and spouting off in public when the silence became too much to bear. I took my mother's rage and made it my own. Even as a child, I defied authority in any small way that I could—rumpling up the dresses that the school's dress code required me to wear, reading every book in the library (something my teachers frowned upon), and leading protest marches across the playground.

When our straight-laced fifth grade teacher would not allow the girls to wear pants and forbade even the wearing of shorts under our dresses—it wasn't ladylike—my girlfriends and I hung upside down on the parallel bars, our cotton underpants showing under our upturned dresses, until she quickly changed her mind. In another few years I would be going to feminist rallies with my mother—but when my friends and I were on the playground, the women's movement did not yet exist. It was 1969. The following year, having learned the power of showing our (almost) bare asses, we were wearing bell-bottoms. In junior high, I sported a button on my fringed shoulder bag that said BULLSHIT in large black letters, and in my first year of high school I got suspended for wearing a U.S. flag on the backside of my tattered blue jeans.

It was my mother who first instilled the idea of fairness in me—that all people should be treated equally. Long before my mother had ever taken me to my first women's rights march, I witnessed her heckling people from our front door. "No one's home. Go away," she'd yell from inside the house when she saw the Mormons approaching our front door. "Don't you know that's child abuse?" she declared the few times when she opened the door and saw them standing there with a child in pressed and starched clothes and looking miserable. When she slammed the door in their faces, they were already headed in the other direction.

Later, I witnessed her heckling the hecklers at a political rally at the local outdoor shopping mall festooned with red, white and blue crepe paper. It didn't matter that the political candidate my parents took me to hear was Spiro Agnew. (My mother stayed loyal to her mother's Republican views until after Nixon resigned when she was in her fifties, and I in my early teens.) What mattered was that she stood up for herself.

This was something my mother learned from her mother. My grandmother may have been an Episcopalian, a proper lady, and a lifelong Republican, but she was also a divorced woman in the 1920s who went out and stood in line after line during the Depression looking for a job until she found one. She managed to keep her children in a time when many other single mothers were forced to give theirs up. My grandmother was a survivor, something that depended on her stiff upper lip and her ability to toe the line. Unlike my mother, my grandmother did not come from the generation of the silent majority. The 1920s and 1930s were rife with social activism and chief among the ideas of the day were women's suffrage and the labor movement. And the merging of these two fronts created a voice for women workers, a voice that was not taken seriously until women got the vote in 1920, the year my mother was born.

It was fitting that I met Barbara at an Equal Rights Amendment march early in 1982—before the defeat of the proposed amendment to the US Constitution that was written by suffragist Alice Paul and in 1923 introduced to the Congress for the first time. We were marching through the streets of Center City Philadelphia and were chanting loudly, "What do we want, ERA and when do we want it, NOW!" Barbara and I were among the loudest in the crowd of women—many of us lesbians if not most—chanting in the street. In the early 80s, we still needed to fight for basic equality for women in order to live our lives freely—especially as lesbians. They were heady days, with rallies, conferences, and endless meetings held in homes, the YWCA and in universities. At one ERA strategy meeting held at the University of Pennsylvania, someone had posted a handwritten sign that said "Women's Room" over the "Ladies" sign. I had read *The Women's Room*, written by Marilyn French, a few years after it was published in 1977. The story took place in the 1950s and in academia, but I identified strongly with the characters. The lives of women in the working class landscape where I grew up in the 1970s were very similar to the 1950s in terms of the second class citizen treatment of women. In fact, a woman who could call herself Mrs. Someone—as my childhood best friend went on to do, several times—considered herself lucky. The book resonated with me so strongly that within a year of reading it, I had broken up with the boyfriend I was dating the four years that I was in college, plunged myself into the women's liberation movement and came out as a lesbian.

Barbara and I first talked to each other at the rally near Independence Hall in Philadelphia, after the ERA rally, and went out for a drink afterward. Later, when we were getting to know each other, one of our early dates included going to a NOW meeting on gender equality issues in car insurance. The meeting was yawningly dull—but I when I looked at Barbara, I was drawn in by her sparkling, deep-set blue eyes. Later, Barbara told me that she didn't understand a word that was said about gender parity and insurance and that the only reason she went was to be with me. The next time we got together was a walk-a-thon to raise money for the ERA. We walked from the Philadelphia Art Museum down West River Drive in Philadelphia and then back to the art museum on the other side of the river. Afterward we went out to dinner with some older lesbian friends. After dinner, Barbara and I took a walk, just the two of us, back to the river, with the city lights sparkling on the dark water. We had yet to become lovers, but that was the night

I fell for her. She wasn't my first woman lover, but she was the first woman I had fallen head over heels in love with. She was my forever.

Later, after we were a couple, Barbara and I were in Pittsburgh, visiting her family of origin, as she called them, and attending a wedding of one of her cousins. An older unmarried woman, a family friend, remarked to Barbara and me that the defeat of the Equal Rights was a shame.

"We're going to do what we want anyway," remarked Barbara.

Our mothers and grandmothers didn't have the freedoms that Barbara and I had, but these women were the bedrock that we sprang from. My dream of my grandmother was the American Dream—represented by the figures of Mother Jones and Norma Rae, where the victims are victors. They triumph over the disasters of their lives and deserve not compassion, but admiration. Under the surface of this dream is the fact that admission of weakness, of inevitable human vulnerability, is not tolerated. Hearing working-class people described as "the salt of the earth" always irritated me. People who have no recourse but manual labor are no different than other human beings. They are not pillars of sodium chloride. They may become strong from enduring, but they endure only because they have to. And when they can endure no longer, they are trained to blame themselves. When a friend told me that in the Ohio coal town where she grew up, some of the laid-off miners shot themselves because they were too proud to accept unemployment compensation, it sent chills up my spine. When I made the mistake of mentioning this to my mother, she had a physical reaction—as if someone had hit her.

Most of the people I know have never been pushed this far. But still, seeing the tight lines of compressed lips—old and young alike staring from the porches of urban row homes—I felt like I knew their stories. Those same compressed lips were in the photos of my grandmother and great-grandmother. Every now and then when I looked in the mirror, I saw the same expression on my own face. It was the same expression that my mother turned toward me—when, during our visit, she had tired of telling me about my grandmother's life.

I wondered if it was fair of me to continually ask about the past. So many people run from it, burying themselves in the American Dream, the accumulation of more, more, more. My mother, on the other hand, was clearing out, making trips to the Goodwill, preparing for the inevitable.

My mother looked at me. A feeling of shame passed through me—the guilt of having more freedom than my mother—but it passed.

Freedom was something my mother always wanted for me. I smiled at her and she smiled back.

She looked out the window. A cloud passed from in front of the sun.

"Before I got sick I went outside and your father was kneeling next to the driveway. Then he bent down to the ground and stuck his butt up in the air. I asked him what he was doing, and he said he saw a spot under the car. Then I got down on my knees and there we were—the two of us with our butts up in the air, bowing down to the car."

My mother and I laughed.

"See," she said, "the car and the almighty dollar—these are the things we worship."

CHAPTER 3

Somebody

"For chrissake, will you stop calling me 'Your Wife.' They know who I am, believe me. I'm Somebody in that office. I'm important—even if I have to die to get that way."

My mother's voice addressing my father was a cold razor. Somebody. My mother defined the concept according to the commentators on the news hour, "Viewpoint," that she watched on public television each week: "They are all women," she had said to me, "black women, white women, young and middle-aged, journalists, editors, TV personalities. They are all Somebody. They have position, title, influence." My mother's definition of the opposite of Somebody: *nobody, invisible, nonexistent, unimportant, herself.*

My mother had suddenly become everything to me.

The rest of my life suddenly dropped into the background.

My relationship with Barbara.

My work—as a freelance writer and editor.

Myself.

My mother who had become everything to me—in the few minutes that it took for her to tell me her diagnosis—was telling me that she had always thought, until now, that she was nobody.

My father's hand trembled as he held the phone to his ear.

She glared at him from the dining room table.

"You're still mine," he said when the receptionist at the doctor's office put him on hold.

"Your what? Your garbage can? Your car? I'm not an object. I'm not a thing called Your Wife."

"You're still mine," he repeated, his attempts at a smile swallowed by the graveness of his features.

A year, a month, a week ago this would have been a spirited banter between the two of them. No one was laughing now.

"I saw it on her face," my mother told me after my father had cleared the table, done the dishes, and gone out for his walk. "After the doctor helped me sit up on the examining table, she looked at me, and I could see it on her face. When she gave me the results of the first MRI, I told her I wasn't surprised. But I just said that. It was a way of protecting myself. Of course I was surprised. How could I have known?"

I told myself that I couldn't have known either.

But what about my mother's air of resignation? Her drawn look every time I suggested something? Had she known? Had I? Wasn't my dream about my own body being filled with tumors really about my mother? I came out of my mother's body. I was suspended between knowing and not knowing—between disbelief and belief.

I called the macrobiotic counselor with the urgency of saving my own life.

He told me that he was afraid of this.

I asked him for a guarantee that she would live.

I asked him to promise me a miracle.

It was close to a month since I helped my mother select her new doctor and two weeks after my mother's first visit with her. On her first visit the doctor had scheduled some tests. Afterward my mother called me. "The doctor looks like Barbara," she said. "She has a round face, deep-set eyes, and salt-and-pepper hair. I like her." When she told me this I relaxed. My mother had found a woman doctor that she could trust. The doctor reminded her of Barbara, someone she loved. Surely this doctor would help her. Then my mother told me that the doctor had found a mass in her abdomen. I heard the dread in my mother's voice, but I didn't allow it to register. I didn't even think about what it meant. My mother had always been healthier than me. And the fact that she was my mother meant that she couldn't die.

I would come to think of that week between my mother's tests and her diagnosis as my last small stretch of innocence.

Barbara and I took a trip to the beach one day, walking along an endless expanse of nature preserve shoreline, delighting in the long-legged terns and scuttling sand crabs. Later in the afternoon, when we had walked as far as we could, we put up an umbrella on a deserted stretch of beach. As I sat in my chair, turning the pages of a book in my lap, an unwritten dread loomed from between the lines. But with the gulls careening in the blue sky, the crash of the waves, and the warm sand curling around my toes, I managed to push the terror away.

I told myself that my mother would be okay.

I told myself that she would get better.

When the doctor got the results of the MRI, she told my mother she had fourth-stage cancer. When my mother called and told me she had something to tell me, I insisted that she tell me on the phone instead of in person like she wanted to. I had been out with some friends earlier in the evening, and it was late when I called her back. I hung up the phone in slow motion. Everything was red. My face felt like it was pressed in a vise that someone was slowly tightening.

"I'm not ready to lose my mother." My voice wavered between a wail and a scream.

Barbara came downstairs and somehow got the story out of me. She tried to console me but I was inconsolable.

I cried so much through the night that when I woke in the morning my face felt like it was stuffed with cotton. I put an ice pack on my face and Barbara and I drove to my parents' house. My father greeted me at the door with a shaky firmness in his hug that I had never felt before. Everything had changed.

"Your father sat there and cried," my mother told me later. "I was so touched. I know he cares for me, but it was a shock to see him cry. The first thing I said to the doctor was that I would have to tell my daughter."

Barbara had already planned a visit to her own aging parents who lived across the state. Since it was hard for her to get time off from work and since she was always worried about her mother living with her emotionally abusive father, she decided that she would still go. After she left, I settled in for a long weekend with my parents. First on our agenda was a visit to my mother's new doctor. In her office, I felt like I was swimming underwater through the wavy sea-green wallpaper of the small waiting room into the even smaller examining room. Around me, the pale yellow walls were shafts of light filtering down to the depths. The waters parted momentarily when the doctor entered the room: her eyes were compassionate, reflective of our fear and grief.

She was a little older and rounder than Barbara. But I could see how my mother thought she resembled her. Her curly salt-and-pepper hair fell to her shoulders, the way Barbara's did, in a loose perm. Her eyes were deep-set like Barbara's (her mother was Italian American) and reflected a well of compassion. Surely she had some hopeful news, a weighted rope ladder she could toss down for us to grasp. I sat on one side of my mother, my father on the other, our backs to the yellow wall. Shafts of light illuminated the doctor's words.

"I wish you had been my patient sooner." She looked gravely at my mother. "Before things got this far."

Light bounced from the pale yellow walls onto the crisp, clean paper stretched across the examining table, back to the walls, reflecting off an anatomy poster, each muscle, organ and bone precisely outlined and colored accordingly: ruddy pink, purplish blue, bone white.

As the doctor talked, I gripped the metal arms of my chair. My white knuckles were the only thing between me and the sea that threatened to submerge me in an underwater canyon. The doctor's words—Cancer Fourth Stage Terminal Metasticized Oncologist—were pushing me under. Terminal. I tried in vain to hold back the tears that threatened to pour out from the ocean inside of me. Nothing had prepared me for this.

In the car on the way home, my mother shuddered each time we drove over a bump. As we drove over a smooth stretch of road, she turned to my father and said with a snicker: "Janet knows plenty of women. Maybe she can fix you up with one."

My father's hand trembled on the wheel as he stopped at the red light. He turned to her and gruffly said, "You're the only one for me."

The light changed. From the backseat of the car, I watched my parents as if they were in a movie. The final images of an almost fifty-year marriage: my mother's joke, my father's gruff response, his large, calloused hand placed over her smaller, weaker one. My mother turned her attention to me. I saw her face looking at my reflection through the rearview mirror.

"My mother's last words to me were, 'It's okay.'" Her eyes reddened as she repeated this several times, "It's okay. That's what she said, and I believed her." She shook her head, and said, "I was so stupid, I didn't even know she was going to die."

We pulled into the driveway of my parents' house. My father was careful to ease the car to a slow stop, but still my mother groaned from the motion. It was almost unbearable for her to be driven anywhere. I got out of the car first and opened my mother's door. She leaned on her cane, slowly, very slowly, pushing herself up. By the time she stood, the next-door neighbor, a woman my mother's age, had made her way across the lawn.

"I was just on my way home from the synagogue," she said. She stared intently at my mother and asked if there was any news.

"Not good," said my mother. "We just saw the doctor. Terminal." My mother gasped after she said this, as if saying the words aloud made them true.

The neighbor, who had known my mother for thirty-five years, was visibly shaken. She grasped my mother's hand and then turned to me. "You were a good daughter, Janet," she said. Then she caught herself and said, "You are a good daughter."

This woman saw me grow up. Was she right? Was I a good daughter? Would I continue to be my mother's daughter after she was gone?

For the first time in many years, I stayed overnight at my parents' house. My mother always wanted me to stay, but I found one excuse after another to restrict my visits to one day. Even before Barbara and I got together, my schedule was always busy. That and the fact that I lived an hour away seemed reason enough not to stay overnight. But now I wondered why I didn't when my mother had wanted me too. Was I afraid of being sucked back into the quicksand of my adolescence? Or, of reverting to my childhood? Was I afraid of losing control—or of suddenly not being my own person?

None of that mattered anymore.

Earlier, on the drive to my parents' house, Barbara had remarked that she heard a woman on a radio show say that taking care of her dying mother was the best gift she could ever have given her. Unable to hear the words "dying" and "mother" in one sentence, I broke into sobs.

"Maybe you should pull over," said Barbara. I usually drove to my parents' house, since I knew the way intimately.

"No," I said, stubbornly, still sobbing. "I have to get there as soon as I can."

"It's okay for you this weekend, but you can't go to your parents' house all the time."

"What?!" I looked at Barbara as if she were a stranger.

"Watch the road," she demanded.

"My mother is dying," I screamed.

Barbara looked straight ahead. She was probably fearing for our lives as we roared down the turnpike, with me behind the wheel screaming and sobbing. It was early on a Sunday morning and traffic was light. We were fine. But being on the road forced me to calm down. I took a deep breath. I stopped screaming. I stopped crying.

"My mother is dying," I said again, this time calmly, as if I were talking to myself. "Of course I will need to be with her more."

Barbara was quiet. But the obstinate look on her face dropped away.

We both sat staring straight ahead into a future that neither of us could imagine.

The only caregiving I had done at that point was tending to an old cat and reading poetry to the patients at an AIDS hospice, called Betak, that was in our neighborhood. A friend of ours, who was a harpist, had started a volunteer arts program for the patients. She played the harp, Barbara came and brought her drum sometimes, and I read poetry. These were poor people—mostly African American men—who were in the advanced stages of AIDS and close to death. The experience let me see how fast the disease could move.

One week in particular we were sitting in the activity room, and I was reading aloud from the *The LeRoi Jones / Amiri Baraka Reader* to a small circle of men gathered around me on a sofa and a few comfortable chairs. They were familiar with Amiri Baraka and especially loved his early work when he had written under his given name LeRoi Jones. I had the thick tome opened and was reading his line about doing splits at the Apollo Theater in Harlem. Barbara and I had become friendly with one of the patients named Bill, a black gay man who had been a jazz dancer before he became ill. He had lived in one of the old high-rises in Center City Philadelphia and was a neighbor of Nina Simone. Bill was equally impressed that I had met Amiri Baraka a year before at the Naropa Institute in Boulder, Colorado, where I had spent part of the summer with our friends Maggie and Jean, an artist/waitress and nurse/photographer who lived in the foothills of the Rockies for a few years. The five weeks that I spent attending the writing program was the longest time Barbara and I had spent away from each other. This was before cell phones, so we kept in touch with letters and occasional landline calls. Two weeks later, Bill, whose dancer's body had wasted away to skin and bones, was confined to his room, turning away from us on his side, his head toward the wall, nodding to let my friend know that he liked the gentle harp music she was playing. It was too painful for me to witness the deterioration of the patients, watching them go from having some semblance of normal lives to being living skeletons.

I left the hospice program after several months, not knowing that the experience had prepared me to care for my mother who would ultimately be in the same state six months later. I was always squeamish. When I was a child and my mother told me stories about her training to be a practical nurse—emptying bedpans, giving patients their sponge baths—I had squirmed in my seat.

After we came home from the doctor's office, I retired to my old room for a rest. I rubbed the tears from my eyes as I tossed and turned, my ankles hanging over the end of my old bed, the mattress so narrow I had to be cautious when I rolled over. I looked across the room at my old bureau and desk: tiny pink flowers painted around the shiny white knobs. Through my preteen years the walls had been hung with *Tiger Beat* centerfolds, Davy Jones, The Partridge Family, these replaced in my teen years with spike-haired lightning-bolt David Bowie and black-eyed Alice Cooper *Welcome to My Nightmare* posters, along with the silk-screens I made in high school, Robin Trower, my oversize marijuana leaf, the Statue of Liberty sinking in a sea of bubbling pollution, in place of the torch her outstretched middle finger making its final statement.

The posters had gradually come down in my college years. The walls became checkered with blank spots, and when I moved out, the thumbtack holes and tape marks were covered with a fresh coat of primer and an outer coat of ivory paint. My mother moved her things upstairs into my old room: her bookshelves, sewing table, a few framed prints on the wall, one with three horned owls sitting on a log. "That's us," my mother would say, before the stairs got too hard for her to climb and she left her prints and books upstairs and moved back downstairs into the smaller bedroom. "Those three owls sitting like bumps on a log. That's you, me and your father."

The next day we had an appointment to see the oncologist whose office complex was next to a shopping mall. As I sat in the backseat of my parents' car, I felt lost in long loops, off-and-on ramps that seemed to go nowhere. I was subsumed in a hard glittering sense of doom—deep in the center of a nightmare that would not let me wake.

My parents and I were across the parking lot from the shopping mall. The bituminous surface of the asphalt soaked up the September heat and spit it back. We were searching for the entrance to the oncologist's office—through a maze of brick and glass. Finally, we found a chrome door handle. I pushed but it didn't open. There was no sign pointing the way. We walked to the other side of the building. My mother's featherlight body leaned on her cane. My father and I were on either side of her. We placed our helpless hands under her elbows. "You're only making it worse," she said. "Let me walk by myself." She took one slow step after another past what seemed like miles of red brick and silver chrome. Finally, on the other side of the building, a glass door opened.

Inside, six receptionists sat in a black rectangle that was in the middle of other rectangles, separate waiting rooms that interconnected. One receptionist took my mother's name and insurance information and directed us to the waiting room on the far left side of the building. We passed a wall of fish tanks on the way. Large carp with ruffled fins hovered in blackness. A few swam to and fro in spacious confinement—slow-moving blobs of iridescent light. The waiting room was full of silent people. We found three seats together. With my father's help, my mother eased herself into the center chair. We sat down beside her, our backs resting uneasily against black vinyl.

A wide glass and chrome coffee table held glossy magazines about health and wellness, positive living and positive dying. I picked one up and fanned through its oversize glossy pages. I let one page fall open on my lap, then another. A large quote divided the page between columns of text: "Death is the final destination. We are, all of us, each day, moving one step closer..." My vision blurred. The columns of text turned into rivers. I sensed the silence around me, the absence of any outwardly expressed emotions, no grief, no rage, no stifled sobs. I willed the tears back.

"Look." My mother turned her head to me, then to my father.

The magazine on her lap was opened to a glossy photo spread of people on a beach standing in a circle. They were wearing colorful but muted winter clothes, one with a maroon and white striped scarf, another with the side flaps of a dusty pink South American knitted cap pulled down over her ears. Inside the circle they formed with outstretched arms and clasped hands, lay a loose garland of flowers. Hibiscus, dark, vibrant, tropical, a sacrifice dropped at their feet. Their faces, unguarded in their vulnerability, were as familiar to me as their clasped hands, reminding me of a tai chi class I once took, a Wiccan circle where I joined the others in calling the directions, North, South, East, West, echoing the circles of my childhood: "Ring Around the Rosy a pocket full of posies, ashes, ashes, we all fall down."

Another photograph was the side view of a woman sitting in the prow of a small motorboat, the blustery sky as gray and foamy as the waves that slapped the sides of her small vessel, her hair blown back, revealing a mottled profile that combined disbelief with tranquility. Her outstretched arms swept the vastness and her fingers, forever frozen in their uncurling, dropped a single rose into the choppy waters. The caption read: "This woman has surrendered her husband's ashes to the bay." On second glance, I saw tiny flecks of white dotting the waves, dust, grit, sand, and the shell-like fragments of what was once bone and flesh: a life.

My mother ran her outstretched index finger under the words at the bottom of the page: "It's important for the survivors to have a ritual, to come together and air their grief at the passing of their loved ones."

I looked back at the photos. There was something about the people, something tribal, at least unconventional, that made them look familiar to me. They were honoring death and grieving their losses openly, without apology. In doing so, they dropped the veils of the church, the pomp and circumstance, the empty prayers and palliatives. They did not cast their gaze down. Instead they opened their eyes and gazed up into the sun and, at the same time, looked into the pit of their own grief. They were alive even in the presence of death.

Even as I recognized this, I felt myself pulling away. The tears in my eyes suddenly dried to anger, my nerve endings retreating to a safe, hard place. There was only one thing I knew for sure about the mourners spread before me in the glossy pages:

They were not us.

We were surrounded by light. The walls of the rectangular examining room were covered with opaque white light panels that darkened as the oncologist clipped my mother's MRI films into place.

The top view, side view, frontal view, rear view. The insides of my mother's body were displayed like the cross section of a diaphanous tree. The oncologist, a large middle-aged man, stared hard at each panel and, with a solid black magic marker, circled the cloudy white spots, amorphous blobs and solid white masses, which he named as he moved around the room from panel to panel: all throughout the pancreas; at the bottom of the liver next to the gallbladder; the top of the kidneys near the adrenal glands; a five-inch tumor in the abdomen; the long white ridge in her sternum deflecting into her ribs, the left pelvis where the bone had eroded. My mother's face was as white as the disposable gown the oncologist had her change into in the adjacent dressing room. He'd asked if she'd like my father and I to stay. She nodded, and he helped her onto the examining table.

"It's definitely not breast cancer or colon cancer," he said, when he finished examining her, pulling the rubber gloves off his hands.

When she was dressed, we filed across the hallway to the oncologist's office. The comfortable leather chairs might have been beds of nails. The oncologist sat behind his mahogany desk, the walls behind him lined with gold-framed diplomas. The afternoon sunlight filtered through the window and flashed in his diamond pinkie ring as he lifted his hands and folded them under his chin. Deep lines were etched into his face. His cheeks were jowly, his chin square, his forehead furrowed. He had the build of a man who watched what he ate, who exercised methodically, yet everything about him was massive: the cigar-shaped fingers folded under his chin, his elbows resting like tree limbs on his desk. His oversize coffee cup rested solidly on the desk that seemed hewn not from a single tree but a forest. Each word he spoke was ponderous.

"The next step," he said slowly, "is a biopsy of the tumor."

My mother stiffened. More tests, more pain, more climbing in and out of the MRI tube, overnight hospital stays, long needles poked into her frail body.

"Couldn't the biopsy disturb the tumor and cause the cancer to spread?" she asked.

He unfolded his hands, dropped them from under his chin and refolded them again. His square knuckles were stacked in a slightly crooked vertical line. "There are no guarantees. But even though your condition is inoperable, it could be managed, controlled. Unfortunately, we're not talking about a cure. If the origin of the condition is ovarian, which I don't think it is, there's a fifteen percent success rate that it could be controlled for a certain period."

"How long?" The question blurted out of my mouth before I could stop it.

"With treatment, a year, at the most two years. Do nothing—" He picked up his hand, palm up and dropped it back down on his desk—"six months, maybe." His deep voice tapered off, a slab of rock sliding into a quarry.

I was immediately sorry that I asked how long my mother had left to live. I twisted and turned in my seat. My breath was alternately shallow and gusting through me in huge gales that were impossible to catch. The bottom started to slide out from under me. The bright glittering chrome glass walls of the office closed in on me as what I thought of as reality shattered. There was nothing real about this place. Nothing I could touch that would touch me back. My mother sat uncomfortably in her chair. She was small, vulnerable, and now broken, a death sentence hanging over her head.

The tears I had been collecting in the reservoir of my anger—shored up by the luster that the oncologist had surrounded himself with, the deep finish of the mahogany, his glittering diamond pinkie ring, the polished gold globe that was his paperweight, his world, his gleaming tie tack, his tailored suit, his buffed manicured fingernails—suddenly burst forth in an undeniable sob and streamed down my face.

He reached across his desk and handed me a box of tissues. "You're an only child?"

I blew into the deep pile tissue and nodded. I felt reduced to a three-year-old who had lost her mother in a supermarket. I was diminished not by his age but by his status, his sacrifice of everything for his narrow education, his profession that sliced people into categories and body parts without any thought of the whole. I wanted to hate him. But when I handed back the box of tissues and looked into the lines of his face, I saw a deep sadness, the result of too many patients who couldn't be saved.

"I have these two to think about," said my mother as she held my father's hand on the armrest between them. "They're not ready to let me go."

He regarded her with a ponderous silence. "It's very important," he finally said, "to make this decision for yourself. The treatment can be invasive, trying on your patience. If you do it for someone else, you're bound to have some resentment." My mother closed her eyes and nodded.

"I felt a lump in my abdomen ten years ago when I was in the hospital. I told the doctor but he wouldn't look at it."

A day after our visit to the oncologist, my mother and I sat in the backyard. The sky was an iridescent blue. The dogwood's last petals of the season had long since dropped to the ground, once white splashes against green, now invisible. The dogwood was a volunteer, its seed dropped by birds in the middle of what used to be my mother's organic garden marked now with only a few shaggy patches of oregano, rosemary, mint.

My mother was remembering the week she spent in the hospital ten years ago, after she had gone to a doctor complaining of fatigue. He had taken an X-ray, found a dark spot in the intestinal area, and put her in the hospital for a colonoscopy. It was the same year that Ronald Reagan had the procedure done. The dark spot was just a shadow and her fatigue was caused by a mild case of anemia, cured by vitamins. After she was discharged from the hospital, she went to the library, looked up the doctor and found long unexplained absences in the conduct of his medical practice. Then she ran into another patient of his who said she believed he was an alcoholic.

"I always say that the hospital is no place for sick people. If you're not sick already, you start to think you're sick. I was faint from all that sugar water they fed me all week. I had to fast for the colonoscopy and all I could eat was Jell-O. Jell-O! For a week! It's a wonder it didn't kill me. I took my walk, though, every day. I tried to time it so the nurses wouldn't see me because they told me it wasn't allowed. In the morning, when they were changing their shifts, or later in the afternoon when they were taking their coffee break. I'd walk from my room to the patient lounge and then sneak out the fire exit and walk up and down the stairwell. The stairs were made from a metal grate, so you could look down and see the bottom floor. Your father came with me sometimes and other times I went by myself. Up and down those stairs, ten times each way before I was finished."

My mother turned serious.

"I never saw the doctor, just his associates. He had every doctor in his practice stopping in to see me. And when I told one of them that I thought I had a lump in my abdomen he wouldn't even look at it. All he was interested in was my asshole. Assholes were in that year. Ronald Reagan's was on the front page of every paper."

A gust of wind swept the laughter from us.

"When I was in the hospital, I shared a room with a woman who was dying. She told me her life story. People do that when they're dying. The poor thing. I opened the window so she could breathe some fresh air. Her husband came to see her and sat there like a dummy and watched the football game. Her two daughters never showed up. Then I woke one morning and her bed was empty."

It was time for us to go inside so my mother could rest and I could start making lunch. She leaned forward on the seat of her chair and placed the cane solidly on the ground between her legs. Before pushing herself up, she looked over at the garden.

"Your father won't know what to do with them." She motioned toward the oregano patch, the stalks of mint, the shoots of the rosemary plant. "He might as well mow them down."

I stared silently at the oregano patch, contemplating my mother's comment. I thought about protesting. Both to the fact that my mother would die and that the herb patch would disappear. Some things would always be eternal in my mind: My mother. Her garden.

But the moment weighed too heavily on me and I could not say a word. I looked back at my mother and nodded. Another level of disbelief fell away.

My mother decided not to have the biopsy.

"But Mom, what if there's a chance?" I was talking to her on the telephone a week after our visit to the oncologist.

"I can't take anymore," she responded. "No more hospitals, no more tests. It's too painful."

I was silent, wanting to respect her wishes, at the same time needing to beg her to live.

Then I said, "But a doctor I know told me about a patient who had the same condition that you have. She had the treatment and surgery for a hip replacement. Two years later she's still alive."

Now, my mother was silent.

"What if I went ahead with the biopsy? What if they stick a needle into that tumor that's been there for God knows how long and the cancer spreads throughout my body? What if I die early? How would you feel then?"

I had no answers to her hypothetical questions. There were no answers, no magical patterns in the tea leaves that I was too defeated to even attempt to read.

"Good for her," said one friend, then another, when I told them of my mother's decision. Both had watched parents die drawn-out-painful deaths, two, three years, in and out of hospitals, the treatment so invasive, it was unclear whether it or the disease killed them. Several other friends told me that their mothers, also old women invisible to the medical establishment, were misdiagnosed and ended up in the hospital with fourth-stage cancer. Both had died almost immediately after going through with the biopsy.

My life had changed overnight. Even though I had known most of my friends for many years, I hadn't known their stories. Some had lost their parents before we met. Others were reticent to talk about their own experiences until they overlapped with mine. Suddenly, when anyone asked me how I was, even casual acquaintances, my own story came spilling out. Most people were sympathetic, but sometimes there was an awkward silence.

"I can't believe it," said a lesbian my own age. "My mother's so young and healthy. I can't imagine losing her."

I quickly did the math. If my mother had been twenty when I was born, instead of forty, my mother would be younger and most likely she would not be dying.

In several encounters, the chance question, "How are you?" was a conversation stopper.

The pain was etched into my face, my body. "How am I? My mother is dying. I am taking care of her. It is killing me."

The older women in my life—twenty, thirty years my senior—were the most helpful. Their mothers were the same age as mine. The ones who had already gone through the deaths of their mothers told me that it was hard at any age, that there were things they wish they could have done. Several insisted that under different circumstances they could have saved their mothers' lives.

My mother wanted to die at home. At her request, I got her a living will through a local senior group. She checked every box—no forced feeding, no life support, do not resuscitate—and had my father get it witnessed and notarized.

Barbara and I decided to get our legal documents done, too. We owned a house now and needed extra protection. It brought us closer together. We had been together for ten years. Neither of us was raised in a religious family—which may have been the reason that we didn't feel a need for a public commitment ceremony. Though, on one of our early vacations to Mt. Desert Island, Maine—where we had gone camping in Acadia National Park, the same part of Maine that I had camped in with my parents when I was a child—we sat together on a boulder at the edge of a bay and formally pledged our lifelong devotion to each other.

Neither of us saw the point in having a marriage-like ceremony that did not provide legal rights. It could have been that we were put off by the experiences of friends who had commitment ceremonies only to be deeply disappointed by their families of origin who "didn't approve" and refused to attend. Of our two sets of parents, mine were the ones who approved. Barbara was out to her mother but she feared her father might go into a rage about it and take it out on her mother. When I came out to my parents, my father told me he wanted me to be happy and that he loved me, but then he said not to tell anyone that I was a lesbian.

Barbara and I joked about having a commitment ceremony in my parents' backyard in Levittown. As a young lesbian feminist, I found the idea and history of marriage to be oppressive. When I came out, I was actually relieved that I would never have to marry or have children. I did, however, come to see the value in having the right to live as you choose, including the right to marry and have or adopt children. And even though we weren't legally recognized by law like heterosexual married couples, we had legal protection—papers we had copied from a lesbian and gay book of legal documents and that we had notarized at the nearby Weaver's Way Food Co-Op.

The next time I visited my parents Barbara came with me. While we were there, the HMO hospice program representatives came to talk to my mother. My mother was feeling weak and could not get out of bed. With the two nurses and my father and mother in the small room, there was no room for me and Barbara. We sat in the living room and silently eavesdropped. One of the nurses told my parents that when she found out her father was dying, she took him gambling at the casinos. This was what he liked to do best and it was his dying wish.

My mother refrained from commenting.

After some more small talk, my mother pointedly said, "I want to make sure my husband knows exactly what to do. If I slip into a coma he's likely to panic and have me taken to the hospital. And then I'll get stuck on life support."

My father was silent for a moment. Then he blurted out, "What else am I going to do?"

My mother. Right as usual.

The nurses explained the HMO's hospice plan procedures. A nurse would come in three times a week for several hours at a time to check my mother's vital signs and chart the progress of the illness. And a nurse's aide would come in on the alternate days.

When the nurses left, my father went outside to talk to them. I went into my mother's room, and plumped up the pillows behind her head. She smiled wanly, then closed her eyes, saying, "That really wore me out."

I asked her if she was satisfied with the answers they gave her and she nodded.

My mother had taken what control she could over her own destiny.

Like my older friends, I became convinced that I could save my mother. I talked to the macrobiotic counselor morning and night, reporting on my mother's progress, listening to his advice. I repeatedly asked him for assurances I knew he couldn't give me. All he could say was that refusing medical treatment was a difficult decision for her to make. Then he added that studies had proven that people with macrobiotic lifestyles live the same amount of time as people do who pursue traditional medical treatment, but with a higher quality of life. Holding my breath, I waited for him to say that she could be cured, like one of macrobiotic success stories I had read about in the books I was bringing home to my parents: *The Macrobiotic Miracle*; *To Live Again*; *Recovery from Cancer*.

"Perhaps," was all he would say. "Perhaps."

The counselor told me about some natural remedies, including buckwheat plaster for my mother's feet, which had been swelling from edema caused by water backing up when the kidneys weren't doing their job.

"This will never work," she said.

Then forty-five minutes later after we removed the oatmeal-like paste from her feet: "It worked. I can't believe it."

I grated the ginger, squeezed out the juice, and mixed it with sesame oil, then rubbed it onto her hips when they began to ache.

"It's better than aspirin," she said, astonished.

Other remedies I was not so sure of. Shiitake mushroom tea, to shrink tumors. I went to the health food store and bought several fresh shiitake mushrooms. Twelve dollars a pound—but the mushrooms were very light.

"Use dry mushrooms, not fresh," said the counselor when I talked to him. "Fresh too strong."

My mother was diligent about her diet: a scoop of brown rice, adzuki beans to help her kidneys, fresh greens, organic collards, mustard greens for calcium; miso soup and Wakame seaweed for special vitamins and minerals. With my mother I chewed my food twenty times, remembering the counselor's words: "Drink your food and eat your drink." Before our meals, we held hands, my mother, father, and I, and chanted, "Suuuuu." I suspected that my father was just mouthing the words, but he went along with it. It may sound crazy, at best "New Age," but the chanting before each meal was a soothing frequency, a kind of grace acknowledging that the food we were about to eat would form our bodies. My mother took a walk around the block almost every day, nothing compared to the four miles she used to walk, but it was still enough to get her outside into the fresh air.

"Isn't this day beautiful!" she exclaimed as we looped around the drive, next to the hill that led down to the creek which ran between the two sections of houses. The creek was hidden behind the treetops that we looked down on, magnificent in the green textures of leaves turning to yellow and red: maples, elms, ashes. Between the leaves, we could see the different patterns of the trunks, a smooth ash, a wrinkled beech. She stopped walking for a moment, hung onto my elbow, and with her good arm pointed her cane up to the translucent bell of blue sky. "I'm so glad I didn't kill myself months ago when I woke up with this thing and felt like dying. If I had, I never would have seen this beautiful day!"

My mother decided to try and stop taking her prescription painkillers, and instead take just the extra strength Tylenol, to allow her body to better heal itself. Some days were better than others. But she was still losing weight. And the pain was increasing. I started reading *The Tibetan Book of Living and Dying*, carefully outlining the Buddhist exercises in each chapter, and came across one called "Tonglen." With this exercise, I developed compassion by putting myself in my mother's place. I breathed in her pain and breathed out tranquility. I breathed in the trauma of her childhood, the frustrations that bound her. Breathing in, I felt her life filling me. Breathing out, I felt myself releasing my mother's pain and also the part it had played in my own life. In doing so, I released my grandmother's frustrations and my great-grandmother's also.

A friend lent me *Many Lives, Many Masters*, a book written by a medical doctor about past life experiences. I gave it to my mother. "It seemed so real. I could hardly believe it," she said, her eyes moist when she handed me back the book. "But everyone died a violent death in each lifetime. It doesn't seem worth it. Can't I sign up somewhere not to have to do this again?"

A day later when I mentioned the book again, she said, "The woman was always a servant. Didn't you notice that? In one lifetime she was a servant and in the next one she was a secretary. I'm not coming back unless I can be a college graduate." Her voice was perforated with lost opportunities.

I didn't bring up the book again.

Every afternoon when I was visiting, we put on a meditation tape and sang along with it. My mother sat in her gold velour rocking chair, me in the middle of the couch, next to her.

"I am whole. I am filled with light."

We sang the entire song a few times, breath moving through us in a circular motion. When I closed my eyes, light swirled up like colors dabbed on a palette, a chalky yellow, muted green, and at the bottom a deep tranquil blue.

"That's good," she said. "It takes the pressure off my sternum."

And we both breathed deeply to begin again.

CHAPTER 4

Everlastings

"I always wished that I could have done more for you," said my mother, leveling her gaze at me. Several weeks had passed since her diagnosis. I had been staying at my parents' house on the weekends and also visiting several afternoons during the week.

"What do you mean?"

"Other people's parents have connections, they know people. They help their children with their careers."

"But Mom…you helped me just by being who you are."

"That never got me very far. I just wish I could've helped you more, that's all." By now the hollows of her cheeks had become gaunt and the look she gave me was piercing.

Suddenly everything had changed—not only with my mother but in my relationship, too.

Barbara and I were trying to keep up some of our old social life and we had invited our friend Nakasha to our home to have dinner the previous evening. I had just sat down at our small wooden kitchen table, after I put down a casserole dish of vegan "macaroni and cheese" in front of us and a plate of steaming greens. Nakasha, who is blind, had just eaten some of the vegan "mac and cheese" and was commenting on how much she liked it. I had been holding my breath, since Nakasha was a picky eater. She had lived for many years in a home for the blind and was used to conventional food.

"What kind of cheese did you use?" she asked. "It's different than anything I ever had before."

"It's tahini cheese," I answered, winking at Barbara who smiled back at me. If we told Nakasha that the dish was made with tahini (ground up sesame seeds), a vegetarian staple commonly found in Middle Eastern cuisine, she undoubtedly wouldn't have eaten it.

"Mmmm...tahini cheese," said Nakasha.

Then, characteristic of her direct nature, Nakasha asked, "Janet, have you considered moving back to your parents' house to take care of your mother? That way you wouldn't have to travel back and forth so much."

Nakasha couldn't see the stricken look on Barbara's face, but I could.

"Yes," I answered. "I have thought about it."

Barbara, who had not sat down to eat yet, was standing next to the kitchen sink holding a blue glass dinner plate. It shattered against the kitchen floor.

"I'll get it," said Barbara tersely when I stood up to help her. I handed her a broom and sat back down.

My answer about moving in with my parents to take care of my mother must have come as a shock to Barbara since I hadn't told her what I was thinking.

"I did think about it," I said, continuing my answer to Nakasha's question, "but I decided it would be too much for me. There's my freelance business to consider. I can do some of the work at my parents' house, but I need to use my computer and would still have to go back and forth."

Then I looked at Barbara, bending over and sweeping up the shards of the shattered blue glass plate and felt suddenly guilty. I realized that my attention had shifted so much to my mother that I was putting Barbara last. We hadn't made love since before my mother was diagnosed. We didn't talk about it, but Barbara didn't complain. She seemed to understand.

"Besides, who's going to make Barbara dinner?" I was attempting to make a joke, but there was nothing funny about the tension between us.

Still, I barely gave the fraying rope of my relationship with my partner a further thought. I was in crisis mode with my mother. She had been given six months to live. Half of one precious month had already gone by, and I was frustrated by my mother's comment that she wished she could have done more for me. Why was it that my mother—the woman who gave birth to me, who made sacrifices in her own life to accommodate mine—could think that she didn't do enough for me? I was angry. Not at my mother, but at the world that made her feel inadequate. I was angry that she had gone through life being made to feel like she wasn't good enough.

For years I, too, felt I wasn't good enough. Even after I had achieved what was defined as "success," I walked around for a decade feeling like an impostor, as if the young woman whose photo appeared in the *Chicago Tribune* and whose byline materialized in national magazines coast to coast was someone else. Her accomplishments graced my résumé and portfolio, but the *real* me was struggling—lost in confusion, self-doubt and chronic feelings of inadequacy. Through all these years, my mother was my biggest fan.

Now, as we sat in the living room talking, I looked over at the breakfront against the wall near the front door—the gold framed photographs on the top shelf, my parents on their wedding day, my high school graduation photograph and under that, on a lower shelf, the journals and anthologies where my writing was published.

My mother took pride in my work, commenting on the other pieces as well as on my own, and seemed oblivious to the fact that the plumber or the next-door neighbor might come in the front door and see the purple cover of *"By Word Of Mouth: Lesbians Write the Erotic,"* the first anthology I published in. I had given my mother copies of the other anthologies that I had published in also, although at first I was hesitant. I was worried that she wouldn't approve of the sexual content, not because it was lesbian but because some references were explicit.

"I was afraid you might think it was dirty," I once said to my mother a few years earlier when we were in the city shopping at Giovanni's Room bookstore and I came across *Wanting Women: an Anthology of*

Erotic Lesbian Poetry—a collection that included my work.

My mother read the poem and, to my surprise, simply shrugged. "Who do you think taught you dirty?"

I laughed. When she was in grade school in a one-room schoolhouse in the country, my mother used the word "bitch" (she had one at home—a Great Dane misnamed "Hector" who had just given birth to a litter of puppies) and her teacher had told my grandmother that her daughter swore like a "drunken sailor." My mother had lived up to her teacher's description of her and was still one of the most creative swearers that I knew.

Standing next to the periodicals rack in the bookstore, the slim anthology still open in her hands, my mother read the poem one more time and said, matter-of-factly, "Well, your dirty is different than mine."

Of all the places I had seen my work, bookstores, libraries, I always felt proudest when I saw these publications on the shelf of my parents' breakfront. My place on my mother's shelf reminded me that my work was important.

In my twenties, first when I was working as a staff writer for a business magazine and then when I was freelancing, I would frequently give my mother copies of the magazine articles I wrote. "I don't believe it," she said about an article I had written about the health hazards of video display terminals that had been translated and published in a Russian journal. "All my life no one ever listened to me and your article is published in the Soviet Union!"

Each accomplishment was followed by another. I was blasé about all of them. I told myself that lots of people did what I was doing. Each success was a rung on an endless ladder. I thought I was proud of myself. But when I told my mother about my accomplishments, nervousness crept into the pit of my stomach. I might have felt guilty because I was living out my mother's ambitions. More than anything else, my mother had wanted an education. This wasn't possible for her—beyond going to secretarial school and then later finishing her high school degree in night school—so she did the only thing she could. She passed her dreams down to her daughter.

Perhaps I feared her resentment. I had succeeded in doing what she had not been able to. At the same time, I always felt that I needed to do more. No matter what I did, it was never good enough.

In my neighborhood, no one ever hurled the epithet "trash." But my friends and I learned early that our lives were disposable. No one I knew with the exception of my teachers—who were mostly content to let their working-class students slide into oblivion—had been to college. My friends and I had no road maps to follow other than the one that led to the military, the steel mill, the chemical plant, the assembly line, the fast-food counter. And the few union jobs that were left would be gone in the eighties and nineties when the steel mill closed and the other plants were cut back to skeleton crews.

As I sat with my mother in the living room—the minutes ticking into hours—the silence between us grew into stillness. I looked out the front window to the house across the street, painted a garish bright blue. My parents' house had ocher bricks on the exterior bottom front, under the windows, and white siding. But the construction of the house, its basic shape, was identical to the one across the street and the others around them. My parents had moved from Philadelphia to Levittown—with its sprawling miles of identical ranch style tract houses—in 1963. I was four years old. None of the houses or other buildings, the stores, schools, churches, were more than ten years older than me. Everything was built out of plywood, at best brick and chrome. No wonder we became atheists. Nonbelievers. Nothing existed except tract houses and the memory of cornfields.

Every Sunday until I was twelve, we went to visit my grandmother in her row home in North Philadelphia. When my mother was a teenager, the neighborhood was mostly inhabited by European immigrants. She would always tell me about her Polish and Jewish friends, and my favorite was the Swiss woman who covered her kitchen table with a paper-thin layer of dough every time she made strudel. Gradually, the European immigrants moved away or died, and they were replaced with poor black families who migrated from the South. "Grandpop," my mother's stepfather who died when I was eleven, was really just a shadowy, senile presence lurking in my grandmother's home. After his death, my mother wanted my grandmother to come live with us in Levittown. My grandmother steadfastly refused. She insisted on staying in her own home.

The race riots of the 1960s may have been raging around her, but she befriended her next-door neighbor. Mr. Harvey, a middle-aged, heavyset black man, who frequently looked in on my grandmother. The few long-time friends she had left, lived in the neighborhood—old women hunched over their shopping carts walking to and from the A&P. On Sundays, black mesh veils covered their heads in St. Simeon's Episcopal Church, a majestic stone building—with iron bars on the outside of its stained glass windows—that was the bedrock of my grandmother's existence.

My weekly visits to my grandmother's house were full of deviled eggs and bags of candy. High kitchen walls of white ceramic tiles with raised white ridges reeled around me as I threw back my head and spun around on the rotating kitchen stool. I remember my grandmother's open-throated laughter, her absolute delight in my company, the white lace tablecloths that she put on the table when we came, the hot baked rolls covered with a napkin in a basket. I could still see my grandmother, even though she had been gone for more than a quarter of a century, bending down in her garden, wearing her plaid house-dress, pulling some weeds near the back fence.

That tiny inner-city flower garden in her postage stamp backyard was my grandmother's oasis. The pale pink petals of the spider plant reflected the pink plaid of her faded housedress. And the tiny stars of everlastings grew toward my mother as if she held the sun in her hands. My mother took cuttings of these and planted them in her own garden where they grew and multiplied around the edges of the patio, and in a large flower pot that sat on the stump of the old apple tree in the backyard. When Barbara and I bought our house, one of the first things my mother did was to give us cuttings to plant in our garden.

Like the everlastings, my grandmother's dream for basic human dignity took seed in me and grew. During my turbulent adolescence, when I was attempting to erase myself in a blitz of drugs and alcohol before society did it for me with an assembly line of dead-end jobs, this dream was dormant, but nonetheless it was still there waiting for me to recognize it.

In my young life, retaining my dignity somehow got entwined with stepping over the line of my own existence. In rebelling against what my female socialization dictated I should be, I became a kind of hybrid between James Dean and Twiggy. I was a rebel with the cause of alternately destroying and saving my own life.

When I was sixteen, I attended modeling school. This was my mother's idea, entirely. She probably thought that learning poise and confidence would be good for me. I had recently sprouted up to nearly my full height of six foot two inches. I felt—and most likely looked— awkward in my gangly body. At the modeling school graduation, I teetered down the runway—looking more like a grown woman than a teenager in the low-cut dress my mother had sewn for me. I was unaccustomed to wearing high heels and was also slightly drunk.

That same year, I was a member of an unofficial girl gang that hung out at the roller skating rink. A year before, two women's roller derby teams came to my junior high for a special program. This was the first generation of roller derby women—decades before the "roller girls." The two ends of the rink, constructed for the occasion, were raised, providing a sloping and elevated runway for the women to pick up speed, swearing loudly at each other as they hurled each other into the padded guardrail. The other mothers were making tsk tsk noises and shaking their heads and my mother was squirming in her seat and looking nervous. She was the only person I had ever heard who swore almost as much. One woman smacked into the padded rail with her stomach and spun all the way around in a kind of somersault. It was the most exciting thing I had ever seen.

Less than a decade later, after I came out, I met the roller derby captain. She was the coach of Barbara's softball team. This woman was not out, but she was extremely butch, on the short side with a square muscular body, and had short hair that ended in a duck tail, and she was a smoker. Her partner—they had met in the hardware store where they both worked—not surprisingly was very femme. When Barbara's softball team played in the barrio, a group of Hispanic young men recognized the coach from her televised women's roller derby days in the seventies, about seven years earlier, and called her name from the sidelines. Barbara found out about the softball team through her ex-husband (the company that he worked for had a women's league) when they were still married and four years later, when she was separated from him, she came out. Her teammates were all lesbians, but since they worked with her ex-husband, they were surprised to see her at the now defunct Rainbows, a mixed gay and lesbian bar in Philadelphia with a backroom for the men. Her teammates, most of whom lived in South Philadelphia, a working class Italian American neighborhood, were a rough-and-tumble bunch. A few months after Barbara and I had got together after she had already met my parents, they came to watch one of her games. It was 1984, the year that the photographs of the fallen Miss America Vanessa Williams having "lesbian" sex were in the centerfold of *Penthouse*.

The team members were careful not to be out—they didn't want to "tarnish" the team's reputation or to get beat up. They didn't wear their team jackets into gay bars or hold hands in the street. But one of Barbara's teammates had brought the issue of *Penthouse* to the game and the women in the stands began passing it around a few feet away from the end of the bleachers where my parents sat. I was mortified, of course. But my parents, watching Barbara playing shortstop between centerfield and leftfield, seemed oblivious as they sat under the lights that illuminated the game in the South Philadelphia night.

When I was a teenager, I was too terrified (and self-medicated) to be in touch with my lesbian sexuality, but the roller derby women provided me with endless inspiration. At the roller rink, on Sundays, my girlfriends and I would lock hands on the skating floor, one of us speeding by and pulling the other one until she shot out in front. And just where the rink turned its sharpest curve, I squatted down on my skates and stuck out my right leg to trip the girls from the rival gang. On one occasion, this resulted in a fractured left arm, which swelled up and turned purple until I saw a doctor several days later. When the doctor told me that I had to wait six weeks until the cast came off until I went skating again, I burst into tears.

I went to Roll-A-Rama every Sunday and spent the entire afternoon. The shafts of light filtering down from high rectangular windows were filled with sunbeams kicked up from the dusty floor. The 1970s country rock music was gravelly with the sound of wheels turning round and round.

It didn't matter that the music—my favorite piece was "I Shot the Sheriff"—was mostly bad, or that the girls had to wait to be picked by the boys during couple's skate when the lights were turned down low and clammy hands connected. It didn't matter that our parents picked us up and dropped us off, or that we weren't yet too cool to stand in a circle and do the Hokie Pokey, putting one foot in and the other one out. It didn't matter even that the short balding men who worked there were the biggest geeks on earth. All that mattered was the rush of air turning into wind rushing past me as I sped around that dusty rink.

The faces changed between junior high and high school, but the girls I ran with were a wild bunch, as bad as I was and then some. We were searching for something, and then we were ourselves lost. In my junior and senior years I cut almost as many classes—hanging with my druggie friends in the girls' room—as I attended. My grades were abysmal, and college—which most students from my high school did not attend—seemed to be out of the picture. With the help of my high school guidance counselor, I decided that the army was my ticket out. My mother warned me that the military was no place for a woman.

"My friend Mary joined the WACs looking for an adventure," she told me. "They put her in a basement ironing uniforms and after a few months of that she stuck her head in an oven and killed herself."

"Oh Mom, that was ages ago. This is the seventies. Things are different."

"See for yourself."

The recruitment center was horrible. I felt like a slab of meat on a hook. I stood naked against a gun-metal gray wall in a large room full of shivering women waiting for our physicals. Afterward, the uniformed man who took my fingerprints joked that my black-inked hands wouldn't look pretty for my date that night. And at the end of a day that seemed to last for a week, the recruitment officer told me that the army occupations I had applied for, the positions of photographer or darkroom technician, were not available to me. "Why?" I asked the uniformed stocky black man who sat behind the desk. He breathed heavily and without looking at me said, "Neither position is open to females."

That was the summer I worked in the paper box factory. I was one of the workers who worked alongside the assembly line. We were called "line workers." The operators—one stood at the head of each of the assembly lines and sped up the pace as fast as they could—were men. The line workers were women. Some were young, but most were middle-aged. Many of them had what I later would come to identify as the "butch" lesbian look—they were rough around the edges, direct and had short hair. But, most likely, the majority of these women were straight. They looked older than their years—no doubt exhausted from their second and third jobs, going home to husbands and kids, cooking, cleaning. Most of them smoked. Their faces were prematurely wrinkled from the residue of cigarettes combined with lines of pure, unabated laughter. They traded wisecracks across the room, above the machinery's roar, without missing a single box as they kept pace with the operators.

One woman in particular took me under her wing. Estelle. Her hair was a bright orange flame. My first day on the job, the line down, I grabbed a broom and began sweeping the floor, mountains of pulpy cardboard dust in front of short stubby bristles. Estelle's cackle danced like lightning on an electric wire from across the room. "She's here for a day and she knows our tricks."

Estelle taught me the ropes. Warning me not to scoop the boxes too quickly from the line, she pointed out the operator's secret hand motions—as he pulled the gear into full throttle behind a high pile of cardboard flats—to the other operators and the foreman. With a jerk of her head, Estelle sent my glance in the direction of the foreman who gave a slight nod to another operator who then sent the boxes flipping even faster from the feeder onto the assembly line. The women bent and scooped as fast as they could, then a little faster.

There was something magical about Estelle. With her bright eyes and quick wit she could have been one of the good fairies in a tale about the wicked witch of industrial capitalism. Many of the other women shared her qualities. They were thick around the waist, their legs muscular enough to be called haunches, and yet their movements were nimble. Their fingers were short, stubby and arthritic, but they soared. As much as I liked these women, I was determined to be different. At the same time, I did little to change my destiny.

After my days at the factory, I hung out with my old high school friends and polished worn barstools with my dirty dungarees. My glass was bottomless, my dreams unquenchable. I carried a small spiral notebook with me and wrote down things that were most often unintelligible the next morning. One night, my friends took me to a neighborhood bar to see a male go-go dancer on "ladies' night." I was underage—as were most of us in the group that I came with—but they let us in without carding us. Since it was "ladies night" the drinks were discounted and most of the patrons were female. I stood in the back of the room with the throng of younger women—many of them most likely under the legal age for drinking (which in Pennsylvania was twenty-one) like I was—waiting for the music to start again so we could dance. During the first set, a woman had asked me to dance. I was unaccustomed to women I didn't know asking me to dance, but I quickly said yes, and joined the sweaty throng on the dance floor. Now, between sets, I stood in the back and peered over the crowd to the center of the room where a table of middle-aged women, who looked like regulars, sat next to the stage grasping dollar bills in their hands, gleefully anticipating the second set when "Sammy the Sunshine Boy" would reappear, maybe this time dressed as a cowboy or construction worker before stripping down to his G-string.

Since the idea of a male go-go dancer was a novelty at the time, in the late seventies, the idea came to me that I should interview Sammy and sell the article to the local newspaper, the *Bucks County Courier Times.* After some persistent phone calls from me to the editor and after I had gone back to Sam's show to take some black-and-white photographs, the article eventually ran under the headline, "Male Dancer Shows He Can Make a Living by Exhibiting His Body." In the first line of the article, I wrote, "You've come a long way baby." When it was published,

I took a copy of the article to the bar after work and cried in my beer. They were tears of joy, but also of desperation in an almost pathetic attempt at gaining a sense of self. The article was proof of my existence. I flashed it around the factory like a wad of bills.

Seeing my name in print gave me the idea that anything was possible.

When the bosses started insisting on mandatory overtime, two hours every day, no extra breaks, no overtime, just straight pay in the sweltering summer heat, I led the women line workers in a walkout. The operators refused to stop working and the paper boxes spilled onto the floor as we filed down four flights of stairs. The manager stood next to the time clock, arms folded across his chest, lips pursed, glaring. "No mandatory overtime. State law," I stated as we filed by. The manager nodded slowly. He may have been surprised to think that any laws applied to his workers except his own rules. It didn't occur to him that "his" workers had rights. But he backed up and let us pass. I turned around. Estelle was right behind me. Seeing her head held high, her smile flashing like a piece of flint in her chiseled face was worth every particle of cardboard dust I had inhaled on that job.

Pride is a difficult thing to swallow. It took several more factory jobs to finally wear me down to the point where I could admit that my mother was right. I took her advice and enrolled in the local community college where the SAT scores that I didn't have weren't required. My friends were doubtful. "You—a college girl? Let's see how long that lasts," my best friend's mother retorted. Her negative comment was a spur. I decided then and there that I would show her. When the end of my first semester rolled around, I was on the dean's list.

The Triangle Shirtwaist fire was little more than a footnote in my college history book. But the fact of it raged under my life and the factory floors I stood on were hot with fire. In my memory, the fire exits of the paper box factory I worked in were blocked. I did not know that this was accurate, but I did know that our visits to the bathroom were timed, and the workers were of less concern to the bosses than the machinery we worked on. I did not share my grandmother's experience of going to work in a factory when I was thirteen and having little else to look forward to in my life. But I did share her outrage at being treated as less than human.

I was forged by the conditions of my grandmother's life. Despite the opportunities afforded me—higher education, professional jobs, time for artistic pursuits—I have lived most of my life on assembly line time, driven by the clock.

When my mother became ill and I saw my father taking care of her I understood how his work patterns fueled him. One day when I was in the kitchen helping him make lunch, I put the spoon I had been using to stir vegetables on top of the stove. I wasn't thinking about what I was doing—getting the stove-top dirty, picking up germs that would go back in the food. But my father noticed in an instant. "Pick that spoon up and wash it off," he commanded. "I'm the guy who has to keep this stove clean." My father was devastated by my mother's diagnosis. On several occasions, when the two of us were alone together, he broke down into sobs. But for the most part he was able to cope by clinging tight to his old work habits.

When someone was with my mother and he could go out, his walks were punctual, precisely timed. My mother took his dedication—as well as his stubbornness—in stride, realizing that he was attempting to take charge of what none of us had any control of: the so-called "progress" of my mother's terminal illness. The HMO nurses who visited had wry smiles on their faces when they commented on what a good job my father was doing with the cooking and cleaning. But my mother was not the type of woman who would feel apologetic for the fact that her husband was at her beck and call. She accepted his dedication as a fact of her life.

Each time I visited, my mother continued to hold court. One afternoon she told me about her "carrot and the stick" approach to life. We had been talking about artists, how some of them work for decades before their work is appreciated. My mother told me that when she worked full time, the "carrot" was her paycheck. Knowing she would get it at the end of the week was the motivation that kept her working. This is how working people are taught to think—how they are tied to a system that cannot exist without them.

I knew this, because it was also how I had been educated. After graduating from community college, I attended Temple University. Because of its relative low tuition and convenient location, Temple was a magnet for students who were the first in their families to attend college.

Getting an education there was an entrée into the world of professional employment, a way out of the mind-numbing screech of the assembly line. So intent was I on the task at hand, I barely noticed that the studies requiring the greater expanse of mind and time—the classics, literature, history—were, for the most part, reserved for other students, namely more affluent ones who attended the Ivy League schools.

Education is shaped by our circumstances as much as we are shaped by our educations. My education may have been limited, but still it offered me the privilege of escape. And with this privilege, it was sometimes difficult to imagine myself in the shoes of my grandmother as a girl or the other factory workers of her time who did not have that privilege. Still, I know that the struggles of these workers made my life easier. Isaac Harris and Max Blanck, the owners of the Triangle Shirtwaist Factory, by way of restitution offered to pay one week's wages to the families of the one hundred forty-six workers, most of them teenage girls and young women, who had been killed. More than a few of the families, out of a fierce and determined pride, refused this offer.

Still, the workers did not die in vain. Prior to the 1911 fire there were no regulations for starting a factory. In 1928, a State Commission of Safety was formed in New York, and FDR's New Deal was around the corner of the next decade. But for the masses of workers, my grandmother as a girl, the mostly non-English speaking immigrants who filed into the Triangle Shirtwaist Company's newly opened firetrap, the gains were nothing but a glimmer. They accepted the conditions that they were given and set their shoulders against the mortal wheel.

When I asked my mother what my grandmother was like as a girl, she told me mostly happy stories. When people are told they can't have much, they adjust their expectations. My grandmother always said, "It's not what you have, it's what you do with it." My grandmother made the most of what she had—from when she was a girl. Her religion was handed down to her from her mother, and my grandmother took it a step further.

"Your great-grandmother was Methodist Episcopal," my mother told me as we sat in the living room. A few hours had gone by and the late afternoon sun slanted across the room, illuminating the golden highlights in the brown carpet.

"When your grandmother was a girl she became friends with a group of shop girls and decided to join their church which was high Episcopalian. It was her way of moving up in the world, and of getting away from her mother and her brother."

My mother paused for a moment and added, "The high Episcopalians are as bad as the Catholics with all their ritual and rigmarole. Burning incense and chanting in Latin, the men prancing around in their robes. It's a regular party."

Since my grandmother was not a shop girl, she may have lied to better fit in with her new group of friends. I could imagine her telling them what she would have called a little white lie—"Yes, I work at the candy factory, but in the office as a clerk, of course." I could see her as a young woman, her hair brushed a thousand times until its shiny chestnut brown held no trace of the caramel dust that coated it during the week. The white gloves she wore would have covered the cracked red hands of a factory girl.

There was shame in this, the shame of being something other than what she pretended to be. But there was also hope. My grandmother must have thought her life could be different. She could get away from her mother who was forever favoring her brother, the "little man." If she could do this she might be able to escape the candy factory, too. Her future might have something wonderful in store for her.

Hope became a prayer.

Sitting on the sofa across from my mother in her chair in the living room, I stared down into the cup warming my hands.

"Don't read too much into that."

"Into what?"

"Remember I told you your grandmother told me her mother used to read her tea leaves? My mother wanted to read mine, but I refused to let her. Nothing her mother ever told her came true. It's just like anything else, people tell you what you want to hear."

When I stared down into my cup, all I could see was the reflection of my own face, but in my imagination I saw my grandmother, Ethel, as a girl of sixteen. I wondered how she felt when her mother told her fortune. She might have been mesmerized or frightened, maybe both. She might have had goosebumps on her arms as her mother poured the boiling water onto the loose leaves.

Her mother would have told her to think hard about her destiny and then turned the cup three times from the left to the right. Like other teenage girls of her time, my grandmother was probably thinking about her only chance of escape, a handsome man in a dazzling white uniform—her prince or sailor—who was coming to take her away. When she was done drinking her tea, her mother would have tilted the cup over the saucer, letting the liquid drain. She would have stared into the cup for what seemed like an eternity and then tilted the cup toward her daughter.

There were the signs of good fortune—heart shaped clumps, a ring. Perhaps there would have been symbols of birds and flowers. My great-grandmother would have wished that my grandmother could have the happiness that she had wanted for her own life. She would have read in her daughter's tea leaves a husband who didn't die young, two children who made her life complete, happiness ever after. Finally, she would have taught my grandmother to read her own tea leaves. If either of them saw the bad omens, the clouds and crosses, they would have ignored them.

I looked into my own cup, and thought about my mother's diagnosis. If the tea leaves were loosed from their bag, no doubt they would be full of bad omens. The only thing I could be sure of as I stared into my own reflection was that my mother's life—and her mother's before her—was converged with mine in a timeless arc.

The silence that surrounded my mother and me was crystalline.

Eventually, one of us would break it.

This time it was my mother.

"I don't know why you bother to come see me. All you do is stare into that damn cup."

CHAPTER 5

The Big White Wolf

"You won the jackpot," my mother would always say, accusingly, to her younger sister.

"What do you mean by that?" my aunt would retort. At seventy, she parted her pale blonde hair into pigtails and was still wearing jeans, not Kmart jeans like my mother, but designer jeans from Macy's. Still the adored and adorable baby sister.

"You've always had everything."

"Like what?"

"Like *what*? Men and money. What else is there?"

"Every single one of the men was an alcoholic. They'd come into a room and zero in on me. Like flies on shit."

"So? You always had them. Husband after husband and probably lots of others, too."

"You're the one who always had the stable marriage."

"Big deal."

Barbara, who had come with me and my mother (before she was ill) on several of these visits to my aunt's house in South Jersey, near the seashore, said to me later in a hushed voice, "I could see your aunt and mother together in a book."

I nodded. The idea had already been planted. My aunt and mother were the characters in a book that was the story of my life.

My mother and my aunt, who lived two hours away, were enough alike and different to be opposite sides of the same coin. As adults they saw each other only several times a year, and marked each other's birthdays by sending greeting cards with sarcastic messages about getting older. When the two of them talked about this, my mother snickered and my aunt would say, "At least we stayed in touch all these years. Our mother didn't even speak to her brother."

A week after my last visit to see my mother—when she told me that she "wished she could have done more for me"—we were sitting outside in the sun talking when my mother turned to me and said, "I'll have to call my sister and tell her." That fast the phone rang. I ran inside and picked up the telephone to hear my aunt's voice. When my mother got off the phone she said I must have called my aunt and told her to call. It had been at least six months since we had seen my aunt, and I hadn't been in touch with her since. "I guess she really is psychic," I offered.

My mother didn't dignify my comment with a response. But the next day when my aunt arrived at the front door, my mother had tears in her eyes.

The three of us sat in the living room. My father was there when my aunt first came in, but as usual when surrounded by family where he was outnumbered by the women, he made himself scarce. Suddenly there were chores to be done in the backyard.

"My God Jane, you really have lost weight," my aunt said as she came in and hugged my mother. They both had tears in their eyes. My mother, using her cane, sat down slowly, grimacing as she eased herself into her chair. After I said hello to my aunt an awkward silence fell between the three of us.

My aunt had brought some vegetarian sushi with her, and I went out to the kitchen to put it on a plate and to pour us some tea. In the background I heard the two of them talking, my aunt mentioning that she drove through Philadelphia on I-95, which cut through the industrial neighborhoods where the two of them grew up.

"I passed Allegheny Avenue, Roosevelt Boulevard, and the old cookie factory. Remember how good that always smelled?   I couldn't hold back the tears."

I made several trips back and forth to the kitchen—bringing out the plate of sliced sushi, followed by three cups of tea. By the time I settled back down on the sofa, the two of them had fast-forwarded from discussing the landmarks of their childhood into their favorite activity— arguing with each other. After they were done accusing each other of having had the better life—when the fact was they were both more suited for the lives they had, my mother in a long-term relationship with my father, and my aunt with the glamorous veneer of exchanging husbands—they each took a piece of sushi and chewed silently.

My aunt looked at the books lined up on the eye-level shelf of the breakfront—some anthologies that included my work, next to Barbara Walker's *Crone*, a book I gave to my mother several years ago. "I'm in a coven," said my aunt, after she wiped her mouth with a napkin. "My group meets at my house every Wednesday night. We light candles and follow the exercises in Starhawk's book."

I nodded, swallowing my last bite of vegetarian sushi wrapped in a sheet of Nori seaweed. It was my third piece. I was starting to acquire a taste for it, like I did years ago for straight-up scotch.

My mother's eye rolling was virtually audible: *A coven? For chrissake.*

"I've always been psychic, Jane."

"Yeah. I remember that mumbo-jumbo about the parking spot."

"I still do it and it still works. I hold my index finger and thumb together when I'm looking for a parking spot and say my mantra."

"I have a mantra, too. I learned it years ago in my Transcendental Meditation course at the mall."

"See Jane, you're psychic too."

"No I'm not. I tried to get a parking spot that way and it didn't work."

"You have to be patient."

"Patient smatient."

My mother and aunt were at a standoff. Round two. Instead of a buzzer, there was a long silence as tautly drawn as the skin above their lips. My mother turned to me, smiled, then turned to my aunt. "I am really lucky," she said, "to have such a devoted daughter." She reached over and pressed her hand down on my wrist.

Touch in my family was always tentative. The first time I

remembered hearing either of my parents tell me they loved me was when I was twenty-three and I had just come out to them. Reluctant at first, ultimately they were both accepting of me being a lesbian. However, it took this event—which potentially risked our family relationship—for us to be open about our feelings.I had long suspected that this absence of touch went back generations in my family. My aunt once told me that her mother rarely touched her or my mother. "How could she know how to be warm to us when she never learned from her own mother?" My mother's touch on my wrist was firm enough to feel like it left an imprint. It was as if she were trying to make up for three generations with that one touch.

Barbara's family, on the other hand, was—the opposite. The first time I had met her first-generation Italian American mother, I extended a hand at the end of our weekend long visit. I felt a gentle shove from behind and got the message that Barbara wanted me to hug her mother. I bent down to hug her tiny mother goodbye. Her name was Carmella, and she was the woman Barbara had come from – the origin of Barbara's own creation story.

We were both close to our mothers but they were pretty much polar opposites except that they were both gardeners and in our childhoods they both took on the very realistic personas of a witch. Between the time I was six and ten my mother would sneak up on me in the living room, put her index fingers together in a triangle over her head and start to cackle. "Ha, ha—I'm a witch! I'm a witch!" Barbara had a variation of the same story from her own childhood. She had three siblings. She and her sister shared a small bedroom and when their mother was saying good night to them, she would tent her index fingers over her head, and say, "I'm a witch, I'm a witch, a son of a bitch." It seemed that our mothers were in touch with something ancient passed down to them and their daughters in fairy tales and goblin stories that they used to terrify us into recognizing their power.

My aunt's visit marked three months since my mother's diagnosis. At times, I was despondent. Other times, I was in deep denial. She *could* still get better. Sometimes I was angry. Not only was I pissed at the doctor who had misdiagnosed my mother, but I was also angry at the woman internist, who my mother liked, and also at the oncologist, despite the fact that he had been honest with my mother. They were all part of the medical establishment that staked its claim on my mother's life.

My ear was tuned to success stories—people with cancer who outlived their doctor's prognosis. I figured that if anyone could extend her life through sheer will-power, it would be my mother. I told myself that there was a chance she would continue to live past the six months allotted to her.

Now, as my mother retrieved her hand, the firmness of her touch stayed with me. I was the devoted daughter. I went to the kitchen and brought out the ceramic teapot to infuse warmth into our cups.

My aunt's current husband had stayed home, but as I walked through the dining room—a small room between the kitchen and the living room—I was remembering a different time. Of my aunt's string of husbands, she had been married to Frank for the longest time, for more than twenty years, and he was the one I thought of as my uncle. I remembered when I was a preteen, twelve or thirteen, and my aunt had just given me my first tube of lipstick, a pale rosebud pink. I liked the smoothness of the cool lipstick when I ran it over my lips, but when I was finished I felt like I had wax lips clamped over my own.

"You should leave that stuff alone," said Frank. He was sitting at the dining room table, straining the chair with his girth.

"What do you mean?" I had been transfixed by the lipstick, at the thought of taking my first giant step into puberty, but for some reason—perhaps because of his authoritative voice that issued forth in a low growl—I stopped to listen.

"When women fall off a boat," he told me, "you can't tell one from another when you drag them back in because their makeup has washed off."

Despite the fact that my uncle had children from a previous marriage, he was more accustomed to throwing back some cold ones with his buddies than offering paternal advice. In retrospect, I think he may have meant that all women basically looked alike to him. But then, when it mattered, I took his comment to mean that my own face was preferable to anything I could put over it. It was a few more years before my mother started allowing me to wear makeup and a few more to when I was instructed in modeling school to tastefully pile it on— but eventually, even before I came out, I came to see the wisdom of his advice.

Frank owned a clam house and my aunt, after they started dating, kept the books. He always said that if he had met her earlier he would've been a millionaire. My aunt's motto always was, "It's just as easy to marry a rich man as a poor one." When I was fourteen, I went to stay with my aunt for several weeks at her home near the Jersey shore. Her son, my cousin, was already grown up and had moved away from home. I was the apple of my aunt's eye, and the two of us went shopping at the finest stores where she bought me a denim swirl skirt, a multicolored patched cotton midriff and a slim leather belt. When she turned me toward the mirror, my tall gangly body had magically been transformed into a fashion model's dream. I was all wide shoulders and slim hips. At the beach, I went into a boardwalk five-and-dime store and bought myself a rhinestone necklace that read *sexy bitch*. I caught the eye of the head lifeguard, the adult beach bum son of the town mayor, a fact that my aunt bragged about when she took me with her to the beauty salon. In passing her aspirations along to me—that of attracting a wealthy male—my aunt may have been transferring her dreams to me as a substitute daughter.

But I could see things for what they were. A rich man might be as good as a poor one, but he could also be as bad. I knew that not all men fell into this category, but by my early twenties I discovered my affections and attractions taking me in an entirely different direction. My aunt's motto still echoed in my mind, but I had reached my own conclusion: why bother with either a rich man or a poor one?

Since my aunt had lived her life with such a heterosexual credo, I had been a little worried about coming out to her. I had already come out to my parents several years earlier. I knew my mother would respect my privacy and that it was up to me to come out to my aunt myself. I had been reading Anne Cameron's collection of native myths, *Daughters of Copper Woman*, and decided to pass the book along to my aunt. "I think you would like 'Song of Bear,' I told her when I gave her the book. The story was about a girl who falls in love with a bear only to find out that the bear was female. "I did love the 'Song of Bear,'" my aunt told me the next time we talked. "I passed the book along to my friend June. I had to think of who I could pass the book along to. Not everyone can appreciate that story." That was the way Anne Cameron's underground classic found its readers, and it was also the way I was able to come out to my aunt. My aunt, who had already met Barbara, came to love her as a member of the family.

"I used to belong to a group that was kind of like a coven," I said, sitting down midway between my aunt, at the other end of the sofa, and my mother who was seated in her chair. "We called it a shaman group. It was mostly women but there were a few men, too. All of us were artists of one type or another. We burnt sage, saluted the geographical directions and danced around my friend's loft, pretending we were animals."

My aunt nodded. "I have a power animal, too."

My mother shifted uncomfortably in her chair.

"Our group fizzled out after a few months. Half the time people never remembered when we were meeting." I punctuated the end of my sentence with a shrug, a half-hearted attempt to please both my aunt and my mother. The conflict rooted inside of myself: Yes, I am spiritual. No, I'm not a basket case.

My mother wasn't buying it. Her eye rolling escalated, back and forth, from her sister to her daughter, from her daughter to her sister. Two nuts, loose from the bowl. Power animals indeed. Hocus-pocus, priests and incense, lipstick on the Pope's ring.

"None of that for me." My mother's tone was absolute. "I sneezed in line at the health food store last week and some nut whips a crystal out of her pocket and starts waving it around my head. I told her to get that goddamned thing away from me."

My aunt had moved from the sofa to a sitting position on the floor where she inched her right foot into the lotus position she practiced each week in her yoga class. "Why are you afraid of the crystal? Some of them have healing properties."

"We got enough of that shit from Pop!"

"Pop? What does he have to do with anything?"

"I figure he would've stayed around if it wasn't for his Baptist preacher father. All that Mississippi backwater hell and damnation pushed him right out our front door."

"Baptist preacher? Pop's father was a Baptist preacher?" My aunt pulled her legs up in front of her, locking her arms around her knees. "Why didn't you ever tell me?"

My mother shrugged. "It never came up."

My aunt measured her words. "That may have had something to do with it, but he didn't leave on his own. Mama got sick of him drinking the store's profits and beating you with a strap and she pitched him out."

"You're crazy. He just up and left and never came back. What do you know, anyway? You were only three when he left. I was seven."

"That's what Mama told me years later. She said Pop came back once. And you went out into the hallway, stomped your feet and told him we didn't want him anymore."

"I don't remember that." My mother clenched her teacup.

"That's what Mama told me."

"You two always were a pair."

The glare between them receded into recognition. Their memories of their two separate childhoods were in constant collision.

For the moment, the fact of my mother's life ebbing away did not change anything. For as long as I could remember the two of them were arguing about the past. Listening to them, I was drawn into a deeper sense of myself, its genesis reaching far before I was born. At the same time I felt a lack in my own life. An only child, I had no one to argue with about my childhood. Decades after my mother was gone, I would have no siblings with whom to remember her. My mother and aunt were so entwined I could not imagine one of them without the other.

I had been visiting my mother so frequently that I didn't really notice the changes. But my aunt was right. My mother had always worn loose clothing, but now her cotton shirt and blue jeans hung on her. My mother was folded in on herself, seeming to inhabit less than half the space she had an instant ago. When I looked at her, I felt a strong, vital part of myself withering away. My aunt, too, seemed noticeably older, despite the fact that she was four years younger than my mother. Suddenly, I saw what my mother meant when she looked into my aunt's face and saw my grandmother.

My mother turned away from both of us and looked out the front window. "When we moved to the city, I used to look for Pop all the time. I knew he wore a brimmed hat and drove a black car. So every time I saw a man in a hat driving a black car, I'd chase him down the street yelling, 'Are you my father?'" My mother scrunched up her face, snickering behind her hand. "Of course, that was before I knew how someone got to be a father."

My aunt threw back her head and laughed, tin cans rattling. "You're kidding!"

"No, I'm not."

"You were always the brave one."

The two sisters beamed at each other through the distance of place and years. Then my mother shrugged. "I just wanted to know."

My aunt peered down into her teacup. "Remember that charcoal drawing you did of me when we were kids? That was the best drawing anyone ever did of me. And I bet you don't even have it anymore. I'll bet someone threw it out."

"It was probably the only picture anyone ever drew of you."

"Maybe so. But it was still the best. I'll never forget it."

As the two of them talked, I looked at the photograph on the divider and saw them as children. My aunt with flyaway blond hair, rag curled, pale wisps around her long pale face. Dark-framed glasses drifted down her nose and she wore high-top corrective shoes, her toes turned inward. She stared out of the photograph with eyes that wanted everything. One arm clutched the other, giving herself the hug she desperately needed.

My mother taller, infinitely more serious and self-possessed. A girl-boy in a dress: short hair, her eyes pieces of flint. Her skinny body hinged with clothes hanger elbows and knobby knees. One ankle sock drooped. Her body language, her hand on her hip as she glared into the camera, was defiant.

Despite their obvious difference in age and appearance, my mother always insisted that her little sister got away with murder. Forty, fifty, sixty years later, telling me the story when I was a child, an adolescent, an adult, my mother said, "She hit me over the head with a mop, not just the soft part, but with the stick that had a nail in it. And Mama didn't do a thing about it."

In the photo album I grew up looking at, my mother's father was a missing space. There was no dot of glue or ragged piece of photo backing where a picture fell off. His absence was more insidious. The photo album was only half full. Empty black pages mark the years that he might have spent with his family. His absence was so strong, I could feel his presence.

He was a tall thin man with a mustache. His hair was the same burnished red brown as my mother's. And the tattoo on his right forearm—ropes coiled around an anchor—rippled with muscles every time he swung one of his girls up in the air, drawing their names out in the long vowels of his Mississippi twang.

Their father's absence was the frayed rope in a constant tug of war between my mother and my aunt. "She makes it up as she goes along," my mother always said about my aunt's childhood memories. When my mother talked about her father, I saw anger coiling in the muscles of her neck and shoulders. The tension from my mother's childhood was stored in her bones, in the tight wire that pulled through her, in the stern hands that raised me. For years I couldn't walk by her without flinching, a body movement that was met with an upturned hand, as she threatened another stinging slap: "Stop it. Stop flinching. Just stop it." When I was growing up, parents still smacked their children as a matter of course. Children ate what was put in front of them, and lived in mortal fear of breaking things. As a child, I was often afraid of my mother. Decades later, I had more insight into her life, the injustices that shaped her lifelong torments and rages.

My mother was constantly probing her past, searching for an answer that would explain her father's departure. "Sometimes economics can explain a lot of things," she once said to me, out of the blue. "Not always. But people can get harsher when times are hard." Once when I was alone with my aunt, she told me her mother thought that if she had had a son, her husband would have stuck around.

"After she had me and saw it was a girl, she wanted to kill me," my aunt said to me once, several years before my mother was diagnosed, when we had met for lunch in the city. "There's a word for it now. After a woman has a child, she goes through a period when she loses sanity. I used to visit my mother on Glenwood Avenue after I was grown and had moved away. She told me after I was born my four-and-a-half-year-old sister would walk into the bedroom where I was sleeping and say she was going to put me out in the garbage. She wanted to please her mother, and she knew Mama didn't want me."

It had always been up to me to venture into this minefield alone. I defended my long-deceased grandmother to my aunt: "But she took care of you. She didn't give you up. Lots of women lost their children during the Depression." My attempts at mending the past were in vain, but that didn't stop me from trying. "Maybe your father wanted a boy, maybe that's why he left," I said to my mother several weeks after I had lunch with my aunt. I was careful not to mention my aunt or her allegations that my mother had wanted to put her out in the garbage. Still, my mother sniffed the air, and smelled a rat. "That's *her* version. That's what my sister says. But I was a tomboy. I climbed trees, beat up the boys, smoked cigarettes, slid down the roof. You couldn't have had a better boy."

The contradictions inherent in my mother's and aunt's stories shaped my life.

Now I sat in the living room, listening to their voices. The rhythm of their speech evoked conversations of decades past. "Remember how Mama hid the money from Pop?" my aunt asked my mother. This was a conversation I remembered from my childhood. "Remember? She hid the money in the potbelly stove to keep him from drinking it. Then Pop came in and lit the stove and burned up all the money. Mama must have gotten a lickin' for that." To my childhood ears, this story cast my grandmother as a rebellious child getting a "lickin'" for doing something bad. A "lickin" in my mind linked to a firm swat on the backside, at worst a stinging slap.

As a preadolescent, I laughed along with my mother and aunt, the story at once hilarious and awful: a grown man, my mother's father, striking a match and dropping it into the potbelly stove, burning up in seconds the cash that took months to earn in the country store that he ran with my grandmother. The "lickin'" my grandmother received was secondary. What caught my attention was the instant disappearance of the money, the curl of flames around a stack of bills, the smoke that wound its way through the stovepipe and wafted out the chimney into thin air. A few years later, this story and others began to sink in and the meaning changed. The "lickin'" was a beating. My grandmother was battered, her husband a batterer, a brute to his wife and daughters.

The other story I remembered best was the one about my mother's organdy dress that her aunt, her father's sister, made for her graduation from the eighth grade. Whenever my mother described it—its taffeta slip giving her curves she didn't have, its puffed sleeves falling in a perfect arc from her shoulders to her wrists—her face was radiant. It was her first new dress, made just for her. Most of her other clothes came from the church rummage, ill-fitting charitable hand-me-downs.

In my youth, when my mother described opening the box the dress came in, as she smelled the scent of jasmine wafting from the tissue paper, I always pictured my mother as a girl. Between the layers of tissue paper were warm breezes from the Gulf of Mexico blowing through Biloxi where her father was born and where his father, stepmother and two sisters still lived after he left. I pictured the dress falling over my mother's head and fitting her like a glass slipper on a slender foot. It didn't matter to my mother that her pale freckled face staring back to her from the mirror was still the face of a child. This was her first glimpse of herself as a woman.

"That dress was the most beautiful thing I ever saw," said my aunt as she sat cross-legged on the living room floor, leaning against the bottom of the sofa.

My mother shrugged and then winced from the pain. "I liked the foo foo in the tissue paper as much as the dress." She closed her eyes and took a deep breath. She did this now periodically, in an attempt to control the pain coursing through her body. But this time she was also inhaling the memory of jasmine.

"You never cared about what you wore. I was the one who loved pretty clothes." My aunt's words were an accusation. Her big sister got a beautiful dress and she got nothing.

"You always had nice clothes," countered my mother, who once told me that when she started working she gave her mother most of her paycheck for household expenses and her sister blew every cent she earned on clothes.

"That wasn't the same. That was after I was grown."

"Grown? You weren't grown. You were only sixteen."

"I was a married woman a year later."

My mother arched her right eyebrow. *She didn't tell her sister to get married.*

"It was harder for me. I was younger. It was hard on you, too, Jane. You never wanted to admit it, but you had the burden of taking care of me."

My mother rolled her eyes. "I never took care of you."

"You did too. I remember when we were at a camp. You wanted to go off and play with the other kids, but you were stuck taking care of your little sister."

"The kids were separated by age. I was with the older ones and you were with the younger ones. All I had to do was help you brush your teeth in the morning."

"I remember. You had to take care of me."

My mother's shrug was little more than a twitch of her shoulders.

My aunt stared past her sister, her eyes searching for something she still yearned for. "I remember that dress. It was the most beautiful thing I ever saw."

My mother turned her head and stared out the front window.

My aunt cradled her cup of tea in her hands, stared into it, then looked up at me. "I wanted to tell you about my power animal."

I nodded.

"I have a shiatsu masseuse who comes to my home and gives me treatments. One day when she was working on me, I got so relaxed I thought I was nodding off, then out of nowhere a large white wolf loomed up in front of my very eyes."

My mother rolled her eyes. Then she cocked her head like a bird, staring at her seventy-year-old little sister. My aunt's face was a long oblong, pale like the moon. Her blue eyes were faded, framed by wisps of whitish blond hair that had escaped from their pigtails.

"That's you," my mother said to my aunt. "That big white wolf is you."

CHAPTER 6

Violin Lessons

"Sympathy pains." My mother examined me, owl-like, with shrewd intensity.

Conscious of the iron grip I had on myself, I dropped my hand from my shoulder. It landed leaden on the cushion next to my right thigh. A tension wire pulled through me—loosening, tightening, as she spoke.

"I had them when my mother was dying in the hospital." Her eyes reddened with a sudden welling of moisture, a sponge being squeezed.

"But Mom, it's not like—"

"She had a pain in her chest; I had a pain in my chest."

"But, you're not—"

"She had a pain in her leg. I had a pain in my leg."

My words wavered with dread. I still could not accept the fact that my mother was terminally ill. A few days ago when I came to visit for the afternoon, I found her stretched out on the sofa with a red plaid blanket over her. She had just woken up from her nap, and looked up at me with startled curiosity. "I don't know why I have been given this extra time," she said. Then, taking my outstretched hand, she said, "I'm glad I have it to spend with you."

At times like this, when she waxed philosophical (perhaps bordering on the religious—who was giving her the extra time?), I could not deny that my mother was dying.

That afternoon, shortly after I arrived to find my father in the kitchen using the pressure cooker to make brown rice, my mother decided to eat in the living room. She said that sitting up to the table made her back hurt, but I suspected that she also had been feeling too weak to move around. My father and I sat at the dining room silently, except for an occasional failed effort on my part to make conversation. My mother was only about ten feet away in the living room, and even with my back to her we could have included her in a conversation. The fact of her absence, however, was too depressing. This was how it would be after she was gone. My father and me, an enormous silence between us.

After lunch, my father did the dishes and I sat with my mother in the living room. The afternoon light glinted off the shiny clear plastic cover of a library book resting next to the lamp on the end table. My mother's hand-held barbells, covered in purple plastic, sat on the floor at the base of the table. The barbells had been part of her daily routine, with her lying on a mat in the middle of the living room floor, lifting and twisting, crossing and turning, straining for the definition she admired in the fitness magazines she looked at in the supermarket—until everything changed.

As my mother shifted in her chair, trying to get comfortable, anguish flashed across her face. I felt a stabbing pain in my own left shoulder. Bright hot tears rose in my eyes. I looked away, unable to witness an agony so strong I felt it in my own body.

"I have a control room in my mind. I go into this room and find the dial to turn the level of my pain down." As my mother spoke, she entered another dimension. It was as if she really had entered this room that she pointed to, somewhere behind the furrowed brow of her forehead. She had learned to use visualization to lessen the pain that was taking over her body.

Still, there was something odd about this—my mother receding to an actual place that existed only in her mind.

The semi conversation my mother and I were having about sympathy pains—hers for her mother and mine for her—had taken on the proportions of a lead balloon.   I sat on the sofa staring out the front window, watching the afternoon sun turn to shadows. I felt my mother scrutinizing my face.

I knew that for the rest of my life I would never outgrow the fact that I came out of her body. I sometimes studied my mother's face, seeing no trace of myself and wondering who she was. I noticed that she did the same thing to me. I must be just as much of a mystery to her, I thought, the stranger she gave birth to.

Why did you want to play the harp?" she asked.

Starting in kindergarten and through the third grade, I had attended an Episcopal private school. The girls all wore blue and white jumpers, the boys suits and ties. We learned French, went to chapel in the morning, and in the afternoon at recess showed each other our bare asses in the bushes. When I was in first grade, my mother enrolled me in violin lessons with the school's music teacher.

"Remember when you took me to see the Suzuki violin players?"

My mother nodded. "They were on tour from Japan. I think your favorite part was when one of the kids fell off his chair playing the violin."

I laughed. The student falling off his chair was what I remembered most. "Yeah. He fell off his chair twice. The second time was when he turned to the kid next to him to show him how he fell off the chair, and then he did it all over again."

My mother and I were both laughing. "I'll bet the conductor was ready to kill him," she said.

I shrugged. "What did they expect? They might have been great violin players, but they were still kids."

After my mother had signed me up for lessons, she took me to the city to talk to an old man who was a well-known violin teacher. He showed me his collection of violins, had me sing the notes of the scale, and asked me what instrument I wanted to play. I looked into the smiling lines of his creased face and said, "The harp. I want to play the harp."

"Why did you want to play the harp and not the violin?" my mother asked me, thirty years later.

I was quiet for a moment. "I guess playing the violin wasn't really my idea," I said cautiously. "I liked the harp better." What I didn't say was that playing the violin was my mother's idea. It was her dream, not mine.

My mother was quiet.

I felt guilty for telling her the truth. Playing the violin may have been her idea, but it was something she wanted for me. The child-size violin she bought, and then sold a few years later, was expensive. But it was worth it to my mother. She wanted me to have a well-rounded education, to experience the things that poverty had denied her as a child. I may have cried my way through ear-shattering violin practice sessions, but those lessons instilled a deep appreciation of music in me. I love the violin concertos, in particular Mozart, Tchaikovsky, Vivaldi, and especially Mendelssohn. I learned the musical scale and to read and write music. A few years after the failed violin lessons I was playing Beethoven's Ninth Symphony by ear on the xylophone. In first grade, I developed romantic feelings for another violin student, a fifth grader, who was a more accomplished violinist and also a girl. Those early violin lessons gave me my first glimpse of myself as a girl who loved another girl, as a girl who would grow into a woman who loved other women.

It wasn't surprising that I fell in love with Barbara—Barbara who sang in the tub, whistled melodically and tapped her fingers incessantly until she finally started playing the drums a few years after we had gotten together. She'd performed a few times lately, with a spin-off group from the drum ensemble she had been in a few years ago, but I was too emotionally worn out to go with her.

I felt a pang of guilt as I thought about this. My life had been revolving around my mother, and I was too emotionally exhausted to be a better partner. Barbara seemed fine, however, spending time with her friends, doing her music.

As I sat quietly musing about my own life, I looked over to see a faraway look on my mother's wizened face. She too was thinking back and putting together the puzzle pieces of her life. She had always had a habit of doing this, of bringing up something in her childhood as if it had happened yesterday. But my mother was beginning to retreat into the past, a past that was preferable to her present.

"My mother always wanted me to work in an office," she told me. "She always said that no daughter of hers was going to work in the mill. So I did. But it wasn't enough for me. Then she'd ask me why I wasn't content. 'I'm not a cow, Ma,' I'd tell her. 'Cows are content, not people.'

She was right. Nothing was ever good enough for me. But she taught me that."

"Mama always said, 'Art doesn't put food on the table.'" My mother was talking softly and shaking her head as she repeated her mother's words that I heard so often over the years. My mother was never resentful when she told me this. Being an artist was not a realistic possibility for a poor girl whose mother worked in the mill. This fact was repeated to me about my own life in various ways throughout my childhood and adolescence—most memorably when I spent too much time on my silkscreens in high school and when I wanted to major in fine art photography in college.

"The only one who understood me was my father." My mother looked out the window far into the distance as she spoke.

One night when I was in my early twenties, not long after I moved away, the two of us were sitting in the living room watching a movie on the TV about a young woman whose father was dying. My mother broke down, gasping between sobs, "At least she knew her father died," she said. "I never knew what happened to my father. I don't know if he's dead or alive."

I had grown up listening to my mother tell me stories of her childhood, but this was the first time I had seen her shed a tear over her father. When I was a child, I rarely saw her cry at all. But it seemed I was always crying—my own tears and those my mother had never been able to shed. This infuriated her. My tears were too often met with a stinging slap. As the emotions from her past seeped into the present, my mother shifted in her chair, wincing from the pain of moving her hips, her shoulders. I could feel her tension at being trapped in her body. I was trapped too—in the helplessness of my inability to make things better.

My mother launched into another story. I had heard this one so often that I could see the land and country house of her childhood. When my grandparents were first married, they moved to Bucks County, an hour away from Philadelphia. My mother was born a year after they married. At the time, Bucks County was still a rural area. When I was growing up, the country road where she had lived wound up a hillside across from the newly built shopping mall and the four-lane highway. My mother used to drive me through her old neighborhood and point out the house. It was small, but in my mother's imagination and in the stories she passed on to me, it was larger than life. My mother and her little sister and their parents lived there for seven years until their father abandoned them, when they moved back to the city where their mother found work as a spinner in the textile mill.

The front room of the white painted wooden house was converted into a country store. Its shelves were lined with canned goods, bags of grain and glass jars full of candy that my mother and her sister were not allowed to touch. Once, when my mother was older, about seven, she managed to sneak some soda pop and cigarettes out of the store to share with her gang of friends.

Behind the store was the family room. Like the rest of the house it had an unfinished wooden floor with a braided rug in the middle of its sparse furnishings. "I used to sit in front of that rug for hours tracing its coiled pattern with my eyes," my mother told me. "After Peggy, the Airedale, had given birth to seven puppies, I took my stick of charcoal and drew a big picture of her on the living room wall. There she was, larger than life on the white wall, stretched out on her side with seven scrawny puppies suckling on her teats.

"I had just finished the drawing when my mother came in the room. She looked at it, and she was so angry her face was as white as the wall. I thought she was going to kill me. Instead she went and got my father. 'Look what she did,' my mother said to him, 'Speak to that child.' My father looked at my drawing for a long time and then he said to me, 'Jane, that's a very good drawing.'"

I went into the kitchen to make us both a cup of tea. My father had finished drying the dishes and gone out for his walk. He didn't go out unless someone was there to stay with my mother. The last time I visited, he told me he would not have been able to take care of my mother without me. He also said that if he wasn't able to get out for his walk when I was there, he might not be able to go on.

I poured the tea into my mother's teacup and into my own, considering the fact that when my mother told me her childhood stories I was remembering my own childhood as well.

"I always remember the story about putting the blue chalk in the chickens' water," I said to her after I settled back down on the sofa, and had put our cups on the coasters on the end table next to her chair.

"In the well," my mother said. "I put the blue chalk water in the well. I poisoned the entire water supply. I didn't mean to. I just wanted to make the chickens' water pretty. When I brought the water up it was blue as the sky. My mother was busy in the store. She was always dusting or waiting on the customers or taking care of the baby. And my father was off somewhere, probably in town drinking. I was happy to be on my own. The wildflowers kept me company—the Queen Anne's lace, the chicory root with the pale blue flowers that grew by the side of the road, and the mullen stalks that grew even taller than me by midsummer. The chickens were my friends—Chickadee and Blue, and their baby chicks. Those baby chicks were just little fluff balls the size of my fists. Every time I tried to pick them up, they ran away."

My mother turned to me, and I saw the face of a grief-stricken child staring out from her moist eyes. "The last thing I wanted to do was kill them. My father came back from town and found them dead right next to their water bowls with the blue water in them. Their tiny webbed feet were sticking up, and there was a blue stain around their beaks. They were only chicks, but he had counted on them growing up and laying eggs. He was planning to sell them. I never forgot the look in his eyes when he stood there with those tiny dead chicks in his enormous hands. I thought he was going to kill me."

I stared down into my cup, turning it between my palms. The leaves that broke loose from the tea bag swirled into the broken spiral of my mother's childhood. As I began to understand the terror under her words, I saw her father blocking the light, casting a shadow across his skinny six-year-old daughter whose legs felt unhinged, a china doll with a rubber band down the middle that had snapped.

Something was wrong. It was all her fault.

In my childhood, my mother's stories ended before the strap lashed into her child body, before her father's redfaced anger lashed into her, leaving welts, binding her dreams no matter which way she turned. But now as we sat facing each other, my mother took the story further.

"I was always tense as a kid," she said. She winced and her right hand moved protectively to her left shoulder. "I never knew when my father was going to hit me. I didn't know what direction it would come from."

Still, her father's violence didn't stop her from dreaming. And in her dreams, she soared. I grew up hearing about the catwalk her father had built around the outside of their house.

"My father never did finish it, but I climbed up on it anyway. One day I stood on the roof and spread my arms like a bird. Then my mother came out of the house. She looked up and screamed at me to get down. I was so startled that I damned near fell off the roof.

"My mother called my father and told him to speak to me. He came out of the house and yelled up at me: 'Hello there, Jane, you'd better come down before you scare the life out of your mother.' After the way she yelled at me, I was scaring her? I walked to the back of the house where the catwalk slanted all the way to the ground, sat down, put my hands behind me, pushed, and slid all the way to the ground."

"Weren't you afraid?" I raised my eyebrows and looked at my mother.

"I wasn't afraid," she said resolutely. The ridges of her neck stuck out. Her shoulders turned in on themselves. Bony wrists jutted from her cotton sleeves. Her fists clenched. "It didn't matter to me. Nothing mattered at all."

It wasn't her father's beatings that broke her. It was his leaving, this point of evacuation, that became the dividing line of her life, her before and after. She had never spoken of when he left. When I was a child, my imagination filled this blank slate with a picture that was clean and neat. He left. Without screaming, without violence. He simply left, like my father getting into the car and going to work. Except he never returned. I didn't see my mother in this picture, standing at the window, age seven, her cheeks streaked, her knuckles whiter than the windowsill she gripped, her heart a plum that burst its skin.

A few years ago my mother gave me a small hand-held mirror with a photograph of her framed on the back. The mirror was no more than two inches high and an inch across. In the border of the photograph, the year 1928 was printed in white against a black background. It was taken when she was eight years old. Every now and then I took it out, held it in my hand, and turned it over to see how my reflection compared to her picture. Our hair was different. Hers at eight was bowl-cut, bangs straight across dropping down in a round dome just below her ears.

I've had my share of bad haircuts, especially in my teens when I let my best friend cut it. My childhood best friend was short and tough. She had quarterback shoulders and had often defended me against the schoolyard bullies when I was in a jam. We were no longer in touch; we had gone our separate ways, me on to college and then coming out and her into bad marriages with one husband after another. We tried to stay in touch sporadically over the years. After I had graduated from college and was living in a studio apartment in the city, we were talking on the telephone. "What are you, gay?" she asked. This may have been in response to the fact that I was living alone as much as to the fact that I told her that I wasn't dating any men. "Well yes, as a matter of fact, I am," I responded. She came with me to a party—where she embarrassed me by interrupting a conversation about a local election by saying, "I don't know how yous can be interested in politics—the whole thing disgusts me." And later she volunteered to go with me to a lesbian bar. "But you better keep the women away from me," she said. "Because, damn, I know I'm hot." I let the invitation slide. In many ways, my childhood best friend was the prototype for the women I would later fall in love with. They were usually shorter than me—not hard since I was six feet two inches tall—and tougher than me. In many ways, Barbara reminded me of my childhood best friend. She was shorter and tougher, too. She was direct and down-to-earth and she always knew how to make me laugh. For a while, she even wore her hair in a loose perm which brushed the tops of her shoulders, the same style that my childhood best friend had worn for a time. It took me a long time to become happy with my own hair – but finally, in my mid thirties, when it was short and styled with points in front of the ears, shaped against my head like a cap, I was happy with it. In my twenties, I spiked my hair. And even though I hadn't touched the mousse tube in years, there were times—especially when I slept on it wet—that it stood straight up.

I once thought my mother and I looked nothing alike. But as I approached midlife and witnessed my mother slipping away from me, I reconsidered. Maybe my face was growing into itself, reflecting more of who I was. Perhaps it was simply a matter of perspective. I had the same full lips that solemnly turned down at the edges, the same wary eyes that my mother had when she was eight. The lines of my mother's childhood grief had etched themselves onto my face.

Fortunately, neither of our expressions were static. Our facial expressions were fluid as our emotions—running the gamut from outbursts of laughter to quick summations of anger. But this somber expression was our rest position: disappointment sloping downward in the lines of the mouth as watchful eyes waited for yet another disaster. My mother was my mirror.

As children, both my mother and I dreamed.

My mother dreamed blue chalk water dreams, musing on charcoal pencil outlines, a bitch and her seven pups swirling across the blank walls of her childhood. And I hummed incessantly. I hummed my way through my parents' arguments, through the Vietnam War raging on the television news during dinner. I hummed my way through church services until my mother decided that the whole thing was a waste of time. I hummed so much in elementary school that I became known as "the hummer." It was true that I hummed to shut things out. But I also hummed to tune myself into the vibrational frequency of the grand celestial symphony.

My humming had musical scores. My violin lessons had led me into a wholly encompassing, exhilarating and deeply riveting attraction to another violin student. I was in first grade. Marcie was in fifth grade and a much better violinist than I. She was the student taking lessons before me, and when I peered through the tall double wooden doors into the music room and saw the intensity of her dark eyes, the distinct tilt of her chin, and the arc of her arm as she held the bow, my heart thudded all the way down to the soles of my saddle shoes.

I had what my mother called a boyfriend in first grade. Jimmy used to chase me around the room and try to kiss me. I always got away, but eventually consented to let him button my coat after he promised to show me his six toes on one foot. The fact that two of his toes were webbed together like a duck was an oddity I couldn't resist. But it was Marcie, with her searing eyes and tomboy ways—recklessly waving her violin case around as she ran down the front steps of the school at the end of the day—who captured my heart.

I wrote in heavy letters on the cover of my phonics notebook with a number two pencil: I LOVE MARCIE. Too late, I realized what I had done and tried in vain to erase my letters. I rubbed my green notebook cover to white with my pink eraser but the incriminating words could still be read.

"What does that say?" my mother asked when she saw the notebook. I don't recall that my mother was angry, but her strained curiosity caused a pounding in my veins. "Lassie," I said.

"I love Lassie." It was 1964. Fear and hatred of people who loved the same sex was in the air I breathed and the water I drank. Already, in first grade, I knew that it wasn't even safe to tell my own mother that I loved another girl, no matter how wonderful she was.

There were other signs over the years. Once, a stab of recognition curled my toes in my blue Keds when I met the eyes of another girl in the lobby of a restaurant where I went with my parents. I was a preteen by then, and there was something about this girl, something dark and forbidden, that made me recognize that she was like me. I also had strong emotional attachments to my girlfriends. But for the most part, I managed to block this forbidden love out of my psyche.

The omens of love that were available to me then, the hearts and rings, the promises of "I shall" and "I do" were inadequate to prepare me for being a lesbian, a woman who owned the province of her own sexuality. As an adolescent I hated myself without knowing why. In the time and place where I grew up, alcoholism and drug abuse among adolescents was the norm rather than the exception. But my repressed lesbian feelings were one more thing to obliterate.

Alcoholism was a genetic trait passed down to me from both sides of my family. My father didn't drink but his brothers did. His younger brother died of a heart attack by the time he was forty. My mother told me that he drank and danced himself to death. This story—complete with the knife that he slept with under his pillow after coming home from the front lines of WWII—met my childhood ears as a kind of adventure. Soon I was able to fill my own life with the same kind of danger and excitement gleaned from alcohol and drugs.

My first drink, when I was fourteen, slid easily into the next and I was transported out of my body. I drank to escape myself. I drank so my life could be endured. I drank my way through junior high, high school and college. As a young woman, I drank my way through two extremely tumultuous relationships with men—one starting when I was eighteen and lasting four years and the other lasting six months. I drank my way through working on an assembly line and my early years as a journalist. Two-fisted drinking was acceptable in both worlds. Drinking nearly cost me my life, but it never got in the way of my work. As a journalist, being able to drink my male colleagues under the table was a point of pride with me. I probably would have kept it up, except that when I was twenty-three I became involved in the women's liberation movement. A few months later I came out as a lesbian and stopped drinking to excess.

It was that easy.

There's very little about my life that I would have changed. I was happy. When I was twenty-four—the same age at which my mother met my father—I fell in love with Barbara. Like most people in long-term relationships, we've had our ups and downs. But even now—when I didn't have the time to spend with Barbara that I usually did—I had the comfort of knowing she was there for me. Sometimes I felt guilty that I wasn't able to spend more time with her. But deep down, I knew she was there for me. I knew she understood. I didn't need to be with her all the time to know that she was the love of my life, my safe harbor.

My mother was sitting quietly, a whimsical expression on her face as she stared out the front window at the lengthening shadows. Deep from the bottom of my vocal chords, below that even, a small vibration started. It became slightly louder, almost audible, and then crested through the line of my pursed lips. I was humming, ever so slightly and almost unconsciously. I was humming the melody of my childhood and the dissonant chords of my adolescence. I was humming from the belly of the woman I had become. I was humming as I had always been humming. With my mother's help, I hummed myself into existence.

CHAPTER 7

Pipe Dreams

"That's Churchill." My mother sat at the dining room table and pointed out the back window to the jay sitting on the rim of the white plastic birdbath. I stood at the window, careful not to touch the opaque white rayon curtain and startle the bird. A few days ago, I saw this same bird, a warrior in blue feathers, swooping as it defended its territory against a handful of house sparrows.

"Churchill?"

"Churchill." She nodded at the bird as if addressing an old friend. The bird feeder, its plastic pedestal weighted down with rocks inside it, sat on the edge of the patio. An end-of-the-season potted pink begonia still in flower was seated on the basin's raised center.

My mother composed her thoughts and then spoke. "Churchill ate in the bathtub. Every morning the jay swoops down, scares all the other birds away, splashes his feathers in the birdbath, and pecks at the bugs on the begonia."

The thought of a corpulent statesman satiating himself in my mother's birdbath made me laugh.

"Churchill planned entire war strategies from the tub," she added. "Everyone loved him during the war. Then they dropped him afterward."

"Why?"

"That's the way people are." She shrugged with a twitch of her shoulders.

We both stared out the window, contemplating human nature.

Suddenly she turned and said, "I always wish I had known more about my father's family."

My mother's sudden departures into the past took me by surprise. She was still losing weight and it was becoming more difficult for her to walk. She used her cane at all times. In the small bathroom in the hallway next to her bedroom, a red enema bag hung over the shower rod. The HMO nurse now came to visit three times a week, an hour for each visit, to measure my mother's vital signs.

It was Saturday and Barbara was working. I had come the day before and brought my overnight bag, planning to stay for a long weekend. It was my third weekend in a row away from Barbara. A musician friend of ours who lived in Durham, North Carolina was staying at our house. Barbara and Kathleen were rehearsing for an upcoming gig. Kathleen was a compassionate singer/songwriter who was getting over a bad breakup. I had talked to both Barbara and Kathleen on the phone last night before I had gone to bed. Barbara always joked that I didn't have anything to worry about when she was doing music—"my hands are always on the drums," she would say. I wasn't worried. The foundation for our relationship over the years was that our creative lives always came first. We had other passions in life besides each other. Still, part of me missed being with Barbara and our life together. More than anything, I wanted my mother to be better and my life to be the way it was.

More than three months had passed since her diagnosis. My mother's life was slipping away. Her stories resonated in my bones.

After my mother and father were married, fifteen years before I was born, they took a trip to Biloxi, Mississippi where her father had grown up.

"It was beautiful," she told me. Her eyes widened as her thoughts took her far away to a place where palm trees bent over the Gulf of Mexico, fronds swaying in warm ocean breezes.

This trip to Biloxi was her second. She first traveled there when she was six months old with her mother and father to visit his family.

"Mama told me that Biloxi was just one big mud hole. That was *her* version of things. But it was before indoor plumbing. She had to stay in the house with the three women—my father's two stepsisters and his stepmother. She told me his stepmother and one of the sisters called her a 'damn Yankee' the whole time she was there."

My mother paused for a moment and said, "That's the way Southerners were. The Civil War had been over for fifty years and they were still fighting it. Mama told me that one of my aunts was a skilled seamstress. She could walk into a store, look at a dress, and go home and make one just like it. My other aunt, her younger sister, was crazy."

"What do you mean, crazy?" At times like this, my interest in my mother's stories was motivated by pure self-interest. Did I have a genetic history of mental illness?

"You know. Crazy. Like *my* sister."

My mother had laid the transparency of her own life onto her father's relatives. One of the sisters, like her, was a seamstress. She was practical. The other one was like my aunt, meaning she went through life as if on a whim. I thought about pointing out to my mother that my aunt was not, in fact, crazy. I started to say something and then stopped. Anything I said would be construed as taking my aunt's side, something my mother had accused me of in the past. I was also careful to avoid taking my mother's side in conversations I had with my aunt. It was futile to enter the fray of their never-ending arguments.

"Mama told me that my aunt never wrote to us after my father left. But I never believed her. I think she was always afraid my father was going to come back and try to find us. He may have been a louse, but Southerners love their children. Besides, how else did my aunt know where to send my dress for my eighth-grade graduation if she wasn't in touch with my mother? And how did she know my size?"

My mother looked out the back window at the empty birdbath. The jay was long gone. Finally she turned to me and said, "That's what my mother told me. Take it for what it's worth. She always was dramatic."

When my grandmother was a girl, a family friend who ushered for the People's Theater in Kensington helped her get bit parts. The theater was known as "Peeps." As a child, I followed in my grandmother's footsteps. I wanted to be an actress. One day, in fourth grade, my first year in public school, I stated my dreams out loud.

"An actress," sneered Michael, the class clown. Intimidated by my height, he was always intent on knocking me down a peg or two. "Get that, everyone. Mason wants to be a movie star."

"I didn't say that. I said I want to be an actress."

"Same thing."

Michael had a gang of boys at his service, and the laughter of my classmates who had learned the lesson that their survival depended on cooperating with his cruelty. The teacher also took his side. When she had us diagram sentences, Michael always responded with semi-obscene, not to mention ridiculous, noun, object, verb schemes that she found amusing. Teachers were once students, perhaps brainy unpopular ones, and some of them had learned to side with the pack leaders.

Perhaps the teacher did not defend me because she didn't want to encourage pipe dreams. She might have thought female students should not have any hopes of stepping outside their predestined roles: teacher, nurse, wife, mother, factory worker. With the women's movement just beginning then, in the late sixties, she may—consciously or unconsciously—have envied the fact that her female students would have more opportunities than she did. At the time, all I knew was that my dreams were not defended. I learned to keep my mouth shut about what I wanted out of life. But I never stopped dreaming.

That year I volunteered for a role in the school's spring play. I wasn't the star of the show, the androgynous flying Peter Pan, or even Wendy or Captain Hook. I was the crocodile. I was the tallest child in the fourth grade—one of the other teachers had sympathetically told me that "girls always shoot up faster than boys"—and my height no doubt suited me for the role. Michael played the part of Captain Hook.

My new role as the crocodile gave him further fuel for his daily ridiculing. Even though I was the object of derision, I couldn't help feeling, as I looked down at him, somewhat superior. I also grew disdainful about my teacher's lack of intelligence, made obvious when she laughed at Michael's jokes, which were not, in fact, funny.

In retrospect, I think Michael must have sensed my indifference, and this made him more determined to make my life miserable.

As a child, one whose feelings were easily hurt, I had no idea at the time that I would I grow up to have a life that was far preferable to those my tormentors would go on to lead. I would never look back to my childhood or adolescence as my glory days but I would not end up living in a trailer park, working in a warehouse, or in retail endlessly searching for "Mr. Right"—as so many of my schoolmates would go on to do. Even at the time, I did know that I was different and some part of me was happy about that. So I ignored Michael when he taunted me about being the crocodile. I rather liked the idea that I could snap off his head.

My role in the play did not get off to a good start. The first day of rehearsal, I felt sick to my stomach. Karla, the girl standing in front of me—the perfect Wendy, constantly tossing her golden tresses over her shoulder—insisted that I hold her script. "You better take this," I said repeatedly. "I feel sick." She pointedly ignored me. I nudged her again, holding the script in front of me. Just then, the sloppy joe I had for lunch made a spectacular resurgence. Globs hung in her long blond tresses. As mortified as I was, I couldn't help an "I told you" as the music director whisked me off to the nurse's office.

The humiliation was impossible to live down. But I still managed to outdo myself during the performance. When it was time for the crocodile to run off the stage and into the center aisle, the spotlight blinded me. I ran smack into several audience members in the aisle seats.

Despite everything, I remained the star of my own imagination. At recess every afternoon I could be found swinging high into the air, the afternoon sunshine holding me in its light. I was special. And in this small act of defiance, I was united with my grandmother.

The fact of her husband's leaving thrust my grandmother into a part that she might have played on the stage. When my mother was seven and my aunt was three, the bank foreclosed on my grandmother's country store. To the two girls it was as if the moon fell out of the sky.

It was 1927, the latter years of the Roaring Twenties. My grandmother would have seen the cartoon images of the flapper, a woman with bobbed hair and a short skirt daringly showing her legs from the knees down. This was the image of the loose woman—heralded in F. Scott Fitzgerald's *The Great Gatsby*—that came to represent the decade. But this lifestyle existed for only a few—those who belonged to the class of the decadent rich, their excesses based on the skyrocketing stock market that would soon come tumbling down. For the majority of women, especially working-class women like my grandmother, it was still scandalous to be divorced.

With her children in tow, she moved back to the city where they stayed with an old church friend in the Germantown section, the neighborhood I later moved to—which at that point had become a haven for artists, political activists and lesbians—when I moved away from my parents' home in the suburbs. It was evident from the disappointed look on my mother's face, even now, more than a half century later, that regardless of the large house they stayed in she would have much rather been back in the country.

"Even the yard wasn't anything compared to the country. It was just a patch of grass with a wrought iron fence around it. There was a birdbath with a wrought iron bench next it that was painted white. Who sat on a bench?" I looked at my mother—her scrunched-up face framed by her short hair—and I could see the ten-year-old staring out of her seventy-four-year-old face. "My favorite thing about that yard was the elm tree. It had low branches, as low as my favorite climbing tree in the country. It was the closest thing to home that I could find."

She shifted painfully in her chair. "Eventually Mama found a job at the mill, and we rented a row home nearby in North Philadelphia. Our backyard was tiny, a small square yard with a cement walkway between two patches overgrown with grass and weeds. There wasn't a tree anywhere in sight. We moved around a lot. Once or twice we only moved two blocks from where we had lived before. I always thought my mother was hiding us from our father. If he couldn't find us then he couldn't come and take my sister and me away."

My mother held her shoulder and her eyes narrowed as she spoke. "I was a latchkey child. This was before the Lighthouse started a program for the older kids as well as the younger ones. The Episcopal women started the Lighthouse as a daycare and after-school program for the children of single mothers. Do you remember when I took you to the old neighborhood when you were ten?"

I nodded, remembering it well. A new hospital stood on the site of the old Lighthouse, off Lehigh Avenue, in the heart of North Philadelphia. When my mother was growing up, the neighborhood was full of European immigrants. Now it was a mostly Spanish-speaking section known as the Barrio. My mother's stories of the Lighthouse captured my young imagination. I pictured an island jutting from the ocean, a tall cylindrical building with a pulsing light, an actual lighthouse. My memories of visiting her old neighborhood were full of exotic tastes and smells—*arroz con pollo*, plantains, the greasy sizzle of fried tortillas at the Spanish restaurant where we ate.

My mother sat gazing out the front window, looking far away into her own past, full of a different set of tastes and smells. "Before I started going to the Lighthouse with my sister, I came home from school earlier than my mother and had to let myself in with the key I kept on a string around my neck.

"One day I lost the key. That was the time I was homeless. I was out in the freezing cold for hours. It seemed like days before my mother came home from the mill. There was a storefront next to our house, and there was a light in the window so I went and stood in front of it. The store was closed but there was a woman inside. I could see her folding the linens, her outstretched arms looked like a cross draped with a purple sash at Lent."

"Why didn't the woman in the store let you in?" I asked. We had moved from the dining room into the living room, and my mother sat in her gold velour chair. The ottoman, covered with the textile my grandmother brought home from the mill, sat in front of her.

My mother gave me a look of pure astonishment. "In those days children were to be seen and not heard. All my life I've been in the wrong place at the wrong time. First children weren't listened to. Then when I was grown, Benjamin Spock came around and said parents should shut up and listen to their children." My mother's words were deliberate, not angry; precise, rather than resentful. As she spoke, I saw a skinny seven-year-old in a frayed cloth coat, shivering as she waited the long hours for her mother, her teeth chattering as she stood in the doorway.

"Usually, I would take Mama's dinner to the mill. We had ice boxes in those days—every morning the ice man would come with a block of ice and by the end of the day the ice melted down into the tray. I still remember the drops of water beading up inside the wax paper that covered the pound cake. In those days we didn't think about what a healthy dinner was. So we had cake, not for dessert but for the main course. No wonder my mother became a diabetic. I passed by all the factories and red brick warehouses along the way. You'd never know it was the same neighborhood today with all those vacant run-down warehouses and factories everywhere. I still know the names of the lace they displayed in a store window on the corner: Italian Milanese, French Chantilly, English Honiton, Bedfordshire, Antwerp, Point de Lille."

My mother's story entered my imagination and I saw her as an observant child, turning the corner to where the textile mill loomed in front of her, four stories of red brick. She would have passed the night watchman who greeted her by name, to enter the back door into the clanking, whirring factory, which like a large hungry animal blew its hot breath on her neck. As she scurried down the familiar hallway toward the cafeteria, the familiar gray walls weighed down on her as heavy as the flabby arm of an old woman.

She slipped into the cafeteria, unnoticed in the midst of the clatter of flatware against the Formica tabletop and the cacophony of female voices.

"And then that vulture had the nerve to put his hands..."

"Ssshhh." Sitting at the opposite side of the table, my grandmother's lifelong friend, Lillian, put her finger to her lips as she jerked her head toward my mother.

"You sit right down, toots," she said to my mother. "Don't worry about your mama. She's in the loo."

"She'll be back any minute now," said another woman, her voice swirling in a kaleidoscope of sound. My mother sat down and placed the larger piece of pound cake at her mother's place and took the smaller one for herself.

"I declare, this child is growing like a weed."

"You'll be working alongside us in just a few years."

"You better start eating more."

"That's right. A growin' girl needs more than a skimpy piece of cake for dinner."

"Look at those skinny arms."

"The wicked old witch would never want to eat her."

"Fatten her up."

She pulled her neck into her shoulders like a turtle and jumped when Abigail, the oldest of the spinners, reached out and pinched her wrist between a gnarled thumb and finger. When she jerked her arm away, the old woman opened her mouth wide and cackled. The rest of the women laughed also, eyes shining, mouths opened wide, here and there a chipped tooth, the hard resonance of laughter in a small room.

"What's going on?"

My grandmother stood in the doorway, bits of thread sticking to her apron, a strand of royal navy, wisps of red clinging to dusty gray.

"We were wondering when this big girl here is going to start working with us."

My grandmother frowned, turned her back on the women, and walked to the teapot. "She's only ten." As she poured the tea, her elbow was pressed to her side, just above her apron's gray sash. "No child of mine is ever going to work in a mill. She's going to work in an office."

When my grandmother took her seat, her spine was as stiff as the wooden backed chair. Several of the other women raised their eyebrows and one of them spoke in an imitation Cockney accent. "Who does she bloody think she is, anyway, her Royal Highness?"

"That's right," said the woman next to her. "Her Mighty Highness."

"The future Queen Elizabeth herself," said another, "you can tell by her jewels and finery."

Abigail cackled. The other spinners joined in, all except for Lillian who winked and patted my mother's wrist with her calloused hand.

Soon the laughter would disappear into a mirthless whir, spindles filling and refilling, emptying into hours of aching legs and splitting fingers. But for a moment, my mother as a girl stared in wonderment at her mother, as the filaments of light turned the strands of her hair to a golden crown. And that moment, of the daughter seeing a crown of regal self-possession on her mother's head, turned into an eternity.

My mother and I both stared at the iron legged ottoman, covered with a faded tapestry that my grandmother wove more than a half century ago. Whenever I looked at the patterns of the ottoman, the faded edges and the lines of darker colors, I saw my grandmother.

My grandmother was a woman of great dignity. The Episcopal Church, especially after she had divorced and returned to the city, was one of the major pillars in her life. I don't know that she was particularly religious. But I remember visiting Saint Simeon's with her, and I could see the appeal of the church, especially to a poor woman who had little if any luxury in her life.

She might have been saying prayers that she no longer believed in as she sat there, her head bowed and covered, next to her two girls—my mother squirming in the aisle seat and my aunt sitting next to her daydreaming as she stared at the stained glass windows. The shiny brass organ pipes reached to the ceiling and looked as beautiful as they sounded. The pews were polished mahogany, the wood smooth and cool. The scent of incense and flowers permeated the air. All St. Simeon's needed was some red velvet seat cushions and gilded cherubs on the ceiling and it could have been easily transformed into the sensuous lair of an opera house or, perhaps, a bordello.

Sundays at St. Simeon's were a respite from the rest of my grandmother's life. Her days in the textile mill encompassed her like the full spectrum of shadow falling from a sundial. The morning light filtering through the small windows of the dark mill would have been diffuse.

Her hair would have been tied back into a bun as the light fell around her like the fiber of soft cotton. She would have bent over the heddles that kept the warp lines in place as she threaded the machine. The colors on the ottoman—rust red, dusty blue, olive green, black—would have filled the spindles that unraveled furiously into the automated looms as her hands kept pace. When the morning light turned into afternoon and the heat rose in rivulets of sweat dripping from her skin, my grandmother would have reminded herself that she was lucky to have a job. The soup lines were getting longer. The unemployed and the homeless were marching in the streets. Even if my grandmother didn't know anyone who committed suicide, she would have read the listings in the daily papers.

I wondered what it was like for my grandmother, a woman with dreams and aspirations, a woman whose life dictated that her only option was to work in a mill or to clean someone else's house, which was what she did after she left the mill. Did her dreams keep her going through the tedium of her life? Or did knowing that her dreams would never come true make her life close to unbearable? And if her life was unbearable, what kept her going? Had the thought of her girls having better lives than hers made it all worthwhile?

When my grandmother worked at the textile mill, she was a woman who was no longer young but not yet old. She still had her girlhood daydreams of her young adulthood as an escape from the pure tedium of her life. At the same time, the features of her face would have been hardening themselves into the lines of her future. Her lips may have opened easily in laughter, but they were on their way to becoming a stitch in the center of her face.

My mother told me that when she was a girl my grandmother would tell her stories about her own childhood. Her favorite stories were about the People's Theater, where she would sit in the front row with her cousin Adelaide, each of them sucking on a dill pickle, drooling as they tried to catch the eye of the actors. One day the two of them, between nudges and giggles, caught the eye of Romeo and when he looked at the two girls, their lips puckered over their pickles, he flubbed his lines. "Good Goose" became "Goose Goose."

Ethel and Adelaide played Fairy number one and Fairy number two in "A Midsummer's Night Dream." My grandmother's lines —"Hail, hail!"—were less memorable than her dress, filmy chiffon, petals flowing down from her neckline. The dress may have belonged to the theater company, but as she stood on the stage, the dress—and the audience's applause—belonged to her alone.

Her memories would have swirled through her mind as she stood sweltering in the textile mill, reloading the spools that needed to be filled faster than she could keep up. Her back might have been aching and her fingertips numb—she might have been wondering how she could afford to pay the rent—but in her dreams she was stately as a queen as she stood center stage. Her green chiffon dress was a waterfall cascading down her. Ladies in waiting stood behind her. A diamond tiara sat on her head, its sparks of light reflected in Romeo's eyes. He knelt at her side, staring up at her, as rapt as the audience seated in its plush red velvet hall. Romeo reached his hand toward hers, then vanished.

Wherefore art thou, Romeo? The words dropped from her lips, the life that could have been, as the curtain descended in front of her.

Sitting in the living room with my mother, I could hear the distant applause, replaced suddenly by the din of the mill. The noise of the loom, the thud, the thwack, entwined with a ceaseless rhythmic tramp—the tread of hundreds and thousands marching through history.

Like my grandmother, I was always dramatic and thin-skinned, especially when it came to criticism and slights, real and imagined. When my mother decided to transfer me from a private to public school in third grade, she told me that the money saved on my education would send me to college. Like the violin lessons, college was my mother's dream, not mine. College was an aspiration that was not shared by any of my new classmates. I wasn't aware of it at the time, but there was a cultural chasm between my private school years in kindergarten through third grade and the public school I entered in fourth grade. The boys in my fourth-grade class, egged on by Michael, "called me out" after school. I had no idea what they were talking about, but I quickly found out that this meant challenging someone to a fistfight.

These children had not learned French in first grade as I had. They did not go to the symphony with their parents—which I did and enjoyed, even though we sat in the seats closest to the ceiling. They were not children who had led quiet lives reading books. Many of them were beaten by their fathers and older brothers in the front yards of their homes. Corporal punishment was a way of life. It was survival of the fittest and when it came to protecting myself, I was not prepared at all.

One day at recess I stood on the edge of a steep hill. It was a windy day and my arms were outstretched like an eagle, a great wingspan soaring to new heights. As my imagination took flight I felt a thud in the middle of my back and the wind was knocked out of me. I had felt capable of flying but I fell. I was pushed. Four boys on the playground had rammed into my back. My chin and knees were scraped. I had bruises on my torso and arms. The world was upside down and I couldn't catch my breath, but the part of me wounded the worst was my pride.

Somehow, in my ten-year-old mind being pushed down the hill became my fault. When I came home with cuts and bruises I told my mother I had tripped and fallen. Almost every day I was taunted and chased by bullies on my way home from school. I still did not tell my mother. I might have been afraid I would get beaten worse if I told. Maybe I didn't want to worry my mother, or perhaps I sincerely thought that I had some deep-set character flaw that invited this treatment.

Even so, I still had my dreams.

My mother had given me a "School Years" book—a thick spiral bound book, four by five inches, with a white cover—that contained my report cards and my pictures from each grade. She always asked me what I wanted to be when I grew up and wrote it down each year. It didn't matter how ridiculous or remote the possibility was. In first grade I wanted to be a fireman, later a violinist, a gypsy, a scientist, a comedienne, an oceanographer, a guitar player in a jazz band.

My mother let my dreams be dreams. She did not expect consistency or demand a discipline that would eclipse my childhood. No one ever asked my mother what she wanted to be when she grew up. But she asked me every year and wrote down my answers. As I watched my mother slipping away from me—as painful as it was, day after day—the thought of this book, filled with my earliest dreams and aspirations, was something for me to hold onto.

CHAPTER 8

The Girls of Summer

My mother and I were having lunch with my aunt. She was having problems with her eyesight, making the two-hour drive to my parents' house next to impossible for her. For this visit, she had a friend of her husband's drive her and drop her off.

It was late in November. Almost four months had passed since my mother's diagnosis. I had become more stressed. I didn't want to burden my mother with my grief, and for the most part I was able to suppress it when I was with her. But several times driving home from her house, I had burst into tears, the turnpike blurring dangerously before me. Last week I forgot where I was and turned onto the off-ramp exit of I-95. At my parents' house, I tended to look for things in the wrong drawer thinking I was at my own house. When my father and I were both in the kitchen, I forgot where I was and thinking he was Barbara called him "Honey." At the time all he said was "Hmmph." But a few days later when I was talking to him on the phone he told me to stay home for a few days and take it easy.

It had become obvious that I was in danger of losing it.

Barbara, as well, encouraged me to take a break. I sensed she wanted to spend some time with me. I tried, but what was dinner, a movie, compared to my preoccupation over my mother dying? After a few days, I insisted on going back to see my mother.

Barbara was going to come with me—but at the last minute she changed her mind. I suspected she might be uncomfortable around my mother sometimes. The last time, she had brought my mother a large bag of tube socks as a gift. This was Barbara's way of trying to make things better—of buying my mother a practical gift that she could use to keep her feet warm. After tearing off the wrapping paper and seeing the large bag of socks, my mother said, "Barbara, how long do you expect me to live—I won't be able to wear all of these." Barbara's family was always giving each other presents—shopping was a way of expressing love. My mother, though, must have looked at the large bag of socks and saw more work. She had been cleaning out her closets for a few years, and now was trying to get my father and me to take more of her old clothes to the Goodwill.

"I'm disappointed that Barbara didn't come," said my aunt, while we were eating the lunch she had cooked at home and brought with her. Barbara was always making a fuss over my aunt, insisting on taking her out and paying for her meal when we visited her and taking her little gifts and sending her cards.

After lunch, my aunt, my mother and myself sat around the dining room table drinking tea. As usual the two of them were swept up in their spirited banter. Their ongoing disagreements sounded normal to me. This was the way it always had been. But my mother was weaker than ever. Soon their voices faded to silence.

The banter had become a kind of subterfuge—a way of pretending that things were the same. Suddenly the conversation took a turn into the reality of my mother's life. My mother told us that the HMO nurse's aide, Chantel, was there earlier in the day. "It's her job to clean my room—though I really don't see the point in her running a dust rag around the windowsills." Earlier, when my mother and I were alone she told me that my father was so embarrassed at having someone else cleaning her room that he went upstairs and stayed in the bathroom the whole time.

"It took her less than ten minutes and she's here for an hour. She wanted to clean the bathroom, but I told her to sit down and relax. I don't know how much she makes but I'm sure it's not much. She has two young children at home, and all she's ever done is take care of people. When she was growing up, her mother had her take care of her great-grandmother and then her grandmother. Can you imagine that—not a minute left for herself?"

My mother shook her head. She had always been a compassionate person. As her life ebbed away, I could see how this had become a survival tactic for her. The fact that she could get out of herself—asking the nurse how her sick child was, for example—helped her, at least for the moment, to forget about her own pain.

"Chantel's supposed to bathe me too," my mother said, turning toward my aunt. "But I told her that I can do that myself. At least I can do it for now…" Her voice trailed away. The look on her face was frightened, lost. My mother who had always done everything for herself would soon be unable to bathe herself, to brush her teeth, to control her bodily functions.

Tears came to my eyes. My aunt looked away.

The silence that surrounded us was a closeness that in its purity made me feel as if everything, after all, could be okay.

Their conversation moved backward in time. When they talked about the rope bridge of their childhoods, I felt its rough strands unraveling under my fingertips. I hung onto each word.

"Remember that rope bridge that stretched across the river?" My mother was talking about Camp Little Light, the summer camp they went to that was part of the program for children of single mothers.

"Remember it!" exclaimed my aunt. "I was scared to death of it. I wouldn't even cross it. And you were so courageous! You used to stand in the middle and rock back and forth way up there above the water!"

"They really had their hands full with me." The expression on my mother's face was somewhere between a mortified adult and a hellion tomboy child. "Then there was the time I talked Hedwig into hitchhiking into town. A man picked us up in his car, turned around, and drove us right back to camp. It turned out he was a friend of Miss Zollers. Boy did we get a talking to! She told us we must never ever get into a car with a strange man again. In those days no one talked about rape. Rape? What did we know from rape? We just wanted to have an adventure!"

"Boy, you had a lot of fun," said my aunt. I didn't know anything about that, Jane. I was stuck with the other little kids. But I remember your friend Hedwig. I wonder whatever happened to her?"

"We fell out of touch when camp was over. You know how it is after women get married and take their husbands' last names. We can never find each other again. I've often wondered if she kept the name Hedwig or if she went by Hedy when she got older. She was in camp with us because she lost her father too. She told me her father was killed in a car accident with another woman—not her mother. Hedwig came from a Polish Catholic family. She almost died the first day of camp when I took off all my clothes and ran through the woods naked…" My mother paused and then laughed, the lines around her eyes turning crimson. "Her mother was so strict that Hedwig wasn't even allowed to touch herself between her legs with a washrag. She had to wash by pulling a towel back and forth between her legs. Though it seemed like that would have been even more fun!"

My aunt gave my mother an astonished look. "You never told me that you ran naked through the woods."

"Of course not. You would've told Mama."

"I would not have."

My mother shrugged. "You were playing with my toys when I was away."

"I was not!"

"That's what Mama said in the letter she sent me. You were still too little to come to camp, and I was away for the summer and Mama told me you were playing with my toys."

"I was just a kid."

"So was I," my mother said quietly. "And Mama shouldn't have told me that."

"Sometimes I think she tried to pit us against each other. We were all she had and she was afraid we'd gang up on her," said my aunt.

My mother nodded. The three of us were silent.

Finally my mother said, "I went back to Camp Little Light years later and that bridge was gone. But the house where the owners of the camp lived was still there. Remember? It was a long stone house with a patterned slate roof and old, old windows with that glass in it that makes everything look wavy when you look through them."

My aunt nodded.

"When I saw that house, I wanted to buy it," my mother said. "But you never wanted to go back there," she said to my father who had just returned from the backyard.

"What are you talking about?" he said, not waiting for an answer. "We went back there half a dozen times. We were just there a few years ago."

"But you never wanted to stay," she retorted.

"Hmmph." My father exited the dining room into the garage.

"He's in one of his moods," my mother said to no one in particular.

My father was right. He and my mother had returned to Camp Little Light many times. I remember going. The camp was near Collegeville, a small town a half-hour ride from the city. My mother, as a child, had arrived there by trolley, watching with glee as the row homes and cobblestones turned to trees, trees, trees in an undulating carpet of green.

When I went, the camp had been long defunct, but the forest was still there, the house where the owners had lived, and the wide stream with its rocky whitecaps that my mother said was once much bigger, so much bigger that it was a river.

My mother's stories about her adventures at camp were endlessly fascinating to my childhood imagination. Since she didn't have brothers, camp was the first place she saw a boy's penis. ("When I was cleaning the latrine I opened the door and saw a boy sitting there. I laughed and he got mad, saying I was looking at him on purpose. But I didn't care what he had. I didn't care if his penis was purple.") And every Sunday she went to chapel. ("Hedwig and I used to sit next to each other laughing and laughing. Not outside but inside. We'd just about get it under control and then one of us would look at the other one and it would start all over again.") She told me about the lessons she learned, chief among them the virtues of fairness and parsimony. ("Every evening after dinner each child got one piece of candy and one piece only.") While moderation has its virtues, this lesson also extended into self-abnegation. ("The children who had birthdays in the summer, including me, were not allowed to celebrate them, not even to receive presents from their mothers, because it wouldn't be fair to the others.")

To me, who had birthday parties every year with cake and ice cream, and once even a piñata, my mother's childhood was a mystery. She painted her stories with the wild and vibrant palette of her imagination, and what captured my fascination was not the poverty she was raised in but rather her endless sense of adventure. Our childhood dreams and reveries converged, mine made richer by the stories of her youth.

Camp Little Light, which was no longer a camp but simply a forest with a wide creek running through it, became a place of magic and mystery to me, a place where I found a fossilized outline of a leaf pressed into rock, a place where I could see glimpses of my future as I skipped smooth stones across the surface, drops of water fusing into sunlight.

"Whatever happened to Miss Zollers?" my aunt asked as I poured her another cup of tea.

Miss Zollers, the director of the camp, was the woman that my mother always referred to as her second mother, her educated mother. She had taken an interest in my mother's artistic talents, encouraging her to draw figures from the Bible for the class's lessons.

"Don't you remember?" My mother gave my aunt an incredulous look. "We went to see her when she was dying. We were only kids. Mama is the one who should have gone, but she sent us instead. And when we got there Miss Zoller's sister gave us some rags and told us to clean the room. So we did. When Mama found out she was so furious, and she wouldn't let us go back to visit again."

"Now I remember. Mama was so mad I thought I had done something wrong. There we were, a couple of poor kids, and Miss Zoller's sister just thought she would put us to work."

"Her sister had some kind of a job." My mother stared down at the cup in front of her. "I think she was a nurse. I bet she didn't have anyone in her life who cared about her, and she was jealous that her sister had us."

My aunt took a sip of her tea and was quiet for a moment. "Maybe she thought we were just a couple of charity cases. Mama used to pay three dollars a week to keep us both in the light house, but that couldn't have covered much. I ate three meals a day there before I started going to school and you ate dinner there after school, and I don't think Mama paid much to send us to camp in the summer either."

When I was growing up, my mother's stories about receiving charity entered my bones and took up residence in the marrow of shame and resentment. Telling me about a hand-me-down dress she wore from the church rummage, my mother said, "I knew the girl who had owned the dress was looking down her nose at me in church. I didn't want to be wearing her old dress. I wanted my own dress." Later, my mother shrugged and said, "It was just vanity, not wanting to be seen in someone else's clothes. Vanity, that's all." But under my mother's stony countenance, the hurts of her childhood were seething.

When I was a child, my mother also told me that her family received free meals from the Episcopal church they belonged to. The lines of my emotional reality were so blurred that years later I couldn't remember if this was something that happened to my mother in her childhood or to me in my childhood. Finally I remembered that this was my mother's experience, not mine.

When church people did come to our house—like the proselytizing Mormons—my mother always slammed the door in their faces.

The stories my mother told me about the charity she received as a child were double-edged. She wanted the hot meals. But the baskets of food were never given without a judgment taken. Some of the Episcopal church women, no doubt, could not let the fact of a divorced woman with two children go unnoticed or unspoken about. My mother ate the food they brought and swallowed her own mother's resentments.

It's also true that for my grandmother, and countless others, the simple and generous act of charity was what enabled them to keep their children. The educated Episcopal women who ran the light house knew the mothers who needed their services were proud women who didn't want to take handouts even though their economic circumstances forced them to, so they charged each mother a nominal amount, no matter how many children she had in the program. To my grandmother and the other mothers, charity was a word that meant as hard as they worked—dawn to dusk, bringing home barely enough for food and rent—they weren't capable of taking care of their own.

As an adult, I began to understand my mother's resentment. The Episcopal women who provided these services, who ran the centers, sat on the boards, and provided the funds, were, for the most part, associated economically, either through marriage or family connections, to men who made their wealth off low-paid workers. The robber barons and the other owners of the mills and factories found giving money to charity cheaper than paying their workers a living wage.

Still I believe their wives and daughters ran these charitable institutions with good intentions. They saw suffering and sought to ease it. Along with providing food and shelter to the children, they also helped the mothers improve their lot in life. They ran a series of classes to teach the mothers how to handle their household budgets on tight incomes. My grandmother won an award as the mother who could stretch a dollar the furthest.

"Remember the Christmas we spent with the girls at Bryn Mawr?"

My aunt's face lit up. "I'll never forget it. The college girls were pushing us across the floor in wooden chairs and we were having so much fun!"

"Yeah." My mother was beaming. "We made such a racket that the teachers came in and told us all to be quiet and to stop ruining the wooden floor. It wasn't the girls' fault. They were just having fun with us."

"Who thought about the noise or the skid marks?" My aunt's eyes were shining.

"I'll never forget the present I got." My mother had a faraway dreamy look in her eyes. "It was a watch, not a real one that could tell time, but an imitation one. It was a sensuous experience. It came in a powder-blue box and sat on a soft fluffy ball of pink cotton and the copper band was cool and smooth in my hand."

As my mother and aunt talked, I was drawn into my own recollections of Bryn Mawr College. Barbara and I visited the campus—large cathedral-like buildings set on a rolling expanse of green—frequently over the years since there were lectures with interesting writers and feminist music events, like Sweet Honey in the Rock. The college was on the main line, about half an hour from our home in the northwest section of the city. But we frequently became lost when we were driving there. The tiny unlit street signs located at large and imposing intersections and meandering side streets seemed as if they were there for one purpose: to keep outsiders out.

The lives of the students often did not seem real to me. I knew that my feelings were not entirely based on reality. Some of the students attended the college on scholarship. And the programs—featuring writers and musicians from all over the world—were frequently socially progressive, free and open to the public.

What impressed me most about the college was the film I saw in the mid-eighties called *The Women of Summer: The Bryn Mawr Summer School for Women Workers*. It was about Bryn Mawr's summer program for blue-collar women, many of them textile workers, which lasted from 1921 to 1938. If my grandmother had lived longer, she would have been the same age as the women in the film. A single mother with two children depending on her, she was not among the women with the freedom to go to Bryn Mawr's program. But the women, filmed years later at a reunion, were so much like her. They spoke bluntly about their lives. Their laughter was wide open like the vast blue sky above the green campus. They even looked like my grandmother with their plain housedresses and white hair. One of them had a goiter on the left side of her neck, just like the one my grandmother had.

The female educators who ran the program at Bryn Mawr shared the feminist vision of women from all class backgrounds, races and ethnic groups working together. They took risks unheard of at the time, teaching classes on Marxism, encouraging the women workers to become labor organizers, and bringing the first black women ever into Bryn Mawr's educational system. These educators put their jobs on the line. They were called rabble-rousers and communists. When the corporate donors decided it had become too radical, the program was discontinued.

I saw this film in my early twenties at the same community center where I took my women's karate classes. The film was sponsored by a feminist organization in an attempt to raise awareness about class issues. The woman I had gone with—an older friend from my karate class—had attended a Seven Sisters college.

All she could say after the film was how pretty the grounds of the college were. Another woman I talked to, telling her how much the women reminded me of my grandmother, gave me a stricken look and said, "When I see films like this I always feel like I should be more politically active."

At the time, reactions like this made absolutely no sense to me. Eventually, I came to understand that these women were responding from the conditioning they received from their own upbringings. They had probably never discussed, and perhaps never even seriously thought about, issues of class before.

I thought of mentioning this experience to my mother and my aunt, but I was lost as to where to begin. I was trapped between two realities, the largely middle-class world of the women's movement, which gave me the freedom to be myself, and my working-class background which shaped me. There was no starting point for this conversation, no language of translation that I could use without running the risk of being misunderstood as someone who was ashamed of her background when nothing could be further from the truth.

My mother and aunt were awash in their own memories as they talked about the one-room schoolhouse they attended in the country, and then the city school they went to after their father left. "I knew those teachers looked down on us. They thought of us as those awful, dirty children." My mother said this not with shame or resentment, but with precisely defined anger. "I always thought that about your teachers, too, Janet," she said to me. "Things are different now, but when we first moved to this neighborhood anyone could move in who had a hundred dollars to put down. I always felt that your teachers were looking down their noses at you."

My mother's comment took me by surprise. She presented me with a moment I could use as a springboard to examine my past, the intersections of my childhood with hers. Instead I answered with knee-jerk denial—"Aww Mom, I don't remember anything like that." I don't know why I answered the way I did. It could be that this was my way of reassuring my mother that my education was adequate, that she shouldn't have any regrets for anything that happened in my childhood. I remembered the principal of my elementary school—a tall bald man we called "Egghead"—condescendingly asking me what my father did for a living. I don't remember my answer, or his reason for asking. But I do remember my burning face.

In preserving the myth of my childhood, was I trying to protect myself from the past exactly as it happened?

Before Barbara and I got together, I had been getting close to another woman whom I had met on a feminist collective where we both volunteered. She was from an upper middle-class family and had attended a Seven Sisters college. She was witty, attractive and tall like me. We went out a few times, and one night when we were driving by the long defunct lesbian bar called Sneakers, she sneeringly referred to the women walking up to the blue door as "bar dykes." Earlier in the evening when we were at my apartment, this woman had been drinking out of a silver flask monogrammed with her initials. The hypocrisy of her derisive comment about the lesbians on the street, her extremely classist remark, ended a relationship that might have been.

A few weeks later, Barbara and I got together. Barbara, who grew up in a middle-class neighborhood in suburban Pittsburgh, had always thought of herself as middle class. A friend in her drum group laughed when Barbara described herself this way, saying "Barbara, don't you know that you're working class?" Barbara had graduated college with her bachelor's degree in education and worked for a while as a substitute teacher before she married. Teaching jobs were hard to find then so through her marriage and afterward, she had a string of working-class jobs.

She came to Philadelphia when she married her now ex-husband (whose job brought him to Philadelphia) and when she couldn't find work as a teacher, she was a bank teller and then had a series of odd jobs, including selling ice cream bars and popsicles at the Rolling Stones concert in Veteran's Stadium in Philadelphia, before becoming a case worker with the Department of Welfare. After we got together, Barbara took the Civil Service test and went to work for the United States Postal System. However she defined herself—middle-class, working class, or otherwise—Barbara has always been extremely down to earth, genuine and lovable.

As I sat listening to my mother and my aunt talking about their childhoods, I stared down into my teacup. I seemed to have lost interest in reading tea leaves. What was the point of looking into a future that was sure to be clouded with bad omens? I did not need to look into my cup to see the past. It was clearly reflected on my mother's face which, as she lost more weight, became more painfully expressive. The tea in my cup was from a bag that I placed in the pot. Still, some dust had escaped and settled on the bottom of my cup. As I turned the cup around, it formed a long line of dots, a sign that could be read as an omen of taking a journey, or a snake, portending disaster.

I stared into the cup. The lines moved around and it was impossible for me to come to a clear interpretation. Disaster or journey. Journey or disaster. One or the other or both. But as I turned the cup around, something magical began to happen. The stories of my mother's childhood swirled around and converged with my own memories, and the cup became a kaleidoscope through which to reinterpret and reinvent the patterns.

I never felt like my teachers were looking down on me and my classmates as "those dirty children," but something happened in the eighth grade when I was in the first group of girls to be admitted to a shop class in the 1970s. Our project for metal shop had been to make large aluminum funnels. The shop teacher, a short, bald-headed man, was livid about something a student may or may not have done. He stood us all next to the wall and made us watch while he took a pair of metal shears and one by one destroyed our creations. He cut my dreams to shreds. It was devastating.

Making the funnel had taken focus, determination and precision. In home economics I burnt the cinnamon toast and stuffed the bread back in the bag so sloppily that all the pieces had broken in half. I really hadn't been interested enough in the project to think twice about it. Anyone could make cinnamon toast. Metal shop was different. Aware of the importance of being one of the first girls admitted to the class, I had been determined to make the best funnel I could. My face burned with anger and shame as he made us watch the destruction of what we had spent our precious time creating.

This was something I mentioned rarely over the years, if at all, to anyone. It seemed as if the anger I remembered would amplify this memory, not diminish it, so I don't know why I chose to overlook it. Perhaps those precious few good moments from school, the rare times that were actually life changing, eclipsed it. In high school, I was in honors English and the teacher, Mrs. McGonicle, was my role model.

Her class was first period, after home-room, so I had to make an effort to get there. Half the time I was hung over, and sometimes I came to school already stoned, slightly drunk, or both, but nothing diminished my enthusiasm for this class. We read Chaucer and Shakespeare and took a field trip to a cemetery where we acted out parts from Macbeth. In class, she told stories about her days as an advertising copywriter before she had married and become a teacher. She was the first person I met who had worked in a white-collar profession besides teaching (an occupation I had no interest in), and suddenly I could see a path opening up before me.

She encouraged me to go to community college, where my mostly bad high school grades (except for English in which I excelled) and lack of SAT scores wouldn't matter. It took me a while, but I eventually did make it to that community college, and her encouragement was pivotal. In a sea of teachers content to let us slide into oblivion, she was a rarity. My red-rimmed eyes and rebellious ways did not escape her keen perception. Yet she tossed me a life preserver.

How ironic that Michael, my chief tormentor from elementary school on, was her son.

He was at his worst in junior high. He sat behind me in the "M" row in homeroom and was the ringleader in starting every epithet that could be hurled at me—How's the air up there, Jolly Green Giant, Wilt the Stilt, and so on and on. Every now and then I would try to outwit him—"The air's great up here, too bad you can't reach it," or "I'm not a vegetable," or "I should be as rich as Wilt Chamberlain." But he was insecure and relentless, so mostly I just tried to avoid him.

It was with great delight that I bumped into him at my tenth high school reunion. There was never any question about Barbara not coming with me. She had avoided going to her own high school reunions and was surprised that I planned on going to mine. I wanted to face my old demons.

The reunion was held in a fire hall and the parking lot was filled with pickup trucks. Inside a long line snaked to the open bar. One guy I had known slightly in high school asked me if I was married. For some reason, the question took me by surprise. I explained to him that I was partnered with another woman. Without hesitation, he said to me, "So you're pussy-whipped too."

Later in the evening, I ran into my childhood tormentor. Ten years had passed, but Michael was still short and I was still taller. I put my hand on his upper arm, squeezed none too gently and said, "Hello Michael." He was with his best friend from high school, who no doubt was still his best friend, and his wife, a short, cute woman, with long ash-blond hair, who had been on the high school cheerleading squad. When I told him to give his mother my regards and to tell her I had become a writer, he gulped and stammered, "Y-y-you're kidding me." I told him no, I wasn't kidding, and casually named just a few of the magazines I wrote for. When I asked him what he was doing, he started cracking jokes about what could anyone expect when he just got out of prison.

I got the feeling that whatever he was doing just wasn't very interesting.

His wife intervened. "Michael never remembers these kind of things, but I'll make sure I tell his mother." Then she asked my name, wrote it down, patted my arm, and told me not to worry, she wouldn't forget. She knew how to score points with her mother-in-law, and she couldn't have made me any happier.

I walked away smiling and humming an old tune. At that exact moment I was living out one of my dreams. It was a dream that, even though I hadn't known it, I had been living out all through elementary, junior high and high school: I had dwarfed my arch enemy. I was somebody.

CHAPTER 9

Royalty

"Royalty, my arse." My mother hit the mute button on the remote, bringing the television's sound to a halt as deftly as if she were jamming on the brakes at the tail end of a yellow light. "The queen's chambermaid. Maybe."

A week had passed since our last visit. More than four months into my mother's diagnosis, I visited as often as I could. I was holding down my freelance business, getting things done at home, even making time to go out with Barbara and see friends—we were even planning on having a New Year's day party at our house. But my mother remained the center of my existence. Despite the fact that she was dying, my mother was very alive. She may have needed help to stand up, but her will was never stronger.

As I witnessed my mother's strength, I also felt it welling up in myself. The minor colds and infections that once plagued me were absent. Possibly I willed them away. My mother's immune system was compromised, leaving her susceptible to infections that could now end up killing her. Barbara was going to come with me this day but she had a cold, and we both thought it a good idea for her to stay home.

My mother and I sat in the living room watching Charles and Di walk stiffly across the vast grounds of Buckingham Palace, the green expanse limited only by the frame of the nineteen-inch television set, sound muted under my mother's decisive thumb.

My mother was pondering my grandmother's claim to royal lineage, something that made as much sense as my grandmother's brand loyalty to Bayer Aspirin. My mother always told me that my grandmother was convinced that her headaches couldn't be cured by anything cheaper.

My mother had no need for pomp and circumstance. She shopped for generic brands.

"I'll never understand what was in her head." My mother narrowed her eyes. "A *poor* woman who joined the Episcopal Church and voted Republican."

My mother pointed to Westminster Abbey on the television screen. "I was there. It made me angry as hell. You can't walk two feet in there without tripping over someone's tombstone, a statue, a monument. Millions of dollars spent on the dead. And people are going hungry in the same city. What about the living?"

She turned the mute button off, but lowered the volume. The narrator droned beneath her outrage, his words clipped, his voice carefully modulated. All was equally important, each coronation, each queen, each king, from the thirteenth-century coronation chair of Edward I to his royal descendants in their white britches playing cricket on the green, never questioning their monarchical birthright to rule.

My mother had traveled to England when she was fifty-nine years old. It was her first trip abroad and she went by herself, unfettered after more than twenty years of being responsible for others as wife, mother, housewife, chauffeur, cook, gardener, housekeeper, and holding down her occasional outside jobs as part-time school cafeteria server and in-season tax preparer for H&R Block.

I was nineteen years old, working a summer job at the chemical plant, saving my money for college so that I could escape my working, class background. The summer workers were, for the most part, college students whose fathers worked at the plant. We were the first in our families to go to college, to achieve what we thought of as a better standing in the world. Just as I was a product of the American Dream, steeped in the myth and reality of upward mobility, my grandmother was rooted in another kind of illusion, that of coming from royalty, while, in fact, her ancestors worked in the textile mills in the industrial armpit of northern England.

I was swept into the swing shift rhythms of the plant—the stench, the screech and thud, steam rising, falling, rivulets of sweat dripping down my face in a steady stream from the inside plastic rim of my hard hat, drenching my face, my neck. I met the first openly lesbian that I had ever known at the chemical plant.

Pat was a short, squat woman who wore men's work clothes. I had seen her around the plant and had thought that she was a man—until she turned up in the women's locker room. At that time, I thought a lesbian as butch as Pat was "mannish." She had short hair, a round face on a fireplug body and adopted the sexist behavior of the men at the plant, apologizing when she swore in front of me. I was offended and let her know I was quite capable of swearing myself, and there was no reason for her to apologize. What I didn't realize at the time was dressing and acting like the men at the plant was a survival skill for Pat. It may have just been shyness, but I felt compelled to change in the toilet stall at the end of my shift when she was in the dingy locker room. Once when I was taking a break, she sat down on a chair next to me on the couch, and told me a little about her life. The chemical plant was in the suburbs, in Bristol, close to where I had grown up but Pat lived in the city with her girlfriend. "We just live in a row home," she responded when I was impressed that she lived in the city. Pat had gone to college and graduated with a degree in English literature. She began working at the plant after taking a class with a feminist group called "Women in the Trades."

I was still young and naïve and intent on escaping my working-class origins—by attending college. It was ironic, perhaps, that the best paying job I could find in the summer was working at the plant. I had turned down a low-paying internship opportunity in my field. It didn't occur to me that anyone who had a degree in English literature would have a hard time finding a job that paid even halfway decently. On top of that Pat would have had an even harder time finding work with her extremely butch lesbian demeanor. In those days, Pat was what an out lesbian looked like. When I looked back on other women in my life who were probably lesbian—including a college gym teacher and a high school English teacher—I realized that none of them were out. After I came out in the 1980s in the context of the women's movement, and heard the phrase "male identified lesbian," women like Pat would come to mind. It was true that Pat was a stereotype—but she was also a pioneer. When I was nineteen and working in the plant, learning to drive a ten-speed flatbed truck and pumping oil into train cars with the old-timers my father's age (one of whom dropped dead of a heart attack on his way to clock out), I barely gave a thought to my mother or the trip she was taking to England. At nineteen, I was still trapped in the Not-Being-My-Mother struggle. Yet, I was always connected to her, even when I thought I was rebelling.

My job at the plant helped me understand my father's life better, experiencing his swing shift-altered reality of day and night. Throughout my childhood and adolescence, my father's schedule left an absence when he was at work and a shadowy presence when he was home sleeping in the afternoons. But my job at the chemical plant also brought me closer to my mother. In understanding my father's life, I could see how the work my mother did at home, rotating our lives around his shifts, underscored it. I was in the belly of the beast that spewed the fumes I grew up breathing, the toxins that may have eventually mutated the cells in my mother's body.

A few years after I had left home, my mother wrote me a letter saying she had been to a lecture by a woman "who had licked cancer." She said she had talked to this woman afterward and that the woman gave her a knowing look as if she had found a kindred soul. This was several years before my mother ended up in the hospital getting a colonoscopy, when she felt the lump that the doctors dismissed as inconsequential. This hospital visit was ten years before she woke up with the metastasis, before she was diagnosed with terminal fourth-stage cancer.

This was one of the few letters where my mother talked at length about herself. Usually the loops and scrawls of her handwriting echoed her concern for me. In my twenties, the letters I sent to and received from my mother attempted to bridge our relationship. My mother had not wanted me to leave home—most of the young women in my neighborhood did not leave their parents' house until they were married—and in later years my mother said that the fact that I went to college made me different from those around me. She also told me that when I was too busy to call she took it as a sign that she had done her job. She had reared a daughter who went on to live her own independent and active life.

The letters she sent me in those early years when I had left home were full of the difficulties between us: we should communicate better;

she missed me; she wanted me to come back for an extended visit, a kind of "vacation" from the city. Often she addressed more personal concerns—that I was too hard on myself; that I started a sex life too soon and it might be making my life difficult. She was also concerned because I had become disillusioned in my job as a magazine editor.

She ended one letter by saying, "Just remember the witch can't hurt you...ha ha ha." She compared our two lives as she saw them—she who lived for daily practicalities and me who seemed to live beyond anything practical. Most often, she ended her letters asking if I needed a dustpan and brush.

My mother always liked to talk, and as a teenager I didn't always like to listen, but when she returned from her trip to England she told me about it in such detail that I felt I had been there. A few hours after she landed at the Heathrow Airport, the cobblestones of London came alive with each step she'd taken. She stood in front of Buckingham Palace watching a parade of red and white uniformed Household Cavalry, the plumes atop their silver helmets cascading like smooth haired dust mops to brush their high-neck collars. Everything about them was the same: their shaved unsmiling beige faces; their gloved hands with wide white cuffs turned back to the elbow; the reins in their hands held exactly at the same perpendicular angle; the spurs on their heels riding above the identical footfalls of the horses.

At first she could hardly see anything from where she stood at the back of the crowd. I'd been in enough crowds with my mother—from rallies for political candidates to women's movement marches—to picture her elbowing her way through. "Pardon me, excuse me, same to you lady," she'd volley, stepping on a few feet, returning a cold stare or two until she stood at the front directly behind the gold tasseled rope. She pointed her camera at the guard in the red coat—standing stiffly at his post—and then clicked the shutter, setting off the flash on her camera. His black bushy hat bristled like an upturned toilet brush and he glared at her. My mother jumped back and laughed at this sudden expression she'd provoked on his wooden face.

Years after her trip when she talked about the Texan she met on the tour bus, she was still fuming. It had all started out innocently enough. The couple across the aisle from her was offering her some Southern hospitality. Then they found out that she was traveling alone.

"What's a little lady like you doing in a foreign country without your husband?" asked the man whose Texas drawl could fill a ten-gallon hat. "He just didn't get it," she told me later, "that a woman might want to get away from someone like him and go off and enjoy herself."

She changed her seat and continued her sojourn through the western seaport of Bristol and northern England into Scotland where they crossed the border into Langholm and then returned. "I almost didn't come back," she told me. "When the bus stopped in Langholm I got out to take a walk and I got so caught up in watching a man play the bagpipes—he was standing on a rock with the fog swirling around him—that I damn near missed the bus."

In each town she visited in England she thumbed through the pages of the telephone directory, running her index finger down the lists of Gadsbys, Washingtons and Farnsworths, the maiden names of her mother, grandmother and great-grandmother. She did this in the dusty corners of pubs where she ate her fish and chips dinners ("the food is awful—too greasy, for starters"); in telephone booths on street corners ("it's surprising no one mistook me for a hooker"); and in the guest houses where she stayed, lace curtains in the windows, and the "To Let" signs outside ("'To Let?' At first I thought the sign meant they had a toilet!"). Throughout her travels she found a handful of Gadsbys, Washingtons and Farnsworths, but the search ended in the telephone directory. What was she to do, call up a complete stranger and say, "Hello. You don't know me but we might be related?"

She traveled through the small towns with their thatched roofs and countryside inns serving steak and kidney pies ("no thanks"); jugged hare ("a nice name for roasted rabbit"); and sweetmeats ("bull testicles, no less!"). Through Bristol and Bath, Birmingham and Coventry, Newcastle upon Tyne and Crewe, Sheffield and Manchester, her mind stayed on one destination: Bradford, the city her mother told her their ancestors had come from.

When she finally arrived in Bradford, she sat on the coach fuming.

"I refused to get off the bus," she told me. "I could see from the window that the whole town was a dump."

From my mother's drawn face and the rage curled in her white-knuckled hands, it was clear that her mother's hopes and expectations about being related to royalty must have, in some small way, lived on in my mother. The home of her ancestors had taken root in her mind, compelling her to fulfill her mother's dream and her own curiosity by visiting Bradford on her one and only trip abroad. As she sat on the bus, her dreams and her mother's dreams came crashing down faster than the old London Bridge in the children's song.

To each side of the Italianate chimney of the Manningham Mill,

Bradford was nothing but one big dirty footprint left by centuries of soot. The coach had toured other industrial cities, Manchester, Birmingham, Leeds, but Bradford was the worst, sootier than the skyline of smokestacks she had grown up under, the poverty more acrid than the stench of the chemical plant where she waited to pick up my father after his shifts. The horizon was a jagged line of sagging stone and failing mortar, some of the houses in the distance indistinguishable from piles of rubbish. Faded pieces of cloth, dusty orange, brownish green, encrusted red, flapped limply from the broken windows of the narrow homes. Children spilled from open front doors and stared at the passing bus with hungry eyes. The people on the bus stared back, speechless. This was not an England that any of them had expected to encounter. As the bus careened down the narrow streets toward the station, they passed entire blocks full of abandoned buildings. These were the hulls of textile mills that in the city's Victorian heyday produced most of the world's worsted cloth. Pieces of old spinning and weaving equipment rusted in twisted heaps under the broken windows to which the well-dressed world turned a blind eye.

My mother feigned a headache to avoid getting off the bus, shooing away her concerned fellow travelers by pressing a moist towelette to her forehead. After the bus emptied, she opened her guidebook. The main attraction of Bradford was Saltaire, a perfectly preserved "industrial utopia" modeled after the town designed by textile baron Sir Titus Salt. Saltaire was built around Salt's Mill, the largest factory in the world when it opened, larger than St. Paul's Cathedral. An entire community, schools, hospitals, wash houses, baths, almshouses, along with eight hundred and fifty houses, surrounded it. The position of each of the houses reflected the family wage-earner's position in the factory hierarchy. The first public building finished was the Church of England, built directly outside of the factory gates. The church was the linchpin of the obedient worker, holding the hierarchy in place.

Thinking about her mother's devotion (which my mother most likely thought of as subservience) to the church, my mother slammed the guidebook shut. There was nothing here that was any better than her mother's life working in the textile mill. The mill was like an evil fairy tale—her mother and her mother and her mother before her had all pricked their fingers on a spindle and the life drained out of them. Seven years had passed since her mother's death. But, in my mother's mind, the final image of her mother, the cold and rigid lines of her face made garish by the undertaker's botched makeup job, was still in her mind. She remembered the waves of fury rolling through her as she stood in the drafty vestibule next to her mother's coffin. It was the same fury she felt as she sat on the bus, pressing the soles of her shoes against the metal floor until the heat felt like scorching flames, mounting higher, higher. Suddenly she was glad her mother was dead. At least she would never find out about Bradford, this home of their ancestors, this place of soot and decay and squalor that held her illusions over the spit and let them burn till they drowned in their own drippings.

"I was so angry at the British when I came back." My mother sat in her gold velour chair, staring off into space, somewhere between the front windows and the flickering but silent television set. "A few years later when I went to see the movie *Ghandi* it made me hate the British even more. What they did to the Indian people! They were demonstrating peacefully, just sitting there, and the British soldiers slaughtered them, gunned them down in cold blood."

I nodded, watching the silent image on the television set—an endless expanse of green inside the castle grounds, the luxury of time and space wasted on cricket matches. The tiny island that tried to rule the world—and at the same time hung its own people for stealing a loaf of bread or, if they could read the Bible, transported them as indentured servants.

My English ancestry was always with me as a remote mythic landscape somewhere in the back of my mind. When I was in grade school the teacher gave us an assignment to do a report on our ethnic backgrounds. Mine was filled with magazine cutouts of stone castles guarded by strangely dressed men with pantaloons and stiff collars. I may have used pictures of the English countryside with its symmetrical hedgerows, and maybe even a picture of Stonehenge with the sun shining through a circle of rock. But this remote landscape failed to fully capture my imagination. I found my best friend's report—full of pictures of spaghetti and lasagna and her declaration that she wanted to go to Italy to taste the food—much more interesting.

Still I knew where my ancestors had come from, and sometimes that made me feel unique. As a child, I would straggle behind my parents as we walked the boardwalk in Atlantic City and stare importantly out to sea. "England's over there," I would say to anyone who would listen, sometimes affecting a very bad English accent. "That's where I come from—way across the ocean." My mother had always told me that the British were boring ("Don't you ever bore yourself?") and also that they were hard on their children. "Your father may not talk about his childhood," she would say, "but the fact is that his father was just about as bad as mine."

When I was a child, my mother was the expert on ethnic backgrounds, mentioning as we walked around the neighborhood where the Scottish family lived, and the German and the Italian, all of whom just looked American to me, so there was no doubt in my mind that what she said about the British must be right. I could see the picture clearly for myself: cold damp foggy weather, stone castles, stiff upper lip, and no lasagna.

I always knew that stone castles, moats, knights in shining armor, and kings and queens were the stuff of fairy tales, and that none of it had anything to do with me. Still, as I watched the disillusionment etched on my mother's face and felt her resentment toward the British well up inside of me, I began to think that more of me was made up of my grandmother's illusions and my mother's indignations than I ever thought possible. I pondered the signs and omens that I had begun to read in the tea leaves. What was once murky was becoming clearer. The dust that had settled on the bottom of my cup, the lines of dots, did not portend disaster or represent snakes. Instead the dots were marking the path of my journey as I circled back to the starting point of my life which had become my destination.

My mother's terminal illness, and my consciousness of it, was always there, even when that old knee-jerk denial kicked in—(She's my mother. She can't possibly die)—or my endless rationalizations—(I could walk in front of a bus and go before her).

Spending time with her in this final stage of her life was the most difficult thing I had ever done. I came close to breaking down every time I saw her. She had become skeletal and was in more pain. But even so, a miracle was taking place between us.

My mother was growing tired. The clock on the mantelpiece was ticking. The silence between the seconds enclosed us. She reached out to me, and I slid toward her to take her hand.

"That was a nice talk we had," she said. "I think we're closer now than we've ever been."

CHAPTER 10

Devotions

I woke from my afternoon nap with a start. My mother, sitting on her chair next to me, blinked sleep away from her eyes. "I thought I heard church bells," I mumbled sleepily.

"Church bells?"—her eyes widening—"There's no church around here." But as an afterthought, she said, "I thought I heard something ringing too."

Both of us were in the living room later the same day of our talk about my mother's trip to England. We had fallen asleep, my mother in her chair and me on the couch, listening to a meditation tape of harp music. Dream images lingered in my mind: A fire blazing on the heels of a distant ancestor running through a dark forest, her breath raking through her, tree branches snagging her hair. The life of this woman continued beyond the end of my dream into the lives of the women whose destinies had come down to my mother and me.

I went into the kitchen to fix us both some tea and a snack—vegetarian brown rice sushi that I'd made earlier in the day. My mind slipped back to the woman in my dream. Her name was not known to me, but her life and her mother's and her mother's mother entwined with mine. Her face, dirt-streaked, broad cheeks, eyes dilated, was filial.

By the time I set the dishes and silverware on the dining room table, my mother had a sudden burst of energy and had managed, unassisted, to use her cane to push herself up from her chair. I kept hoping that she might regain her strength, and for the moment it seemed that she had. In more recent days, she had required assistance to even help her stand.

I watched as she walked the ten feet to the dining room table, the wooden cane in her right hand preceding every step. How had it come to this? Walking across the living room to sit down at the dining room table had taken on the proportions of scaling a mountaintop.

I brought our cups of tea and plates of vegetarian sushi to the table where my mother sat. Her cane leaned against the table on her right. Her face was tilted down, as if in prayer. Her eyes were distant and, at the same time, analytical, the look that possessed her when she puzzled over the events of her life.

My grandmother's myths and illusions never made sense to my mother. It had become clear to me, however, that they were the foundation on which she stood. They kept her spine erect, even when her shoulders were yoked, and her spirit intact as she suffered the small and large humiliations of a woman alone with two children who needed her job no matter what the cost.

I now understood that not only my grandmother's and my mother's dreams and illusions but also their nightmares and chimeras lived on in me. Dreams are not constructed from thin air. They are born of hopes and disappointments, and they fuel both the will to live and the desire to die. They take on lives of their own, spanning generations, crossing great divides from mind to mind. And nowhere does this transmission of dreams, acknowledged or not, take on more complicated meanings than between a mother and daughter.

When I was a toddler my mother and I used to sing together, my small hands in her larger ones, my high voice blending with her lower one, as we pulled on imaginary oars: *"Row, row, row your boat gently down the stream, merrily, merrily, merrily, merrily, life is but a dream..."* This was our favorite song to sing together and in pictures of the two of us holding our hands up in the air on "dream," anyone could see that these were the golden moments of childhood.

These were the years in which I was molded in my mother's likeness. At times the two of us even wore matching dresses, though

I doubt my mother was any more comfortable in a dress than I was, perhaps less so. In an old black-and-white photograph, I was about three or four, standing outside next to my mother, both of us wearing flower print dresses. It was early spring and I was standing next to a lilac bush, inhaling purple nectar. Our smiles were genuine, not forced or artificial as they sometimes were in later years. As a toddler, I was at home holding my mother's hand, just as my mother found her home in mine.

I was a planned child. My mother had been trying to have a baby for years. When no child of their own seemed forthcoming, she and my father thought of adopting, but the agency told her she was too old. She was almost forty. After the adoption agency turned down my parents I was conceived. When my mother first told me this story I joked that I was the "fuck you" baby in response to the agency's ageism.

If the New Age people are right and we do choose our parents, it may well have been that my conception at this time was my own plucky spirit deciding to enter the world. But it was also true that my rebellious spirit was forged from my mother's own heresies. The nest that was waiting for me was lined with ashes. Years before I was born, my mother went out into the backyard and burnt her Bibles and religious books. I imagined her satisfaction as the pages curled to ash and disappeared into thin air.

"I always thought the church would provide me with answers," my mother said. She had just carefully sipped her tea and put the gold trimmed white teacup back down on its CorningWare saucer.

"What kind of answers, Mom?"

She pursed her lips before she spoke. "The larger picture. The meaning of life and the meaning of death. I was always searching for something. I read the Old and New Testament from beginning to end, then I took a Bible study course, and by the time I finished I was furious. It contradicts itself almost on every page. The only thing that was clear to me was the misogyny. Whoever wrote the Bible really hated women."

I grew up thinking that the Bible was written by a group of gay men—the disciples—who hated women. This was almost all I knew about the Bible, which I hadn't bothered to read except in excerpts in high school English where it was taught as fiction. As an adult, when I mentioned my theory about the women-hating homosexual disciples, which I swear I learned from her (however, misinformed that stereotype may be), my mother denied she ever said anything of the kind.

When I was a child, my mother took me to church every now and then—most likely to appease my grandmother. To me, church seemed to be a mystery—one that involved dressing up, sitting in uncomfortable pews, ignoring the minister and gazing at stained glass windows. The one thing that was clear to me was my mother's rage. It was also obvious that she bent over backward to hide her feelings about the church from my grandmother. My mother was a loyal daughter. She was not about to tell her mother that she had burnt her Bibles in the backyard and had subsequently become a card-carrying atheist. Whenever we went to visit my grandmother, my mother would take me aside beforehand and tell me that if my grandmother asked if we went to church that week that the answer was "Yes." This was fine with me. Staying home and reading the Sunday funnies was far more enjoyable than sitting on a hard pew watching my mother twist the life out of her hanky.

"I was so angry at how the church treated my mother when she died." My mother shifted in her dining room chair. A streak of pain flattened the features of her face. In the late afternoon light, the ridges of her neck were more prominent than I had ever seen them. She looked thinner than she had just that morning at breakfast.

I remembered seeing my grandmother laid out. I knew she had died, but the reality of it sunk in when I saw her in the casket. I didn't know what I expected. That she would come back to life? Perhaps in my only-child mind, I thought she would reach out and hug me just because I was there. I was twelve years old and unacquainted with death. My step-grandfather had died the year before but my strongest memory from that day was seeing my mother sit down on a bench in the funeral parlor, slip off her uncomfortable pumps, and fan herself with her mesh hat. Later she told me that my grandmother was furious with her for doing this.

The minute I saw my grandmother in the casket I broke into sobs. When the undertaker, a stranger with a waxy pallor in his face, a villain's mustache and a diamond pinky ring, put his hand on my shoulder, I recoiled in horror. My mother was angry at the undertaker for the lousy makeup job—she talked about it for months afterward. She was angry at her sister for crying. She was angry at the lawyers for trying to charge an arm and a leg to sell my grandmother's house. In North Philadelphia the housing prices had depreciated so much at the time that it would cost more to get rid of the house than they would make if they sold it. My mother and aunt ended up giving the house to Mr. Harvey, my grandmother's next-door neighbor. And my mother was angry—

spitting mad, in fact—at the church for putting my grandmother's casket in a drafty vestibule instead of in the main sanctuary where she had bowed her head and lined the collection plate each week.

Most of all, my mother was furious that her mother was dead.

That my grandmother had given so much of her life to the church fueled my mother's fury. My grandmother felt indebted to the church. But the shame of receiving charity was so embedded in her that when it was time for her to receive Social Security, she was dead set against it. "I don't take handouts," she would say to my mother. "It's not a handout Ma," my mother explained. "You earned that money all the years that you spent working."

My mother kept repeating this and finally my grandmother relented and accepted the Social Security that she had paid into for most of her life—since the Social Security Act was signed into law in 1935.

In all her years of working, my grandmother put her little white envelope in the church's shiny brass collection plate. Sitting next to her mother in church, my mother, as a child, watched her mother's every movement from the corner of her eye. Except for opening and closing the hymnal, her mother's hands in their white gloves were almost motionless. Then the shiny brass plate was passed. With one deft movement, she opened her purse and took out her small white envelope. My mother didn't know how much money her mother put in the envelope, but she did know that her own shoes were a size too small.

The church was my grandmother's social network. This became especially important when she was older and had stopped working and so many of her friends had died off. After my father retired, my parents became more and more isolated. I was concerned about them, not only because of their lack of a social life—they had always been good friends with each other which partly made up for this—but because they were starting to go to doctors more frequently. They needed a peer group for advice and referrals. At the time, I suggested to my mother that she and my father try going to the Unitarian Church.

I was surprised years later to find out that she had actually gone.

"I didn't like it. After the service everyone stood around eating cookies and drinking coffee. The woman who came up to talk to me let me know that it was her job to greet me. 'Fuck you,' I said to myself, 'if you're not even capable of talking to me on your own because you want to.'"

My mother picked up a piece of her brown rice sushi, then put it down again and shifted uncomfortably. I got a pillow from the living room and put it behind her back.

After she was settled, I asked, "Did you say 'fuck you' to her?"

"No. But that's the way I felt, and she could see it on my face." She shrugged and looked down into her teacup uninterestedly, before looking back up. "That's the way church people are. One makes the coffee, one brings the doughnuts, another one greets the new people. They're very good at doing what they're told—just like a bunch of idiots."

The church was my mother's pushing off-point from her mother. The burning of her Bibles a defiant "fuck you" that wasn't so much directed at her mother as it was to the church that had harnessed her mother's dreams. My mother was a realist. To her, religion was a ruse.

My mother's rejection of religion opened up a world of possibility for me.

After my grandmother died, we stopped going to church entirely. Then after six months or so went by, my mother decided she would take me around to different churches to see if I liked any of them. The Quaker Meeting House—the tie-dyed unisex look (long hair for both sexes) prevailed—came closest. Not being able to tell the boys from the girls appealed to me, but the hippies were all older than me, and the Quaker pews were just as hard as the Episcopal ones. I returned home to read the funny pages on Sunday mornings.

Later that year in my seventh-grade humanities class, we took a field trip to various places of worship including a Greek Orthodox Catholic church and a synagogue. On the way back to the school, the teacher sat next to me on the bus and asked what religion I was. "I'm an agnostic," I told her, a new kind of pride creeping into my awareness. I had chosen my words carefully. I believed in a divine presence, just not in the religious specifics of it. I was different from the religious believers, and I was also different from my mother.

Another six months passed. I turned thirteen. It was time for me to rebel against my mother. I joined a Presbyterian youth group with my best friend, and with my new peers I learned to shoplift and smoke and kiss my middle finger loudly before flipping the bird to anyone I felt like insulting. One of the ministers talked to us about his youth, when he used to drink to make up for his shyness. There were times in his life when the bottle was the only friend he had. Then he found religion, became a minister, and gave up drinking. I got the impression that religion was what helped him most, even though he told us there were times when he doubted the existence of God. I related to his having felt alone in a world where a bottle of liquor could substitute for a friend. As much as his stories resonated with me, they didn't make a difference. Within a year I had gone from blowing smoke rings and shoplifting Twinkies to drinking any kind of alcohol I could get my hands on and smoking dope. It was as easy as graduating from seventh grade into eighth.

During that same time, my best friend went through confirmation in the Presbyterian Church, and she started picking out names for future children she would have with her yet-to-be-met husband. I suddenly lost interest in all things religious. But when I turned eighteen I started dating a good Catholic boy my age, who went to church every Sunday.

Eventually, of course, he wanted me to come with him. Going to a Catholic Mass, given how I felt about the church's stand on abortion, equal rights for women and just about everything else, was not an attractive proposition for me. But, aside from my boyfriend's persistence, going to Mass with him also held the appeal of being one more thing I could do to bug my mother. If I had consciously realized this at the time, I might have reconsidered what I was doing with this boyfriend in the first place. But since I was still drinking, spinning my wheels, and rebelling against my mother, I went to Mass.

Pew by pew, the parishioners lined up to take communion, walking slowly with bowed heads. Sitting in the pew next to my boyfriend and his family, I was a hung-over skeptic. I thought of sheep being led to the slaughter. I stayed seated while my boyfriend and his family went up to the altar. The thought of eating the body of Christ and drinking his blood did nothing for my already queasy stomach. Later, when my boyfriend asked me why I didn't take communion, I told him I didn't want to rush into anything. Trapped as I was in the most conventional of heterosexual relationships with him calling me, deciding where to go, taking me out and footing the bill, this refusal of taking communion was a small victory. But soon it was eclipsed by his expectation that I would go with him every Sunday.

We went out every weekend. I thought I was in love with him, but I was painfully aware that something essential was missing. Even so, he was my ticket to social acceptance. My two closest friends from high school had both gotten married. Unlike my friends, I was in college, commuting from my parents' home into the city. College was a wedge between myself and my friends. My boyfriend, an apprentice in the trades, deeply resented my attendance. He accused me of loving books more than him. Other girls, he informed me, were different.

He was partly right. I wasn't like most other girls—at least not the ones I knew. As conflicted as this made me feel, I didn't want to be like the others. My two best friends had tedious jobs and, in my estimation, came home to even more monotonous existences with their husbands. I had no interest in following suit. But I was still attached to my two best friends with emotional bonds that were stronger than the one I had with my boyfriend. Ironically, the relationship with my boyfriend was the last thing I had in common with my girlfriends.

Having a regular boyfriend also offered me protection. As a young woman, tall, thin, blond, I was constantly under siege from the not-so-flattering attentions of men. In one instance a frat boy followed me for twenty minutes across campus trying to get me to go with him to a party. Dating one man gave me a good excuse to stay away from the others.

As convenient as the arrangement was, I was beginning to get bored. I decided that if I was going to go to church with him, the least he could do was to have sex with me in the bathroom of his house before Mass. He was nineteen years old. Getting it up the night before and the morning after was no problem. In the cramped quarters of the bathroom next to his parents' basement rec room, I loved the guilty look on his face as much as anything else. When he dropped me off later in the afternoon, my mother would apprehensively ask how church was. "It was fun," I'd say, distractedly.

I went to Mass in a hung-over fog, sated with sex, and not giving a damn about what the priest was talking about. Most of the time, I didn't bother to listen. But my boyfriend must have been paying attention. After a few weeks of Sunday morning sex in the bathroom, the guilt-stricken look on his face had spread to the rest of his body. "I can't do it," he groaned.

"Oh Christ," I answered, rolling my eyes, deciding never to go to church with him again.

We stayed together for a few years after that, even though it was increasingly obvious that we didn't have a future together. He wanted a big family. I didn't want children. As a child, I loved my baby dolls as much as any other girl. But books, and the worlds they transported me to, quickly became my passion. When I left my dolls in a heap, their pink arms grubby from the dirt of my childhood hands, to be taken to the Goodwill, my mother did not interfere. She gave me free range with my solitude, letting me curl up for hours, turning pages, intimately involved in the thoughts of imaginary people.

My best friend had spent her teen years updating and revising the names of her future children (her favorite was Crystal). Her mother gave her a bride doll for her sixteenth birthday. With every passing interest in a boy, regardless of whether she was dating him, she began to make plans to grow up and get married. I felt betrayed. Before this, we had always schemed to spend the rest of our lives together. I pictured us as Laverne and Shirley, forever single, making a home with each other. Like Laverne, I would have a large purple "L" sewn on my sweater. It may have been my wish to stay bonded with my best friend that convinced me, several years into my relationship with my boyfriend, to concede to his wishes of having children in the future. One would be okay, I told him, even as I was still trying to convince myself. After all, Barbara Walters had a daughter, and her career didn't seem any the worse for it.

When my boyfriend's older sisters started having children, I watched their lives get sucked into a whirlwind of dirty diapers, baby food, and dashed expectations. Despite my declarations, my stomach began to churn even at the thought of getting married, much less having a child. The fear of losing myself was underscored by my lack of experience. I had no younger siblings or family members. And the few babysitting jobs I took had quickly turned into nightmares of screaming, out-of-control children.

My boyfriend never questioned the expectation of his family that he would be married in the Catholic Church. To me, being married at all, even at sunrise on the beach, was beginning to feel like too much of a compromise. Neither of my two married best friends had been able to conceive children. Even so, their lives were no longer their own. It was the 1970s, but in working-class culture, the 1950s feminine mystique—or "mistake" as I called it—was everywhere. My two best friends vied for my fiercest loyalties, and as a consequence they hated each other. But on this one matter they agreed: I was willing to sacrifice the love of an old-fashioned boy, just to satisfy my self-indulgent whims. They were real women. I was not.

The more I argued with them, the more determined I became. I may have been steeped in internal conflict and alcohol-soaked confusion, but I was fiercely determined to be my own person. There was nothing more appalling to me than the thought of becoming Mrs. Somebody Else's Name, the status my girlfriends had aspired to. The final straw came when I argued vehemently with my boyfriend over a woman's right to choose. I stormed into the house, complaining of what an absolute idiot he was. My mother looked at me and said, "You know how he feels about things. Why even bother to bring it up? Besides, if the argument is about you, I don't think I'd want you to abort my grandchild."

I was spitting mad but managed to assure her that the argument had nothing to do with me being pregnant, and in that moment I looked at her as if she were Judas. *My mother*, who had raised me to be the feminist I was, had taken *his* side. Just a few weeks before, she had looked at a picture of my boyfriend and me and remarked that he looked enough like her to be her son. Now she wanted me to have grandchildren with him or, at the very least, not to abort them.

I broke up with him.

I was graduating from college soon anyway. It was time for a change.

Regardless what my mother did, she couldn't win. A year before we split up, my boyfriend, concerned about my behavior when I was premenstrual, went to my mother for advice. "At least you don't have to live with her," she retorted. Considering how conventional he was, he must have been at his rope's end to bring this up with my mother. I had a raging temper when I was drinking—which was mostly all the time I was with him—made far worse, no doubt, by the hormones in my birth control pills. Whenever he suggested, no matter how politely, that I was probably premenstrual, I flew into a rage. "You men are all alike," I'd say, spitting the words from between my teeth. "It's always my period. My period! Like nothing else is wrong in this goddamn world!"

"I guess it's time to move on," my father said of my breakup. My mother said nothing except, "Well, it really didn't seem like it would work out." I see now that I was far more loyal to my mother than I ever would have thought at the time. My ex-boyfriend never liked my mother. He didn't like that she did yoga, stood on her head, had an organic garden, ate health food, and usually, when not possessed by delusions about her daughter's future security, spoke her mind. In short, he was suspicious that my mother was her own person, unlike his mother who didn't drive, had no life of her own outside of her devotion to the Catholic Church, and let her husband and her children treat her like a doormat.

I was sullen and withdrawn whenever my boyfriend spoke badly about my mother. I was still rebelling against her, but I deeply resented his criticisms. By criticizing my mother, he was, in effect, putting me down. Three years later, before Barbara and I became lovers, she accidentally met my mother at a women's cable TV conference where

I was moderating a panel. In the first few years after I came out, I frequently took my mother with me to feminist events. My lesbian friends, especially the older ones, all found her striking with her short hair, high cheekbones and Katherine Hepburn-like curiosity about the world.

At the women's cable conference, I introduced my mother to Barbara simply by name. "This is Jane Mason," I said. When Barbara asked if we were related, I just laughed and went back to watching the video about the Seneca Women's Peace Encampment. A straight friend of mine from college sat on the other side of my mother as we watched the video. "Boy, Janet," she said, leaning across my mother, "You'd fit right in with those women!"

"That was your *mother*?" Barbara said to me sometime the next day after we had woken up together in her bed and were talking. "I thought she was just an older lesbian friend."

"That's what everyone thinks," I said distractedly, snuggling under her arm and resting my head in a place that already felt like home. We had arrived at her apartment after a harrowing journey from the women's Halloween dance the night before. For starters, my very recently ex-lover, dressed as Wonder Woman, had followed me around all night. Wherever Barbara and I sat, she sat. When we got up to dance, she was right there beside us. Finally, Barbara, who had no idea who she was, turned to her in exasperation and said, "Go ahead and dance with her." I headed for a chair. Wonder Woman followed.

My ex always did have a problem taking no for an answer. But by the end of the evening, her tenacity gave Barbara and me a shove in the right direction. When she asked Barbara for a ride home, I was ready to head for the hills. But Barbara took my hand and convinced me to come with them. After we dropped off Wonder Woman at the group house where she lived in West Philadelphia, Barbara drove back to my car outside the restaurant and hotel where the cable conference had been. She parked on some broken glass, and got a flat. It was too late to change it, so we went into the bar to strategize and decided that I would drive her home and that she would get her car the next day. When we were leaving, the bartender asked us what our costumes were. I was wearing a khaki dress and a wide-brimmed hat. Barbara's attire was a red velvet jacket with a skinny tie.

"I'm Bella Abzug," I told him, "and this is my husband."

Barbara's deep-set blue eyes widened and she gulped. I had a good laugh. Then we went back to her place where I took off my clothes, hopped into her bed, and spent the night.

Six months later when I told my mother that Barbara and I were moving in together, she merely replied, "How long do you expect that to last?" Then she and my father helped Barbara and me move into our new apartment and gave us a present of a hundred dollars. Things were cheaper then and we managed to buy a futon and a set of bookshelves. We had my parents over for a visit and then went out to dinner with them. I knew I was lucky. I had heard many stories from my lesbian friends about parents who couldn't cope. Some parents, like Barbara's, didn't want the nature of the relationship mentioned in their presence. Others forbade their adult children to bring their partners home and some cut off contact entirely.

Barbara, too, had grown up in a non religious family. Her mother was raised Italian Catholic but she married Barbara's father, who was raised Methodist, and married him in the same church where his parents were married. Because her husband would not convert, she was excommunicated from the Catholic Church. This resulted in giving her mother a jaded view of the religion in which she was raised. One time she said to me in a hushed confidential tone of voice, "The priests take donations for the last rites"—implying that they were only in it for the money. Barbara's father, on the other hand, pretended he was more religious than he was and denounced atheists. Barbara's parents were more conventional than mine, but they took no interest in religion when their children were growing up.

That my father called himself an agnostic and my mother embraced atheism helped when I came out. In their eyes Barbara and I were not committing any kind of sin. We were simply two women who loved each other and wanted to make a life together. As my parents' only child, and despite the fact that my father had problems with me being a lesbian, what they both wanted most for me was to be happy.

And I was.

During the first few years of our relationship, when Barbara was getting to know my mother, she always told me with much affection that when I got old I would be just as much of an interesting and attractive live wire as my mother. She said this with what I thought might be a little too much enthusiasm. "What are you trying to tell me?" I'd say teasingly, "You think my mother's sexy?" "Sure," she'd answer. "And so are you." This gave me all the more reason to love her. That she liked my mother so much meant that she liked me, not only where I came from but also where I was going.

Despite my early rebellion against my mother, and my mother's rebellion against her mother—in the form of burning her Bibles—we were both loyal daughters. With my mother's life coming to a close, my loyalty reached its pinnacle. The depth of my emotion was met by the fierceness I saw welling up inside of my mother. As the cancer eroded her body, as her walking, moving and breathing became more difficult, her spirit rose up in mythic proportions. My mother and I were forged from the same molten metal.

The binding ingredients in this loyalty were friendship and mutual respect. When it came to things that really mattered, my mother and I were more alike than different. This included our individual takes on spirituality and religion. As a child, I was always trying to feel the presence of God, something I found impossible to do in a church. The too hard pews, the dark stained glass windows, the sweet sickly smell of formaldehyde and flowers left over from the funerals, the minister's drone, the stifling lack of fresh air.

In contrast, at twelve years old, I lost my way on the beach when visiting the seashore with my parents. The sun was setting and I looked long and hard into the horizon, the thin line between the water and sky disappearing into the dusk, until concentration became a prayer. Something larger than myself enveloped me in a moment that felt like forever. When I turned around, my mother was walking toward me.

It was this finding of God, or of some unnamed spiritual presence in nature, that I learned from my mother. Ever since I could remember, she had a love of gardening in her life.

"Didn't you ever feel it?" I asked my mother as we talked on about my grandmother, about religion and the lack of it in our lives.

"Feel what?" she asked.

I replied, "The presence of nature, of spirituality, in all the gardening you used to do."

My mother smiled. Our eyes connected and despite the words that were forming to come out of her mouth, I knew it was true: My mother had always been deeply connected to the earth.

Then the moment was gone. She scoffed at the idea.

"Gardening has nothing to do with religion. I was growing vegetables."

"But I grew up watching you do it," I said to her.

"You were never interested in gardening," she retorted. "You were afraid of worms."

"That's true," I said. "But I have a garden now."

My mother nodded. "Those were delicious collard greens you brought over. And you knew just how to pick off the leaves, going around the outside to the center."

"I learned that from you, Mom."

My mother shrugged with a twitch of her shoulders. "I think you saw more of my back when you were growing up than my face. I was always bending over the garden, weeding." For a moment her face paled, as if she were thinking of herself as not being a good mother, of not having paid enough attention to her daughter. Then her expression changed to one of well-honed perception. "The good thing about that is that you weren't always looking at my face for validation. You learned to look to yourself for what you needed."

CHAPTER 11

The Funny Papers

"Your father knows where the Memorial Society papers are," my mother told me. "You know I want to be cremated. And don't let them sell you an expensive urn. Take my ashes to the park—remember the clearing where we stood next to the sapling and looked at the moon over the lake?—and scatter them there."

I nodded. I knew the exact location my mother was talking about. We took a walk there several years ago. My father was ahead of us on the path, and my mother turned to me and exclaimed, "This is where I want my ashes to go after I die, right here." It was late afternoon. The sun was out. A pale thumbnail of a moon sat off to the side of the sky. Her comment jolted me into the future. She didn't say why she wanted her ashes there, or indicate any weariness or premonition of her own death.

My mother had always been a talker and, in her observation, much of what she had said went in one of my ears and out the other. But, as I took note of my surroundings, the moon in the sky, the path next to the woods, the clearing that led down to the wide quiet lake, I knew I wouldn't forget this exact moment or the location when I needed to come back to it.

My mother was asking something of me that only I would be able to do.

It was early December, past the halfway mark of my mother's "six months, maybe" diagnosis. Barbara, who had come to visit a week ago, had been looking at the pictures of my mother's calendar with a thoughtful expression. Later, she would show me my mother's chicken scratch scrawl on my father's birthday in March—where she wrote, "Happy birthday Al,"—and mine in May—"Happy Birthday, Janet." Later, Barbara would say to me, "I realized then that she didn't expect to be here in the spring." When Barbara said this a kind of wonderment as well as sadness crept into her voice as if she were thinking, how could it be that my mother would cease to exist? Barbara didn't stay overnight with me at my parents' house but she did come with me now and then when I went over for the day.

My mother wanted Barbara to come and spend the night with me, but I sensed that it was too much for Barbara who always joked that the only intense thing that she liked was me. I understood that being around a dying person is not for everyone. Besides, Barbara had her own vibrant life. This weekend, she was rehearsing for an upcoming gig with members of a percussion group that she had put together called Rhythm Method. "It's how most of us got here," she said sagely after telling me the name she had thought up.

The way I coped—spending time with my mother so close to the end of her life— was by somehow managing to convince myself that by some miracle my mother could live if I were there. But the cold solid fact that she was dying resonated in the marrow of my bones. She had continued to lose weight rapidly, and the tumor in her abdomen was protruding from the surface of her stomach, looking slightly larger than a clenched fist. She began to spend more time in bed. The HMO nurse ordered her an adjustable hospital bed with electronic controls.

My father, who had always slept upstairs, moved my mother's old bed for himself into the room across the hall from hers, the room that served as office, study and sewing quarters.

"She's wanted me to move downstairs for ages," he told me when we were alone, tears springing to his eyes. "I guess I was just used to being upstairs..."

When he broke into a sob, I put my hand on his arm. "It's okay, Dad, I told him. "You're doing the best you can."

He was at her beck and call. At her request, he hung a set of wind chimes next to her bed with a long string hanging down so she could ring the metal chimes whenever she needed him.

There were days when she could not get out of bed. When it was time for her to brush her teeth and she couldn't get up, she called for her "servants" (my father and me) to bring her a toothbrush, bowl and towel. This was her way of making light of a situation that was out of her control. My mother who had always done everything for herself was now reduced to asking for assistance to brush her teeth.

Today she was having a good day, able to sit up in the living room and talk to me while my father was out for his brisk, four-mile walk.

"I've been thinking about your father." She was sitting in the straight back folding chair that she had been using once her gold velour rocking chair had become too uncomfortable. "If he takes care of me long enough he might get worn out. The best place for him might be a nursing home."

I looked at her doubtfully. Both of my parents always hated even the thought of a nursing home. But now that my mother was going and he was staying, she wanted him to check into one? I could just hear my father scoffing at the idea, but I refused to play third party to my parents' disagreements.

"And don't let your father keep my ashes in the house. It won't be easy for him, but he has to learn to let go of me."

The thought of my mother reduced to a silent pile of ashes was too much for me. I broke down into a sob.

My mother rolled her eyes. "Oh God, your father did that same thing to me just the other day. There are things I have to talk about, you know."

I reached for a tissue and nodded. Even at thirty-four I could only attempt to be a grown-up with my mother at times like this. My mother's skepticism left her face and she looked at me with a deepening of her features, a long felt knowing of having seen me come this far through every phase of my life.

"It's not that I'm planning to die tomorrow."

My eyes met hers momentarily and then moved away. The ticking of my father's retirement clock filled the room. Our eyes met in a deep well of compassion. My mother knew what this was like. She had lost her mother.

"I do need to talk about things," she said. "But I don't have to talk about them all right now."

The Sunday paper was a few feet away from where I sat on the couch. For much of my life the Sunday paper had been a kind of religion for me. As a child and as a teenager I absorbed myself in its pages for hours. When I was in journalism school, I frequently read two Sunday papers, limiting myself to forty-five minutes for the *The Philadelphia Inquirer* and an hour and a half for *The New York Times*. A few years later, seriously burnt out from writing all day in my freelance business and working on a feminist paper in the evening, I rarely read the newspaper at all. It was too depressing. Ronald Reagan was president and everything we were working so hard for in the women's movement was being rolled back or denounced by one right-wing politician after another.

Picking up the front page, I suddenly viewed the tragedies of the world as having a new purpose in my life. Now, no matter how gruesome or outrageous, they offered a distraction from my own ongoing misfortune. As they had been for months on end, the headlines were full of news about the brutal murder of Nicole Brown Simpson and her companion. The media had seized this as the celebrity case of the decade. To my mother and me and most other feminists, it was just one more sad case of a battering ex-husband who killed the wife who dared to leave him.

My mother came up with a different twist on this theme.

"I never trusted rich men." A faraway look crept into her eyes as she spoke. "When I worked for the Navy Department, there was a man there who was a big muckety-muck in the accounting office. He offered me a ride home one day in his big expensive car and I accepted. Then he thought he'd try to take me home every day, but I left early and took the subway. He thought I didn't like him because he wasn't in uniform. There was something wrong with him and the army gave him a deferment. But that wasn't the only reason. Rich men think they can buy you. I wouldn't even let him drop me off at my house that one time he did take me home. I would have been embarrassed to be seen getting out of a car like that."

As I listened to my mother, I was lulled into a deeper sense of myself, the part of me that was constructed from her stories. Each time she began to talk of the past, I asked to hear more. I needed to hear the questions she gave me for my life by telling me the answers she found in her own. My listening contained urgency.

"What was the name, again, of the law firm you worked for?"

"Oh no, I don't have to go into that again. Do I?" My mother gave me a skeptical look and then went on talking without further prompting. "Leon and Leaper. There were two law partners." She shifted in her chair, a streak of pain creasing her face, then receding after she paused to take a deep breath. "The one I worked for was just an ordinary lawyer who handled lots of cases. His partner was a tobacco heir, a real Southern gentleman with good manners. It was because of me that he stopped smoking. I would go into his office to take dictation and he'd be puffing away, one coffin nail after another. I'd be sitting there coughing and clearing my throat. One day he said to me, 'You don't smoke do you?' I didn't at the time, so I said no. And, believe it or not, after that he started to cut back and eventually stopped altogether."

My mother's words washed over me, falling into place like the colors of a painting, the reds and oranges reflected in the shadows. After she graduated from eighth-grade, her mother sent her to business school. My grandmother saw it as salvation for her daughter. "Art doesn't put food on the table," she repeated so many times that it entered my mother's mind in a continuous loop. It didn't matter that the sketches and drawings my mother did were already good and getting better, or that she spent hours absorbed in her artwork until her mother interrupted her, saying, "That's never going to get you anywhere. Put it away."

My mother never questioned the logic of her mill worker mother who wanted her daughter to do better. She shut the lid on her art box, the thin charcoal pencils; the chalky pastels; the dusty blue case of watercolors that Miss Zollers had given her; the lightweight paper sketching pad; the loose sheets of ragged edge paper. All of it locked away with the end of childhood, sealed up tight in the unspoken corners of her mind.

Business school was a rustle of dictation and stenography lessons, as precise as the little bell at the end of the typewriter carriage, as orderly as the filing systems she learned. "I always say that the public schools don't know how to teach English," my mother said with a glint in her eyes. "I didn't get a decent education until I went to business school. And it took two foreign-born Jews to teach us. The Strayers were a German Jewish couple who started the school, and you know how they got us in there? They guaranteed us jobs—in the middle of the Depression."

In 1937, she graduated from Strayers Business School and went to work at the law firm that paid her ten dollars per week. She was seventeen years old. The office building where she worked was on Broad Street across from the Pennsylvania Academy of the Fine Arts where she went on her lunch breaks, standing in front of the paintings, analyzing the perspective, the line, the form, the color, the brushstrokes.

"I used to read the cases as I typed them. It slowed me down, but boy were they interesting." My mother continued to talk, sparks flying from her eyes, burning away the years.

I could see her as a stunning young woman: her hair a soft auburn wave, her cheekbones high and defined; her eyes flashing hazel green.

"I'll never forget the case where the husband used to go out and get drunk all the time. Stinkin' drunk. One afternoon his wife had her ladies' club at the house. And he came home and threw up on the dog. Then the dog shook himself all over the ladies! And that disgusting thing came into the office for his divorce case and wanted to date me. He was thirty-five and to me that was ancient. In another case a woman who hadn't seen her husband in twenty years came in and said she wanted a divorce. She wasn't getting remarried. She had finally gotten some money and wanted a divorce. That piece of paper was *important* to her. I should have written a book about those divorce cases."

She shifted again. "My boss used to invite me home to his house to do some typing. His wife was always there. She was his secretary before I was. I bet she *loved* him bringing me around. This naive seventeen-year-old. He may have been interested in me, but I never liked him. He was forty and to me that meant he was a decrepit old thing. The summer after I started working for him he took me to the shore on vacation with him and his wife. I don't know why he brought me, and I'm surprised my mother or his wife allowed me to go. The three of us were walking down the boardwalk in Atlantic City, and he said we were going to the fights.

"'But I don't like the fights,' I told him, screwing up my face. I don't know how I got so fresh. I guess it was because I didn't have a father at home bossing me. I don't think his wife liked the fights either, but she was the type to go along with everything he said. But I opened my big mouth and guess what? We didn't go to the fights.

"When I applied for the job at the Navy Department, it was his wife who told him I was job hunting. A friend of hers overheard me talking about the job in the ladies' room. She must have been in one of the stalls. I was putting on my lipstick in front of the mirror and talking to a friend of mine. I can't believe how stupid I was—talking about my business where everyone could hear me. The next day I was just finishing typing up a brief and was about to pull the page out of the typewriter when I looked up and saw my boss staring down at me. I could tell something was wrong. His face was red and a vein throbbed on his temple. 'Miss Wood,' he said, 'I know you're job hunting, and I refuse to give you a reference.'

"'I'd be ashamed to let anyone know that I worked for you,' I said.

"He was so shocked he didn't know what to say. He never expected his 'girl' to talk back to him. I even surprised myself. I don't know where the words came from. I guess from taking his shit for three years." She smiled.

"That was the beginning of World War II and if you knew the difference between a typewriter and a rifle they would hire you," my mother said about the job she found at the Navy Department, where she tripled her salary from ten to thirty dollars a week.

It was when I entered early adolescence that my mother revealed the long shadow cast over her years at the Navy Department. First there was the promotion she should have received but didn't. "They came right out and told me they gave the accounting supervisor job to a man because he had a family and needed the money more."

Then there was the three million dollar accounting error that she caught and brought to the attention of her superiors, thinking she had helped her department. "I was devastated when they asked me to take a demotion," she says about the cover-up she had unwittingly stumbled onto. "They transferred me to the correspondence department so I wrote a letter about how they treated me and carbon copied the head of the department. When I had my grievance I had to go into a room full of men lined up like judges and sit with my back to them. I was so humiliated.

"What were they afraid of? That I would spit at them or throw something?"

It was 1952, seven years before I was born. The collective outrage of the women's movement was nowhere in sight. My mother resigned from her job. "I grieved about that for years. For a long time it was all I had," she said, looking at me pointedly.

She marched into the rank and file of American housewives who existed in legion yet lived in isolation. Seven years later at the age of forty, my mother gave birth to me. The first breath of air I inhaled was laden with her resentments. After the matching flower print dresses, there were mother-daughter National Organization for Women meetings. Thanks to her, there was no doubt in my mind that girls, at the very least, were equal to boys.

In sixth grade, I marched with the girls across the schoolyard, fed up with being pushed around, taunted and teased by the boys. We stood fifty strong in the center of the playground, yelling at the top of our lungs: "WE HATE BOYS WE HATE BOYS WE HATE BOYS." I wrote the slogans on stickers, pasted them on my bedroom walls, and pointedly ignored my aunt when she said, "That won't last." A year later, as an unpopular seventh grader with nothing to lose except a few sunny afternoons, I entered the smoky basement of a bank in a shopping center with my mother, both of us attending our first NOW meeting.

What I remembered most was the embarrassment I felt as I squirmed in my seat and simultaneously tried to look and not look at the woman sitting next to me who was breast-feeding her baby. I wanted to make myself invisible as I sat next to my mother, the tension in her body a palpable presence between us. When the meeting broke into smaller groups, my mother found out that she was the only one who had not been to college. These women, who were trying to be liberated but had not quite made it, mostly based their self-esteem on their husbands' professional jobs. My mother was the only one whose husband had a blue-collar job.

Some of the women made classist comments, at once snide and revealing of their own insecurities, that left my mother fuming. Their remarks were above my head. But my mother's resentment was not. Again I inhaled her frustrations, this time transforming her anger into my own fire-breath of adolescent angst.

Everything my mother did was starting to embarrass me: dancing in the wide hallway outside the record store at the mall where my friends might see me; having one drink when we went out to a nice restaurant and then pretending she was playing the moving keys of the player piano. Every time she did something out of the ordinary I cringed. Adolescence was a slow furious storm rolling in.

When I was in high school my mother decided I should take a typing course so I would have something to fall back on. My lower back began to ache every time I walked into the classroom and looked at the metal keys that threatened to devour my life. I'm sure my mother, like her mother before her, had my best intentions in mind. Typing was a field in which a woman could always get a job. But I was too busy rebelling to understand this. I saw my mother's demands only as the yoke of eternal tedium. I dropped the typing class for a printmaking and photography elective where I concentrated all my efforts into the four-color silkscreen of a marijuana leaf that I eventually hung on my wall.

Shortly after I graduated from high school, after the army had turned down my request to be a photographer on the grounds that I was female, my mother called a secretarial school and asked them to contact me. "Your mother said you were interested in our secretarial school," said the man who called me. I was sullen, hung over. "No," I said. "I don't want to be a secretary. I want to be a...journalist."

My mother stood next to the sink less than two feet away, dishtowel in hand, her glare as threatening as the cast-iron skillet she reached for. "You better do something with your life," she hissed as I hung up the phone. Her face was dangerously close to mine. Inches away, she could have spit and hit me dead in the eye or, worse, swung the skillet and bashed in my brains.

I took a step back.

She wasn't finished. "You graduated from high school by the skin of your teeth; you come in here all hours reeking like a gin mill; you're wasting your life in a factory; and you want to be a journalist? Smell that." My mother leaned into me, her face jutting forward fast. Her eyes glinted fiercely.

She was right. When the word "journalist" came out of my mouth I was shocked. had grasped at straws and came up with the longest one, the most prominent, most independent woman I could think of: Barbara Walters. Her insightful commentary. Her trip to China. A woman who led an interesting life. I knew instantly that I had to get out of the factory, out of the bars, away from my nowhere friends, the drugs, the alcohol that filled up my hours like buckets of dirty water.

My mother was right. But I couldn't let her know that.

"STOP TELLING ME WHAT TO DO!" I screamed and stomped out of the room.

Six months later I enrolled in a community college. My journalism teacher, Mr. Morton, was a crusty castoff from a career in the wire services. While once UPI and AP were just initials before the dash that started newspaper stories, they were now personified in a living, (barely) breathing wreck of a teacher pacing back and forth in front of the auditorium that was our classroom. Chain-smoking, exhaling in quick excited puffs, he lectured rapid-fire like a teletype machine spitting out the news. When he stood at the chalkboard, writing down the "who, what, when, where," and the infrequent "why" of newspaper reporting, his hands trembled. The red veins on his nose were a road map to his life. Mr. Morton's favorite book was *Drunk Before Noon: The Behind-The-Scenes Story of the Washington Press Corps.*

Enthralled with Mr. Morton's stories, we forgot we were attending a small two-year college. We were involved in something bigger than ourselves. We were beyond the pursuit of grades and the dream of the future accumulation of material wealth. A price tag couldn't be placed on what we aspired to. We were in search of Truth. And if we reached out for it drunkenly, knocking over a few tables at the newspaper banquet as I and a few others did, then so be it. Our senior editor, Tom, a corpulent student who lumbered around with bits of cafeteria food lodged in his shoulder-length stringy, hair, stayed at the paper and the two-year college for six years. Other students were not so tenacious, but had no problem staying longer than they needed to. Not me. I scheduled my time tightly between my classes, my work-study job in the library, and the few remaining hours which were spent in the newspaper office. I was making up for lost time.

My background threatened to suck me in if I took one false step. Becky, the other woman on the newspaper, had a penchant for writing brilliant editorials and snorting methamphetamine. The meth won. First she started cutting her classes. Then she stopped coming into the newspaper office. Soon she was nowhere to be found. One day I stopped for a hoagie at a delicatessen in a nearby town. There she was behind the counter, slicing lunchmeat with the same precision as she had once tapped out editorials. She was putting school on hold, she said, until she figured out what she wanted to do. She looked like she always had, but thinner, more vibrant, like a flame at the end of a wick glowing blue white before sputtering out. The telltale sniff she had developed in the past six months was more pronounced. A month later when I stopped in again, the tight-lipped assistant manager said she had left. No, he didn't know where she was. She wasn't the first in my life who had disappeared. High school friends and acquaintances, girls who hung with the druggie crowd, ended up dead, in jail or nowhere to be found.

A year after we all graduated from high school, my two best friends married within a week of each other. I was the maid of honor at both weddings and after a few double Southern Comfort drinks, went around calling myself "the best woman." Soon afterward I drifted apart from my best friend, the one who had the church wedding and reception at the fire hall with a hundred guests. My short, stocky, tougher-than-nails, tomboy, deer-hunting, *Kiss-Me-I'm-Italian* button wearing best friend had disappeared into her husband's name: Mrs. Thomas Brown was how she signed the thank-you notes to her guests. It didn't matter that a few years later, after she was laid off from the steel mill, her husband's infidelities would push her to the brink of trying to shoot him with the handgun her father had bought her for her sweet sixteenth. The wedge between us had already been driven in.

I still saw my other friend, though, almost every weekend. Diane's mother had given up commenting on the implausibility of my succeeding in college, and had turned her ire on my personal life. "Always a bridesmaid, never a bride," she would say whenever she saw me. I contemptuously ignored her need to validate her own life (she was on husband number three and this one would soon leave her, driving away in her prize possession—an emerald-green Oldsmobile sedan with matching plush seats). We would hang around her mother's house long enough for Diane to drop off her laundry, and then we would tool around town in her powder-blue Firebird. Pulling out of the gas station, Diane chirped her wheels—one last signal to the attendant she had been flirting with—and we hauled ass down the highway.

I lit up a joint, took a deep breath, exhaled, and handed it off to her. Fast-food joints, littering both sides of the road, streaked by. Diane sucked on the joint, held the smoke in as long as she could, and passed it back to me. I held the joint, listening while she told me about her job soldering components in the RCA nuclear satellite division. She had copped the dope we were smoking, some potent Jamaica Red, on her lunch break. She got stoned every afternoon and then went back to work.

I looked up into the slate-gray sky and wondered how long those satellites were going to stay up there before they came plummeting down. When she asked what I was looking at, I told her. "Shut up," she said, "and quit bogarting the joint." I passed it back to her and she took a long drag. "Don't worry," she said, after she exhaled. "Nothing's gonna come crashing down on us. We have quality control. That's what Randolph does. He walks around checking every fifth board to make sure it's put together right." Randolph was her husband, the man she had married in her mother's living room. He was twice her age. When she first met him she was working at Jack-in-the-Box with me, the two of us waiting on customers with glassy-eyed grins under our orange and yellow polyester head scarves.

She stopped at the light and checked out her reflection in the rearview mirror. Her straight blond hair was windblown. She swept it up off her high forehead with a few fingers feathering her hair down either side of the dark roots of her center part. She took a long drag and with a sidelong glance checked out the driver in the next lane. He looked back at her with a long cool stare. He was wearing mirrored sunglasses and had a cleft in his chin. "Not bad." She gunned the engine and smirked. "The weed," she said, when I raised an eyebrow. "I am a married woman you know."

I nodded. She was faithful to her husband, but I didn't know why. Recently, she had confided in me that most of the time when they tried to make love, he couldn't get it up. He felt guilty, she explained, about two children from a previous marriage whom he had abandoned. He never saw them or his ex-wife, but the "kids" would have been the same age as Diane. I figured there must be some reason she was sticking around aside from his pipe dream about sending her to art school. "Does Randolph help out much around the house?"

"Oh no," she said, staring straight ahead as she sailed down the highway. "That's my job. He's a real old-fashioned man. He comes home from work and reads the paper. I make dinner and do the dishes." Three nights a week she went out after doing the dishes to her second job tending bar at a go-go dancer shot and beer joint where I hung out sometimes and shot pool.

"He usually comes in and has a beer, just to make sure the guys aren't hitting on me." A slight smile played on her lips. She was proud that her man was looking out for her.

I stared at her in disbelief: "I'm never getting married, if that's what it's like."

The words were out of my mouth before I thought about their impact. I saw her watching me warily out of the corner of her eye. "It's not so bad," she drawled. "I come home at night, fire up a joint, turn on the TV and everything's fine."

I said nothing but continued to stare at her. She avoided my eyes and stared straight ahead. She pretended to ignore me. But she clenched her jaw and a blue vein throbbed in her pale temple. She laid her foot down heavy on the gas pedal of the Firebird. She had bought the car with money that she got from selling a piece of land in Tennessee her maternal grandmother had left her. The car backfired. She swore under her breath. First one pimply faced boyfriend had driven it and then another, attracted as much by her V8 engine as they were by her bleached blond hair, angular face and the midriff blouses she wore tied up high on her flat gymnast stomach. Now, when she went out with her husband, he drove the car. In a few more years it would be rusting in a junkyard.

We quietly passed the joint back and forth between us. She eyed me warily. In criticizing her marriage, I had insulted the very underpinnings of her life. She stubbed out the joint and handed me the roach to put in the tin she kept in the glove compartment. I lit another joint. She popped out Cat Stevens and put in a Harry Chapin tape. We drove around in an endless loop. I swore we were passing the same fast-food joints two, three times. Turning into the industrial park where I had worked in a factory the summer before, she pulled over to the side of the road. I stared at the single-story factories, the windowless brick walls and aluminum siding.

"Everything looks the same."

"You're telling me," she said.

The joint burnt down between my fingers. I knew I should get the roach clip out of the ashtray, but I waited until the last possible moment. My fingertips glowed red with the embers.

The joint burnt down so close I scorched myself and dropped it in the ashtray. I picked it back out with the clip. We handed it back and forth to each other, our fingers touching, the feathers hanging off the side of the clip brushing our palms.

The differences between us would one day be irreconcilable. But we solved them that afternoon by smoking another joint on the way home. My eyes red and glassy, my mind muddled, I pursed my lips and kept myself afloat with sheer determination. Diane gunned the Firebird. The fast-food places flew by. I was lost on a road that I had traveled most of my life, but at that moment I sharpened my determination to find my way out.

And when I finally did, goddamnit, I was gonna be somebody.

An education and a professional job had been my mother's dream for me, and they had rapidly become my dream. I did find some satisfaction in my work. I interviewed interesting people I otherwise wouldn't have met and traveled to a few places I otherwise wouldn't have gone. But I was always working on someone else's assignments and deadlines.

During my college years, when I briefly worked in a photography studio, I had far more interest in fine art photography than in the staged portrait and wedding shots I had been hired to take. And later, working as a journalist, I became dissatisfied with my work. When I was brain-storming headlines streams of poetry would enter my mind, and when I wrote feature articles, I daydreamed about writing epic novels. In my heart of hearts, I have always been an artist.

It was late in the afternoon. My mother had sent me upstairs to her old room. I was in her closet looking for the clothes she sent me to find when I came across her art portfolio: a plain wooden box tucked in a dusty corner. I knew I was trespassing on my mother's life, but I could not help myself. I took the box from its corner, blew off the dust, and opened it. The bottom compartments were filled with old tubes of oil paints, a box of pastels, charcoal pencils, and a powder-blue case of Sargent watercolors. Used up paints had left their colors—green, orange, yellow, a muddy red—in the bottom of their metal holders. There was also a small index card-size piece of paper with my name written on the bottom. At the top was something that looked like a quote my mother copied, writing over the word "his" with "her": *"Unless the art (student) copes with the anxiety contingent upon her aloneness and helplessness before her own imagination, we do not have the conditions where art is possible."*

In the top of her art box was a divider. I slid it out. I found two pads of art paper and leafed through them. Both were entirely blank. A hollow thud dropped through me, leaving an emptiness in the pit of my stomach. My mother had thrown out her sketches. Even though I could not ask her this question—it was too much of a sore spot with her—I knew this was the answer. As I put the sketchbooks back, I saw a small piece of canvass in the back of the art box. It was diagrammed with brown lines like a tic-tac-toe grid, a few houses along a road, the outlines of bushes drawn in. At the bottom, my mother's handwriting read, "Bristol, England." Lightly written in the outlines were the names of colors—dark green, light green shrubs; brown, yellow grasses; purple brown houses in the background and hills of green tapering into blue gray sky.

I could see the canvass almost exactly as she would have liked to paint it. But other spots on the canvass were blank, devoid of form and instruction. I didn't have to read the tea leaves to see that all the patterns, the myths and lies—handed down to me from my mother and to her from her mother back to her mother and so on—were exploding.

My mother did not want to be an office worker, but she did want the love and approval of her mother. If my grandmother had been able to live her dreams of acting in the theater, instead of working in the candy factory and later the textile mill, she would not have squelched the dreams of her daughter. All my grandmother—and my mother—wanted was for her daughter to have a better means of survival in the world. Survival is necessary, but it too often comes at the expense of dreams.

My grandmother did not want to work in a mill, my mother did not want to work in an office and I—though I appreciated the doors that my education opened—did not want to work in a professional office job. We were all, at heart, artists. The painting my mother started but never finished was proof. It had been neglected for decades, waiting patiently for someone to come along and finish it.

CHAPTER 12

Charcoal Sketches

"I'll bet a lot of women who are housewives get this thing." My mother looked up from the hardback she was reading. "You're always doing a hundred different things, cooking, cleaning, taking care of the kids. It makes you tense all the time, very contracted." She closed the book on her lap.

I nodded. I was painfully aware of the place I held in my mother's life. In my mind, I was the reason her life had consisted of taking care of the kid, rotating her day around my father's shift work schedule, standing in front of an electric range, thirty, forty years, cooking breakfast, lunch, dinner, scrubbing the house clean in the spare moments she could have had for herself, for the artwork she'd abandoned.

The fact that she told me not to feel guilty, that she gave birth to me because she wanted to, not only for me but also for herself, made little difference. Deep in my heart was the knowledge that my mother's empty sketchbook was the evidence of my existence.

My mother was literally shrinking before my eyes. The pain was moving around, from her sternum to her shoulders, her abdomen to her thighs. Every time she winced, I winced; each time her eyes filled with tears so did mine. I might have been too stressed out to remember which day of the week it was, but I always remembered how long it was since my mother's diagnosis. Four and a half months had passed. Her life was coming to a close, and she was tired of living in pain. One day, shortly before her hospital bed arrived, she decided to stage a hunger strike. She lay in her narrow bed, her body rigid, her face unflinching. She refused to speak and resolutely shook her head from side to side whenever I tried to coax her to eat.

"I'm sick of it all. I thought maybe I could just stop eating," she said to me the next morning when I finally convinced her to eat a little soup. I helped her sit up in bed and held the bowl while she spooned the soup into her mouth. She smiled at me when she was done: a gaunt, creased, radiant face filled with love. "You're being so sweet about taking care of me that I changed my mind."

That afternoon she decided to come to the table and eat lunch with my father and me. Gradually over the next couple of days she got a little stronger and spent less time in bed. In the ensuing weeks I actually tried to convince myself that she was getting better.

Two weeks after her hunger strike as we sat together in the living room, my mother told me she wanted to take a walk. It was a beautiful sunny day. Lips pressed together in a firm resolve, she leaned forward, grasping the rounded end of her wooden cane and pushed herself up from the chair. She walked around the end of the couch toward the stairs where she braced herself against the wall with her left hand. With precise determination, she used the straight end of the cane with the rubber stopper to retrieve first one sneaker and then the other.

Every muscle in my body twitched in her direction. I checked my urge to get her sneakers, to help her put her feet into them, to do the things for her that had become difficult but that she was still able to do for herself. Suddenly she was the child and I the mother. I needed to let her do this for herself, to not hover anxiously above the child taking her first steps, or the mother taking what could be her last. She let me go. Now it was my turn.

She held back the tongue of her gray and white running sneaker with her cane, slipped her right foot into the shoe, then pushed down the Velcro tabs with her cane.

Before she started with the second sneaker, she looked up, a gleam of satisfaction in her eyes.

"I always thought," she said, in a thoughtful, faraway voice that sounded as if she were talking as much to herself as to me, "that I could've been a lesbian."

I looked up, startled.

As she stood next to the stairs, leaning both hands on her cane, she looked at me keenly, as if looking into my life and beyond, back into hers.

"You remember my friend Mary from the organic gardening club. I think we would have been lesbians if we had the chance. One day she asked me if I liked sex. I think if it had been another time, we would've just done it. What's the big deal about sex? America is so puritanical. I think that's why the big fuss about gay rights."

My mother stepped out with her left leg, shifting the weight that she was leaning on her cane. She braced herself against the wall again, reaching out with the cane to retrieve her other sneaker. After she pulled it over next to her foot, she looked back up at me.

"Don't get excited," she said. "We didn't do anything." She looked down at her sneaker.

A smile was curling the edges of my lips. I thought about mentioning the difference between "Do you like sex?" and "Would you like to have sex?" But I didn't.

My mother looked up, her eyes narrowed to the pinpoint of a precise memory. "Now Vera, the woman who was in my nursing program, she was something special." My mother looked past me, far into the distance. "She had nice broad shoulders like your father. And boy was she interesting to talk to. She walked like a man, her feet pointing to the outsides. She didn't pretend to be anything she wasn't, so everyone knew she was a lesbian.

"None of the other women wanted to have anything to do with her, even the other black women. They were all cats. But I liked her. When you listened to her talk you knew she had something between her ears. She really knew how to think for herself. When she put her hand on my knee, I didn't say anything. I just pushed her hand away like I would do to a man. Poor woman, I was probably the only one in the program who had a kind word for her."

My mother's eyes reddened, and she looked down. Again at her sneaker. Putting on her shoes, this daily incidental that had become a monumental task.

I had heard the story of Vera before, about the hand on the knee, a reminder in my preadolescence, when lesbianism was still a foreign concept, that all people should be treated fairly, with respect, like the human beings they are. But today my mother's reminiscence put Vera in sharper focus for me, this broad-shouldered black lesbian, this woman ahead of her time who, despite the small-minded women in the nursing program, despite the closed doors of the fifties, could risk breaking all taboos, to place her hand on the knee of a straight, white, married woman, who at forty years old was pregnant with her first and only child.

I imagined myself in my mother's womb, a place I have never dared to think of, curled up tight, growing larger in the amniotic fluids that transmitted the touch of Vera's hand on my mother's knee, perhaps feeling a flutter of excitement, then the light brush of my mother's arm across her stomach, sweeping away Vera's hand, keeping all that she was expected to be in place. It's quite possible that in 1959, the desire that was dormant or repressed in my mother was handed to me, a gift embedded in the vibrational frequency that formed me.

My mother had finished putting on her sneakers. The redness in her eyes had subsided. Vera was in the past, but somehow in the present also: part of my mother's memory of her life and of my memory of my mother's life before me. This memory hovered over us, a nimbus, as I helped my mother on with her lightweight down jacket and grabbed my sweatshirt as we headed outside for a walk. There was a winesap late autumn scent in the air, golden red brown leaves fermenting, carried on a faint breeze that was chilly to me but cold to my mother. She stopped to pull the gold square of her woven scarf tighter around her neck, her normally thin body now a wisp inside the cavernous down jacket. Only last year it fit her perfectly.

We walked in the street, outside the bumpy sidewalk with its uneven blocks of cement uprooted by tree roots and shifting earth, dangerous in the threat of tripping my mother and damaging bones already eroded by the cancer. Our destination was the end of the street, down a hill and back up, less than a quarter of a mile. This was about half the distance we walked a month ago, down from the four miles a day my mother walked before last spring when she woke up with the metastasis. I walked beside her protectively, watchful for sticks on the side of the road that might trip her, for any movement (including collapse) that might unbalance her. My two arms swung freely, but they were alert, ever ready to grab her and hold her upright at a second's notice.

I was strong enough to carry the weight of my mother.

"Did I ever tell you about the time your grandmother met an old man and wanted to bring him home?"

"You're kidding me."

"After my stepfather died, she met an old man and told me she wanted to bring him home to live with her."

I looked at my mother's face. She was serious.

"I said to her 'Aw Ma, you don't want to get involved with that.'"

When I asked her where my grandmother met the old man, she nearly doubled over with laughter. Red-faced with embarrassment, she hung onto my arm with all her weight. "In the park. She picked up an old man in the park. I figured that having had to take care of one old man was enough," said my mother when she regained her composure. "He was senile for years, and at the end when he was sick in bed, she finally gave him a few good cracks."

I looked at my mother with astonishment. "Grandmom? How did you know? Did she hit him in the face?"

"No. I don't think she left any marks. Unless she bruised him where you couldn't see it."

My mother and I had stopped walking. We were standing in front of a house with a pumpkin on the front step, a few orange and gold shiny paper leaves decorating the front windows. The moment of shock dissolved into laughter.

"I guess I did my best not to laugh when she told me that she gave him a few good cracks," said my mother as we began to walk on, slowly, me shortening my long stride to her weakened steps. "He was never any good. He didn't even help her around the house. He just sat around in his suit and tie criticizing everyone—telling us that he was a gentleman—and let her support him. But after he died, she didn't know what to do without him. A year later she was dead."

Tears moistened my mother's eyes, the crinkled skin around her eyes more crimson than the red maple leaf swirling down from the branch of a nearby tree. "When we used to drive past the graveyard, my mother would say 'Someday that's where I'll be.' I'd say, 'Aw Mom, you're not going to die,' and I believed it!"

My mother grabbed my arm, exclaiming, "I was always so dense!"

I laughed with my mother, but then drew into myself, noticeably silent. Twelve when my grandmother died, I remembered very little, except my own numbness and the long tense silence of my mother, exploding into the shattering of dishes against the kitchen sink, an angry blur speeding through the living room before the slam of her bedroom door.

I am my mother's daughter. As close as she was to death, I still could not accept it. She was always the strong one. Even as she walked beside me, gripping my arm for support, I expected that she would fling down her cane and start to take the long crisp strides that less than a year ago fueled her four-mile walks.

"My mother's last words to me were, 'It's okay.'" Tears sprang to my mother's eyes as she spoke, and, even though she had told me this before, many times, I felt my own hot tears welling up.

My mother talked about the end of my grandmother's life, her diabetes and heart attack, the month she spent in the hospital. I nodded, remembering the cold sterile building, a mass of concrete rising up from its inner city neighborhood of row homes, just a few blocks from my grandmother's home. My mother took me to the hospital to see my grandmother no more than two or three times. I remembered my grandmother's white head resting on the raised hospital bed, her lips drawn together in a firm, thin line.

One day when my mother came home from the hospital she was in a rage, her voice hissing as she spat out the reason to my father: "They were prepping her for a GYN. I could have killed those interns. Thank God I was there to stop them."

As we walked on, my mother told me about a night when she went to visit my grandmother in the hospital. "After I saw her, I walked out into the parking lot and noticed a man was following me. I thought he was going to try to rob me, but when I turned around and glared at him, he walked away. He saw the look in my eyes and he knew."

When I asked my mother what the look was, she stopped and turned to me.

"I wanted him to kill me," she said. "I was so miserable I wanted to die."

I looked at my mother, my eyes wide with compassion and something else, a twelve-year-old's fear of losing her mother trapped in the core of a thirty-four-year-old woman. I felt a pang inside of me that was really more like a tear, a piece of fabric wrenched from either side, beginning its long jagged journey, soon to be severed through.

I was looking into the future, my mother into the past. Somehow we managed to match our steps and began walking again.

"I couldn't even accept my own mother's death." My mother shook her head as we walked on. "I remember the night she died. She was slipping into a coma, but I thought she was falling asleep. I was getting ready to leave and I leaned over her and said, 'Mama?' and she said, 'It's okay.' The hospital called me at three o'clock in the morning and I couldn't even go back down there. Your father was on night shift, and he had the car at work."

My mother's eyes were brimming. Mine were too. We kept walking.

We reached a bend in the road. A middle-aged woman driving by in an old Chevy slowed down, smiled, and gave me an approving nod. I saw myself through her eyes: a dutiful daughter. I never expected to face the loss of my mother so soon. Even though she was forty years older than me, I always had the comfort of her vitality: She had always walked four miles a day, eaten tofu, pumped iron and was in better physical condition than I.

I was catapulted into a different stage of my life. I saw myself walking beside my mother, watchful of her movements, holding onto her as she held onto me, and suddenly I was older, the decades flipping past me like chapters, thirty-four, forty-four, fifty-four, a woman in mid-life about to lose her mother. This abrupt shortening of her life closed the years between us, until we were not only mother and daughter, or even a daughter who had become the parent to her mother, but rather comrade and comrade standing on the edge of eternity holding fiercely to the few feet of ground we had left to stand on.

Worlds opened up between us.

"Why did Grandmom pick such awful husbands?"

"Her father died when she was three," said my mother matter-of-factly. "Women who lose their fathers when they are three don't know what to look for in a man. I had my father until I was seven and even then I had to put my foot down with your father."

We were silent. Trees that were young saplings when we moved into the housing development were standing over us, twenty, thirty feet high, some with branches almost as thick as their trunks once were. In tree years, they were still young, thirty-five, forty-years old, since they were planted when this section of Levittown was first built. The identical tract houses, with time and more affluent owners, had been transformed, each with its own piece of originality: a bay window, a second-story extension, a porch added to the front of the house over a cement foundation, the name of a family on a hand-painted wooden sign in the yard. Except for the same curve of the street, the uniformly square front lawns, the cars sitting in the driveways, spilling onto the street, the occasional old clunker parked in a yard, this could have been a different neighborhood than the one where I grew up.

As we neared the bottom of the hill, the place we had planned to turn around, my mother urged me to go on. "I'll be okay," she said. "I can walk farther."

I asked her if she was sure, the tone of my voice resonating with what I think of as caution, but I could see at a glance that my mother interpreted as patronization. "Let me do it myself," was what she always said to me. Now, cane in hand, she was no different.

She glared at me. We walked on silently.

"What I'll never understand is why my mother never stopped my father from hitting me. Why didn't she put her hand out and say, 'You can't hit this child.'"

I shrugged. "Maybe she was afraid of him."

It was my mother's turn to shrug, which she did with a barely perceptible movement of shoulders and eyebrows, as she steadfastly placed the cane in front of her left leg.

"Maybe. But she never stopped Harry from hitting me either. Harry was my mother's Italian boyfriend," she added, answering my raised eyebrows.

Then I remember. Harry. My grandmother dated him before she remarried. He used to tie felt balls onto his belt buckle and have the girls—my mother and her sister—play with them. The story was that my grandmother caught him in the act one day and pitched him out.

"Didn't she leave him?" The road was turning and we were nearing the foot of another hill. My mother's steps were growing shorter. Soon we would have to turn back.

"Yes," she said, stopping and leaning on her cane. "But she never stopped him from hitting me. One time Harry walloped me. He chased me around the room and when I hid under the bed he pulled me out and walloped me. My mother didn't say a word." My mother's face was stony, looking forward into a horizon that receded far behind her.

"Why did he hit you?"

"Oh, my mother did something I didn't like and I called her a bitch."

When I asked how old she was, she said, "Oh twelve, or thirteen, the age when I was starting to get fresh."

I smiled wryly, the right corner of my mouth twisted up, as I imagined the adolescent she was and remembered the adolescent I was. My adolescent years collided with my mother's menopausal years at breakneck speed. My hung-over adolescent hormonal confusion and her hot flashes and headaches churned themselves into monumental screaming matches, screeching two-wheeled around corners, disregarding red lights, crashing through intersections, leading us to dangerous places.

"You wouldn't dare," she had hissed at me when, as a flushed and trembling teenager, I held a lightweight metal-framed laundry basket over my head, shaking it at her. I held it in the air a few more seconds, my legs, arms trembling, as I braced myself against the emotions that coiled through me like a cobra poised to strike. Then I put it down, conciliatory, but still fuming, squared off and glaring at my mother who too was furious, her eyes inches from mine as she leaned forward: "Don't you ever, ever, threaten me again."

"Go fuck yourself," I snarled back and, despite the hostility crackling between us, I recoiled in horror when she spat squarely into the center of my face.

The next morning, hung over again, I woke to her pouring cold water onto my face: "This is not a motel where you can come in here at all hours. You better straighten up, or else."

I walked around in a daze for years, not knowing what divided me from myself, hurling myself against a wall that was impossible to cross over.

The years passed. I turned, eighteen, nineteen, twenty, twenty-one, still drinking to excess but functioning, making the dean's list in college despite working several jobs and spending time with my boyfriend of four years. The night of my breakup with my boyfriend I came into the house and slammed the door behind me. My mother called me into her room. I sat tentatively on the foot of her bed and tried to explain: "It's not just him, I've decided that I'm never going to get married."

My mother was angry, defensive, accusing me of rejecting her life, of not wanting to be like her, a housewife, something she was sure, with my college education almost at a close, I had grown to look down on. Agonizing, crying, feeling the wall soften inside me and begin to twist and tear, I told my mother I wasn't rejecting her life. Just because I was making other choices didn't mean I didn't respect hers.

She was right, of course. I didn't respect her and perhaps, in pushing off from my moorings, couldn't. She was everything I didn't want to be: a frustrated, angry housewife, a woman who had denied her artistic ambitions. I didn't yet understand that for her, a working-class woman, whose mother had been a mill worker and later in life a domestic, who herself had been an office worker (demoted, humiliated, in a job she had once gone to with pride and then left, angry, disappointed, grieving) being a housewife was a step up: a woman who cleaned her own house, the daughter of a mother who had cleaned someone else's.

Despite our closeness and our shared feminist views, it was extremely painful for me to tell her I was a lesbian a year and a half later. I called and told her I had something to tell her, and then broke down into sobs. It had been easy coming out to my childhood best friend, who had guessed before I told her, but my mother was different. I was making an announcement that I was vastly different from her, that I would not, in any way, shape, or form, have a life like hers. When I came out in the early 1980s most lesbians did not have children—unless they were from previous marriages to men. And at that time, my coming out meant, in a very specific way—past my declarations of never wanting to marry or have children—that there would most likely be no grandchildren.

My mother paved the way for me to come out to her by writing me a letter. She knew I had been having difficulties on my job and wrote that she "would love me whether I was a writer, or a waitress, or... whatever." Later she told me that when I broke down on the phone she thought I was either gay or pregnant. When I invited my parents over to my apartment for dinner and told them I was a lesbian, she defused the tension by holding up her right hand and saying, "Is becoming a lesbian like being saved?"

"That's right, Mom," I told her, "that's exactly what it is."

I came out to my parents before I was with Barbara—but she was the first lover who I introduced to my parents. In fact, falling in love with Barbara did save me. She was always able to make me laugh and, beyond that, she seemed to know me better than I did. Barbara saved me from many things—most of all from myself.

But my mother first saw my lesbianism as a betrayal, defiantly different from her, as my father said, just one more way to buck the system. In time, though, she came to see it as a privilege. "And what college did she go to?" my mother asked slyly when I mentioned in passing another lesbian I worked with on a feminist collective. I mentioned a Seven Sisters College, caught in my own feelings about the slights passed to me from this woman, her father a lawyer, her background upper middle class. Her barbed comments—Fishtown is nothing but white trash, she'd said, speaking of the neighborhood my father grew up in—were ingrained enough in her psyche to be unconscious but that didn't stop them from sticking in my side like a thorn.

My mother's point, which she had to explain—that being a lesbian was a privilege, handed out with diplomas and professional jobs—was slow in coming to me, but finally I understood. Being a lesbian, like going to college, was an opportunity that was not afforded my mother. But it was worthy of consideration.

Soon after I had come out to her, I was telling her about a friend whose mother, on finding out her daughter was a lesbian, slapped the palm of her hand against her forehead and said, "Ooh! I think I'm a lesbian too!"

My mother tilted her head quizzically and said, "Do you think I'm..."—then smacking the palm of her hand on her forehead—"Ooh?"

By then she was well reconciled to the daughter being different from the mother.

My mother was not above using our differences for her own gain: namely to antagonize my father. "Keep reading," she said to me sternly, as I sat on the couch reading a passage aloud to them both from *Sisterhood is Powerful*. My father wanted me to go to a psychiatrist and get "fixed." My mother was working on him for me, trying to get him to understand what my life was about. I was reading a passage about lesbian-feminism and sex and had just put the book down for the second time out of embarrassment. "Go ahead. Your father needs to know these things."

My father was noncommittal, hiding behind what my mother calls his fish eye, his stare glassy and absent. Retreating inside himself was the only way to escape being outnumbered by his wife and daughter. My mother nudged me. "You read it or I will."

I picked the book up and continued, "Women together can keep it going longer than we can with any man." As I read, I drew into myself, shielding myself with the book. But I wasn't oblivious to my mother's bald-face snickering as she sat on the end of the couch and looked at my father.

"Watch yourself," she told him. "If you don't behave I'm going to run off with the lesbians."

Everything in life was fair game for my mother's sense of humor.

"There goes your next project," said my mother, after my father had barely left the room. Exhausted from our morning walk, she had retired. I was sitting in a wooden-backed chair against the far wall, just a few feet away from the foot of her bed. My father had served us lunch and had taken away the plates to the kitchen where he would wash them.

I glared at her. I had already told her that I would take care of my father when she was gone. She didn't have to ask. I meant what I said: I loved my father and would take care of him. But the thought of taking on "my next project" while I was already overwhelmed with my mother's illness was too much for me.

My mother sucked in her breath, looking like a child who just realized she had gone too far. She breathed out slowly, lips pursed, and then commented: "That's the problem with having two parents, you have to bury both of them. I never thought about that before."

She laughed, leaning back in her hospital bed, the head of it raised to a sitting position. Her shoulders twitched. The red on her cheeks spread across her face, her nose, chin, flushing up to her high-browed forehead, under which her eyes crinkled and shut as if wringing the moisture from themselves. Tears ran down her cheeks. She reached for a tissue from the box on her nightstand next to the bed, and winced from the pain in her right shoulder. She paused and then took a drink of water from the rubber-necked straw in her bottle of spring water.

"I was just thinking about my father this morning." She held the bottle upright in her lap. "I got to thinking that maybe it wasn't all his fault."

Her voice quieted then she started up again, stronger. "He had a strict, overly religious father who was a preacher, his mother died when he was young, and he had a stepmother and two half sisters who may have been miserable to him."

I nodded, my eyes opening for the first time to my mother's father as an individual, not just a source of her pain and lifelong resentment. My mother's father, a man whom I have never referred to or even thought of as my grandfather, occupied a blank territory in my mind.

He'd left my life before the fact of my existence. In his absence, the blank square in the family tree, I had always seen him as an influence on my mother's life, not mine.

Those rare times when I mentioned my mother's father, the man who battered his wife and children, drank away their money and then abandoned them, my words grew terse, my jaw clenched and shoulders tightened as my mother's resentment pulled through me. Now, as I listened to her talk about her father, doing her best to forgive him for not being the father who would have helped her grow and thrive instead of lashing into her with the rawhide of his own resentments, I felt the tension wire relax from mother to daughter as I reconsidered this grandfather I never had.

My mother grew silent. The tears were gone from her eyes, the red flush across her face absorbed into her ruddy skin tones. She was tired, her eyes closing slightly until she blinked them open again. Wide. Forcing herself to stay awake. Reluctant to lose this moment of understanding her father, of spending time with her daughter, telling me as she had before, "You know things have never been better between us."

I nodded. I knew I should let her rest. But I too was reluctant to lose this moment. And when she asked me in a small childlike voice, to read to her, I quickly obliged, reaching to the top of her dresser and pulling down a hefty paperback. *The Magic Mountain*, Thomas Mann's 700-page tome, which my mother read start to finish years before I was born, "Just because," she told me, "I wanted to."

I turned to the first chapter, and we accompanied the young Hans Castorp from the Alpine station where he boards the train and rides in his little compartment to "regions where he had never before drawn breath..." where "home and regular living lay not only far behind, they lay fathoms deep beneath him, and he continued to mount above them..." I skipped through the pages, following Hans as he visits his cousin in the tuberculosis sanitarium, anxious and intent on returning home. Then the sanitarium doctor examines Hans and finds out that either through contagion or coincidence he is not as healthy as he thought and must stay on with his cousin. Hans trades the world of commerce for that of the ascetic, breathing the thin mountaintop air, his gaze lingering over the hurried valleys below.

As I read, my voice grew low and sleepy. Reading out loud to my mother recalled my childhood, her voice lulling me to sleep, weaving through the worlds of *Treasure Island*, *Anne of Green Gables* and, my favorite, *The Story About Ping*. Now it was she who was wide awake remembering the world of this book that she once inhabited as she jumped ahead, telling me about Hans and the other patients sitting outside every afternoon taking "the cure," wrapped in blankets, inhaling the cold air, attended to by nurses who must have been wondering if they were going to be next.

The book was now face down in my lap, then back in its place on the bureau as my mother leapt from its pages to her life, remarking that the setting reminded her of Mt. Washington, the mountain in New Hampshire we drove up while on vacation the year I was ten.

I smiled, remembering the long winding road that held onto the mountainside like a thread, and the gusting winds that nearly lifted us off the ground when we reached the top. Remembering Mt. Washington led me into thinking about the other camping trips we took, the bear caught in a trap outside the bathroom in Yellowstone National Park, the wildflowers in the foothills of the Grand Tetons, the geysers, the still morning lakes, the streams that ran by speaking a language all their own.

Each summer we packed our bags, the tents, our sleeping bags, with my father just off night shift sleeping in the back of the station wagon, and we began our journeys crisscrossing the country, stopping to feed chipmunks that ate from our hands at Lake Tahoe; listening to pounding hailstones big as golf balls in Texas; and driving the endless flat roads of the Midwest, watching as the stockyards and packing houses of Detroit and Chicago rose up from the plains.

My favorite place, though, was closer to home. Mt. Desert Island, Maine. The campground had wooden platforms for tents to be pitched on and was nestled in a thick pine forest, banked on one side with gently rising hills filled with chalky white boulders between the scrub brush of blueberry bushes, the far side of the campground sloping gently into the bay. As we talked about the campground, the soft brown pine needle-covered hill that sloped down to the chilly water, the long wooden walkways leading to docks, the dinghies we rowed across Sommes Sound, I suddenly remembered the charcoal sketches my mother made as she sat quietly on that pine-covered hill.

When I walked up behind her at the age of ten, eleven, twelve, and caught glimpses of her drawing pad, my mother just shrugged, embarrassed perhaps, at having been caught sketching by her daughter. And for the first time, as we talked I began to lose my frustration with her, for throwing those and countless other drawings away, for dismissing the work that I thought of so highly, the work of *my* mother, who captured so perfectly the late afternoon sun cutting across the woodgrain of the walkway, the exact rough shadow of the barnacles creeping up the northern side of the boulders.

Now as I listened to her talk, I began to see those heavy charcoal lines in the edges of her speech, the lines, the shadings, the contours, the perspective that had always been a part of her even now decades later as she lifted a bony hand and described the exact triangular rise of a boulder that jutted out of the bay at low tide.

My mother looked further back, remembering the trips she took with my father before I was born, the canyon they almost backed the car into, the gorges, the peaks, the endless expanse of waves and beach that she may or may not have sketched, her artist's eye leading her into the deeper seeing of her own life.

"I've been so fortunate," she said, "to have seen so many beautiful places." She leaned back, closing her eyes.

As my mother rested, I thought about how her life had shaped mine. The reading of good books—which my mother instilled in me—and taking camping trips with my parents entered my dreams and made room for more dreams. Both the love of reading and the love of nature cultivated a deep quiet place within me that no matter how bad things got, I could always return to. Both of these pastimes brought the world to me and also shaped the way I saw the world. As someone who had lived all her adult life in a city, I was remarkably tuned into nature. Taking a walk in the urban park near my home, I was in an environment where others would notice the broken glass, graffiti and occasional smell of urine. But what registered for me were the nettles, the stars of Bethlehem, the stalks of mullen, the sturdy leaves of amaranth.

I looked down into my cup and swirled the leaves around.

My mother's eyes were still shut as she wavered between her waking reveries and sleeping dreams. The future was mine alone to contemplate. Past the reflection of my face—my terror and uncertainty of living on beyond my mother—the tea leaves were swirling and shifting. Part of me was reluctant to read the distinct signs and omens. But the other part of me strained to understand the portents. I was beginning to see a clear line between my past and present and into my future. Surely there must be some good omens as my mother's dreams swirled into mine.

My mother opened her eyes and a distant smile played on her lips. "What I remember most is driving cross-country with your father after we were first married. We were in the Midwest, where the roads stretch on as far as the eye can see. There wasn't another soul in sight. Just your father sleeping beside me in the pink Plymouth Fury. I remember the afternoon sun glinting off the low-slung hood, the wind roaring in my ears. Before I knew it, I was going a hundred miles per hour." She opened her eyes and looked at me. "This was back when gas was twenty cents a gallon." Then she closed her eyes again, resting. "It felt like flying."

CHAPTER 13

Racing Stripes

When I walked into the house, it was quiet and felt empty. I put the grocery bags on the dining room table and tiptoed to my mother's room, not wanting to disturb her if she was sleeping. The slight mound that she made on the bed looked like a blanket bunched up under her lightweight quilt. My mother was small enough to almost not be noticed in her bed. My eyes darted to her head resting on the pillow, breath coming out of her slightly parted lips. The short hair on top of her head stuck straight up. Her cheeks were bony ridges under her sunken eyes.

I took a breath, relieved that she was still breathing, still alive. I was relieved, yet suddenly terrified of the fact that the silence—without my mother's breathing—could last forever. I reached down to smooth the quilt over her and my hands trembled. I took another breath, as if to steel myself against a certain future. This is how it would be, I told myself, when my mother...

Tears filled my eyes. I took a step back, knocking the wooden chair at the foot of my mother's bed into the wall behind it. She opened her eyes slowly and her lips curled into a wide smile filling the small room.

"You came," she said, her eyes growing round, childlike. "You're here."

I smiled back, startled, almost, that she was happy to see me.

Just the night before when I called to tell her I was coming, she told me to stay home: "You were just here. You have to learn to live your own life, without me."

The days had been flying by into weeks. My mother's calendar was on the wall at the foot of her bed. Five and half months had passed since her diagnosis of terminal cancer. She seemed to have shrunk to less than half the size she had been six months ago.

The HMO nurse brought a portable commode, which my mother used on the days she could get up. On the days when she could not, even with help from my father or me, she used a bedpan. She was in so much pain she could not sleep through the night. During the day she took non narcotic painkillers, but at night she took prescription drugs with codeine. Still, she was only able to sleep for short periods of time.

Despite the unrelenting pain, she was happy to see me. Her smile spread into mine as I walked over to the side of the bed and took her hand. Her hand was smaller than it used to be, softer too, like a toddler whose bones had not fully formed. Inside my larger hand, cool from just coming in from outside, hers was small and warm. When I went into the bathroom to get the damp washcloth she asked for, I heard the mechanical creak of the hospital bed as she maneuvered it to an upright position. The red control button that hung on a wire looped around the raised rail at the side of her bed was never far from her fingertips.

She patted her face dry with a fresh towel. I sat down at the foot of her bed in the straight-backed wooden chair and asked about her day.

"The social worker was here," she said. She looked at me with wide-awake perceptiveness. The color in her cheeks deepened to a ruddy vitality as the vertical lines between her eyebrows creased, her lips pursed, and her eyes narrowed to a scowl.

"The minute I laid eyes on that social worker, I knew that little prick was religious."

I was startled by the change in my mother's demeanor.

"They sent a man?" I asked. "A male social worker?"

"No. Why? Oh I see, prick equals man. A prickess then. How's that? She was a little prickess."

She ignored my laughter with an unwavering stern expression. "She kept trying to shove Jesus down my throat. They come in here and see white hair on your head and think there's nothing inside. I told her I was very good at asking for what I wanted. And I should've said, 'That goes for Jesus, too.'"

"Yeah," I said. "You should've."

"Yeah," said my mother.

I laughed again. This time she relented and laughed with me.

Increasingly, my mother's moods changed from minute to minute. On my last visit, she was laughing, telling me that she almost put her straw in the urinal which was sitting next to her water bottle on her nightstand. Then, less than ten minutes later, when the HMO nurse came, my mother told her she wanted a black pill. I was sitting in the room with my mother when the nurse turned to me with an exaggerated expression of shocked concern on her face, and said, "Did your mother tell you she felt like this?" I shrugged. My mother, in moments of excruciating pain, had told me she wanted to end her life. But there was no legal way to do it. A black pill, or suicide pill, was illegal in Pennsylvania and almost in every other state. When my mother suggested that I could put a plastic bag over her head, all I could do was suck in my breath.

What could you say when your mother asks you to end her life?

It was impossible for me to consider this, even though her pain was excruciating for me to witness. As she had told me several times, once when I questioned her taking the antidepressant the doctor had prescribed, I "wasn't in her body" and therefore had no right telling her what to do or not do. I understood her wanting to die, to end the pain that engulfed her. Yet, as the helper who was helpless, there was nothing I could do. I wanted my mother to live. My love for her was a profound selfishness.

"You're right," she said finally, even though I had not said anything. "It's not fair to ask you or your father."

I didn't see the point in sharing any of this with the nurse. I had no idea how she felt about euthanasia. She was a compassionate, capable medical professional who came to monitor my mother's vital signs three times a week, acted far too cheerful, and then left. But as the nurse continued to stare at me, I found myself fuming. Once again she was addressing me and ignoring my mother, as if by virtue of her age and illness she was not there, or at best an object we were talking about.

"It's not what I think that matters," I said, and turned to my mother, ignoring the nurse's stare. I had a feeling that the nurse might be opposed to euthanasia for religious and moral reasons. Before she left she asked my mother if she would like to see a priest or minister. When my mother firmly said "No," the nurse responded through tight lips, "I won't ask why."

I was indignant after she left, but my mother said to me, "She's just doing her job the only way she knows how."

My mother was right. The nurse was not a bad person.

From the beginning, she had included me in her process of taking care of my mother, explaining the significance of her vital signs, as my mother's blood pressure plummeted and her weight decreased, always assuring me that "this is part of the process of your mother's condition." The nurse was keenly aware of my attentiveness, my devotion. She told my mother, "There's nothing better than a daughter."

When my mother asked the nurse informed questions about her condition, the nurse narrowed her eyes quizzically and said, "You certainly know your ins and outs of the body."

My mother simply shrugged and said, "I read up on things."

I thought of interjecting that my mother had gone to nursing school years ago, but something stopped me. This was my mother's story to tell and she wasn't telling it.

After the nurse left, I asked her why.

My mother simply shrugged, saying "I don't want her to think I know more than her."

This was characteristic of my mother. She had no need to pump herself up, to put on airs, to feel better than someone else. This humbleness could be seen as self-effacing but, in fact, the opposite was true. My mother was secure enough not to engage in the kind of posturing that consumes most people. But after my mother said this, I saw a hint of something else: her face took on a look of extreme vulnerability, a slight widening of the eyes, the unmistakable look of fear.

My mother was well aware that this nurse who came three times a week had power over her. Perhaps it was not the power of life and death, but still my mother recognized it for what it was, and she wanted the nurse to be on her side. My mother who had always done everything herself was now utterly dependent on others.

When I came to visit I would do my best to cheer her up. I wanted to draw her out of her pain, into her past life, the life that existed outside of this room, before the fact of her disintegrating body. Today she turned to me and said, "I didn't expect this kind of devotion from you." And then, perhaps reading a flicker of guilt in my eyes, she said, "Not that I didn't expect it. I didn't know what to expect...I do get a lot of strength from you. I hope that's okay."

I nodded, feeling the weight of my mother's life and death on my shoulders.

What I would later wish I could have told her was that I also got a lot of strength from her. I was determined that I would see her through, and in the process would get through it myself. But the fact remained that taking care of my mother was the most difficult thing I had ever done. It was beyond difficult. It was devastating.

As I took care of my mother who was dying, the waters of despair closed around me. I felt the life ebbing out of me.

Thinking of how to turn the conversation, I grasped at straws and came up with religion—the topic that my mother said was always good for a laugh.

"Remember," I said to my mother as she pressed the control button so she could sit up further in her hospital bed, "when you asked the minister why God is always a he and not a she?"

My mother turned her head to the side, looking past me, and then back at me. "I never did that. You know me. I don't like to make scenes."

I raised an eyebrow. "Like you did the other day with the electrician? When he was standing in the living room talking to Dad and you yelled at him from in here and told him to shove it?"

"That's different," said my mother. "I didn't like the job he did. Then he tried to charge extra."

"That's true," I said. "But you did tell him to 'shove it.'"

My mother was silent.

"A few years ago you told me you asked the minister why God was always a he and not a she, and that the minister was flabbergasted and didn't know what to say."

"You're crazy. I never said any such thing."

What I remembered was her sledgehammer frustration, the edge of her voice that was just short of a slap, her anger with the world, confronting the minister, shaking her unbent coat hanger at the menacing pro-lifer, bringing home her rage, frustration, banging her fists against the kitchen sink screaming FUCK! FUCK! FUCK! The fact that my mother, out of modesty or denial, claimed not to remember these things, did not make them any less real to me.

I remembered the emotions, long stifled, held back in the tight line of a lip, the white-knuckled clench of a fist, until finally they roared up like a tsunami, a solid wall of water that no longer allowed itself to be pushed back, ripping through whatever was in its way, concrete, steel, severing the bars of a society that had held women like my mother and her mother and her mother caged for centuries.

I was there standing behind her or next to her, sometimes frightened as a child or embarrassed as an adolescent, but keenly observing her actions. I watched her painfully shy insecurities—the paper in her hand that shook like a leaf when she was addressing the organic gardening club, her fingers in her lap tugging nervously at the tablecloth the few times we had guests for dinner. I watched her frustrations building, calling my father who was habitually late for dinner—"What do you want? A fucking invitation?"—but most of all I watched her rage. It welled up inside her with transformative powers until she was a mythological Amazon wielding a sword, hewing a path in the brush so that I could walk into the future.

I knew better than to push my mother further. She would not admit to remembering. The divergence in our memories was immaterial. She had her version of things. I had mine. The differences in how we perceived reality had followed us right up into the present. There was no denying that my mother was dying. But a small person inside of me was still stomping her feet and insisting that her mother would live. In a last-ditch desperate attempt at hope, I'd called my mother a week ago to tell her to watch a television show about a woman who cured herself of cancer. Her weak voice rose in a wave of fury: "Janet, can't you bug off already!"

The truth entered the body slowly, silently, with a modicum of shame and an acknowledgment of betrayal. If I could not accept my mother's death, could I truly embrace her life?

"Where's Barbara?" my mother asked softly. "You've spent so much time apart from her. Did you leave her home alone again this weekend?"

"She's busy this weekend, rehearsing again with Kathleen again, "I replied. "I made an apple pie before I left."

I had been experimenting with macrobiotic recipes—and a fat free, sugar free apple pie was on my list.

My mother arched her eyebrows slightly. "Oh, an apple pie. You two are such lovebirds."

I hadn't been thinking of myself and Barbara lately as lovebirds. We were two separate people living two separate lives. I didn't have the time or energy to spend with her. She had her music, the anchor she held onto. Now I saw that the simple act of making Barbara an apple pie—that she loved even though it was macrobiotic—was a gesture of love.

I smiled as my mother closed her eyes and leaned back against the hospital bed. Her jaw slackened and her mouth sagged. She breathed evenly as she drifted off to sleep. I went into the kitchen to fix myself a cup of tea. When I came back I sat down quietly, cradling the cup in my hands, and watched my mother sleeping. For a moment that was all there was, my mother's breathing and my watching her. I blew on my tea, took a few sips, and looked down into the cup as the tea leaves swirled around.

I was drinking green tea that I brought with me to help keep me awake and give me the extra energy I needed to take care of my mother. This particular kind of green tea came loose in the package and was rolled into tiny bullets that slowly unfolded as my tea steeped. When I first looked down at the tea leaves I saw a dark mass clumped in the bottom of my cup. But as I drank more, the leaves separated. Some stuck to the sides of the cup. As the small twigs twisted and turned and the leaves unfolded I began to see a few patterns. I saw something that looked like a bird, its wings jutting outward, the twig of its head pointed south. Then I saw the spiral of dots that I had seen before and knew this meant I was going on a journey.

With my mother's help, I was taking flight.

The moment wrapped around me like wings. As I sat and listened to my mother breathe, I became aware that her life was rearing up fiercely even as it ebbed away. Something deep within me shifted. I felt a window open, and what I have always searched for outside of myself welled up within me, letting in a long golden light.

My mother opened her eyes slightly and looked at me. "I see you staring at me," she said. "You think I don't, but I see you."

She reached a hand to me, and I moved my chair closer to the side of her bed.

"One thing I always liked about the Bible," she said, "are the Psalms."

She closed her eyes as if contemplating sleep and then opened them again, looking somewhere into the past, into the hymnal of the young girl she once was, searching for the answers to her life.

"The Lord is my shepherd," she began, "I shall not want."

She did not stop until she reached the end: "But thy loving-kindness and mercy shall follow me all the days of my life; and I will dwell in the house of the Lord forever."

When she finished, her eyes were red and wet. She was back in the present, crying, and then laughing at the silliness of it all: an avowed atheist reciting the Twenty-Third Psalm and crying.

I was crying too, as I took my mother's hand.

Laughing and crying with my mother.

Later that day, after my mother had rested, we decided to embark on our afternoon project: washing her hair. The first step was to get her out of bed and onto the walker that I had placed next to her. She tried to get up herself, and then when I offered to help, said stubbornly, "Let me do it." She sat on the edge of her bed, pushing her hands on the mattress, raising herself an inch or two, then fell back defeated. I moved the walker so I could stand next to her, placing my arms under her shoulders, feeling the enormous weight of my feather-light mother in my arms.

I walked backward, my arms under her shoulders, behind her back, holding her, her left foot following my right, my right foot leading her left, the top of her head just below my chin. She looked down at the floor, biting her lip to stifle the pain. The trembling in her limbs entered my body, not on the outside along the ridges of my muscles and fat, but deep inside the marrow of my bones. My heart fluttered wildly, trembling like a caged butterfly, but I was steady as I led my mother to the walker, holding her as she grabbed the walker on first one side and then the other, leaning heavily with her arms as she tested her legs' ability to hold her up.

She walked slowly, slowly, down the hall, gripping the white plastic-covered handles of her silver walker, inching it ahead of her. I walked behind her, my arms ready to hold her up, in case she should fall. Finally, we were in the kitchen, inching across the beige tiled floor toward the high stool my father had placed in front of the sink. My mother had decided she would rather use the kitchen sink than the one in the bathroom because it was deeper with more room for her head.

When we got to the stool, I helped her position the walker next to it, so she could ease herself down. She breathed out heavily, trying to dispel the pain that seared through her thighs when she bent her legs to sit. The shampoo bottle was open on the sink. I ran warm water from the tap. She gripped the edge of the stainless steel sink and tried to move forward but couldn't. White-knuckled, she gripped the edge of the sink and howled. In one swift move, I yanked the walker out of the way and put my arms under hers to lift her up until she was standing, lessening the strain on her thighs. I linked my hands behind her back and walked her back across the kitchen tile, around the corner, through the dining room, the living room and down the hall. My mother's entire body trembled in my shaking arms. Her tears dripped down, mingling with the sweat from my pores.

Her pain, my terror.

We were one.

And then two, as we reached the side of her bed, where I eased her down and stepped back.

She gripped the edge of her mattress and sat, eyes closed, breathing deeply, going into the control room of her mind where she regulated the pain, turning down the dial, gathering her strength for the next step, which she did with first one leg and then the other as she lifted them up onto the bed. She leaned against the raised back of the hospital bed, the control button in her hand as she lowered the mattress to an incline. She sat back and closed her eyes. I pulled a light blanket over her and then, unsure whether to go or stay, sat down in the chair at the foot of her bed.

"The spray," she said, her eyes still closed. "Try the spray."

I stood up and reached for the metal can of dry shampoo that sat on top of her chest of drawers. The HMO nurse suggested that I buy the spray at the drugstore. Earlier, when I gave it to her she said she'd rather wash her hair under the kitchen sink.

I placed a clean white towel under my mother's head, shook the can, and held it a foot away from her head, spraying with one hand, while I shielded her eyes with the other. The shampoo was white and powdery. It left a dusting of synthetic snow on her head. After I sprayed all around, I combed out her hair, wiping the comb after each section. When I came to the back, I helped her lift her head off the towel, cupping the base of her head in the palm of my hand. Her hair was matted from being pressed to the towel, her neck was damp, its pale skin creased with red lines from the collar of her cotton pajama top.

After I combed out the dry shampoo, I ran a tissue over the comb and then combed her hair again until it was clean and shining. I parted it slightly off center, drawing it back from her face, then lifted her head again and combed the back straight down. My mother smiled up at me. I went into the bathroom to wash the comb and on the way out I picked up a silver hand mirror and brought it back with me.

"Look Mom," I said, holding the mirror above her. "Look how pretty your hair is."

Her smile turned into a grimace. "Oh, Janet. Take that thing away."

Too late, I realized my mistake and pulled back the mirror.

My mother did not see her pretty hair. All she saw was her gaunt face fast on its way to becoming a skeleton.

I sat down beside her, sliding the mirror under my chair. "But Mom," I said, "your hair looks pretty."

She shut her eyes and ignored me.

I was as resolute as she was stubborn. "It's clean and shiny."

She relented and opened her eyes.

"Yes," she said flatly. "It feels clean. Thank you."

I was still painfully aware of my blunder of allowing her to see herself. I wondered how long it had been since she had looked in the mirror. The changes that were devastating for me to witness undoubtedly were unbearable for her. I grasped for straws, deciding which way to turn to change the subject.

I began to tell her about the *Divine Comedy*, which I was rereading, starting with Dante's *Inferno*, the circles of hell, populated with thieves and murderers, popes and politicians. When I told her about the demons who saluted by sticking out their tongues and making a trumpet of their asses, she laughed but then turned serious.

"I feel like I'm in hell. What have I done to deserve this?"

I was silent. There was no diversion, no piece of literature that sprang to mind, no great words of wisdom dropping from the sky.

"You didn't do anything...Sometimes things happen with no explanation..." My voice drifted away.

Our eyes were both filled with tears from the same salty well.

My mother pointed to a white book lying down flat on her bureau. "That book says we create our own conditions. That means it's my fault."

"It's not your fault. I think what the author means is that we get trapped in emotional patterns and that sometimes an illness helps people resolve them."

I felt the tension welling up in me, the contraction of my muscles, my blood vessels and my breath, fighting its way down into my lungs. I was angry at the author and others like her for blaming the victim. Yet at the same time I was grateful that some of what they said made sense, that it had allowed my mother to reconsider the circumstances of her life, especially her relationship with her father which had left her with so much pain and resentment. Most of all I was angry that my mother was dying and I could not do a thing to stop it. My anger dried my tears faster than a thick pile towel.

When I looked at my mother, her gaze had drifted into the past as she stared at the blank white wall above the pile of books on her dresser. "After I left the Navy Yard, after my demotion when I quit, I did the housewife thing for a few years and then I started taking self-improvement classes. That was bad self-esteem. I took those self-improvement classes because I thought Jane Mason wasn't good enough."

"Of course you were good enough."

My mother stared straight ahead, looking past me. "That's how I felt," she said resolutely. "Wherever I was, someone was always there first, ready to tell me what to do. When I was in the hospital, waiting to give birth to you, the nurses wanted me to do everything on schedule, piss on time, eat on time, shit on time which, of course, I couldn't do. I was going to have natural childbirth, but the labor pains were so bad that when they put the oxygen mask on my face I told them 'Put something in that thing.' After you were born, the nurse told me that the mothers didn't get to see their babies until ten a.m. No wonder you're a lesbian, the first person who held you wasn't your mother—it was the nurse, a strange woman!"

I smiled wryly. My mother looked past me staring back into her life as a forty-year-old mother with an infant daughter. Then she looked at me pointedly. "I would've liked to have known you longer."

It was my turn to stare straight ahead, avoiding her gaze, until I took a deep breath, willing the tears back. Then I looked back at her as she continued to speak.

"I'd feel better about this if you were fifty. I thought if I waited, I could bring you into a better world. I really thought things would be better and in some ways they were. No one talked about racial equality twenty years before you born, there was no environmental movement."

"And no women's movement." I met my mother's unwavering glance.

"Yes, no women's movement." My mother was silent while she looked at me intently. "I tried not to interfere too much with your life," she added. "I figured once you give someone something you shouldn't try to take it back."

For the first time I saw my life not as a fact, but as a gift. A gift I accepted but had not passed on, at least not in the traditional way of giving birth.

I ventured into unknown territory. "I hope you're not disappointed that I didn't have a child."

My mother shrugged. "It's your life. You're the one who has to make that choice."

I returned her perceptive stare.

When Barbara and I were talking about adopting, I mentioned to my mother that we were thinking it would be nice to have a daughter, "Someone," I said, "to pass down all that has been passed down to me."

Despite the fact that we had long ago changed our minds about adopting a child, I now wondered, for more than a fleeting moment, if I made the right decision. I had no daughter to sit and talk to—to read her tea leaves or have her read mine.

"I don't want you to feel guilty about anything," my mother said, looking me in the eye.

"Not even for having to spend so much time taking care of me when I was a kid?" I was halfway joking, but not entirely.

With a perceptible but almost motionless twitch of her shoulders, she said, "I didn't do it for you. I did it for me. I had you because I wanted to."

"Not because you were supposed to?" I asked guardedly.

"No."

I laughed, partly out of relief. "That's right. When did you ever do anything because you were supposed too?"

"I bought that fox collar coat."

"Your coat?" Suddenly, I remembered the tight poodle curl weave of my mother's silvery beige coat, its fox collar that quivered like a live animal around her neck.

"You bought that because you were supposed to?"

"What did you think, I bought it to wear to the supermarket? I wore it to keep up with the other mommies when you were in St. Mary's."

I thought back to the private Episcopal school I was in for four years, kindergarten through third grade, the somber cathedral-like building, window panes laced with ivy, the matching uniforms we all wore, light blue belted dresses in the spring and fall, navy jumpers in the winter. In my memory, my mother's fox collar coat stood apart from all this. I remembered running my fingers through the fur collar, cool silky smooth shimmering and alive, a bit of magic in our otherwise ordinary lives.

"Whatever became of that coat anyway?"

"I took it to the Salvation Army. I would never have bought it if it wasn't for Marilyn. I never should have said yes when the principal asked me to drive Marilyn's little girl to school with you, but she was in your class. Then when the principal told me that Marilyn's husband was a doctor, I wasn't impressed so then the principal told me that Marilyn was willing to pay me. So I said yes."

I nodded, remembering Samantha, the dark haired cross-eyed little girl who sat in our backseat as we made the twenty-minute trip each way to St. Mary's. My mother drove past the chemical plant where my father worked, the acrid smell lingering in our nostrils. We passed the marshes, the cattails, and finally drove over the bridge, below us the white wake of tugboats and barges, the river bordered with cranes and sand piles dug out from the quarry next to the old munitions factory.

Sitting up in her hospital bed, my mother was looking straight ahead at the wall above me, into the past that we shared.

"Marilyn was always waving her ass in my face, and she treated me like a servant—especially in front of the other mothers. I think she was poor as a child. I noticed she had braces on her teeth. She probably couldn't afford them until she got her doctor husband. She wore that mink coat everywhere. She was ridiculous, a forty-year-old sexpot, wearing low-backed cocktail dresses. She made me so angry that one day I did something I shouldn't have."

I stared wide-eyed at my mother, waiting to hear the secrets she had while I hid my own, the math tests with poor grades that I was supposed to take home but never did, tucking them instead in my messy desk, behind which I sat hiding an open book under the ledge, surreptitiously reading while the teacher talked, defying authority in any small way I could, taking the belt off my uniform, playing doctor with the other kids in the bushes at recess. I looked expectantly at her.

"One day, taking the two of you to school, I had just picked up Samantha in the Country Club section where they lived. Marilyn was pulling out of the driveway as I was driving off.

Both of us had gold cars, the exact same shade, except hers was a big gold Cadillac and I had a little gold GM American car. I had just left her section and was on the highway when I saw her pull up behind me at the red light. It was a two-lane highway. After the light changed and we both started moving, she pulled into the lane next to me. When she first decided to pass me the road was flat, but I put my foot on the accelerator and she kept right up next to me, and before you know it we were going up a hill, nose to nose, a double line between us. I slammed down my foot on that gas pedal and kept on going. When we neared the top of the hill she finally backed off and dropped behind me."

My mother paused, light sparking from her eyes. "I think she started a rumor about me after that. Something about how I endangered her life. But it was her own fault. She was mistaken. She thought I was going to slow down and let her pass but I wasn't. I didn't know she was going to drive up that hill. I thought she had enough sense to know when she was licked.

"Shortly after that, the kids were having a party in someone's backyard, Amy's mother—you remember her, the one who always said "git" instead of "get"—she just loved Marilyn and was always sucking up to her. She decides to clean out the pool while we were there and she just happened to hit me in the head with end of the pool skimmer. She said it was by accident, but she was just lucky that I didn't deck her.

"When the principal asked why I was taking you out of St. Mary's, I just said one word: "Money. Notice I didn't say whose."

My sides were aching from the stifled laughter inside me, held only in check by my mother's composure, from the last shreds of dignity that she held tight to as she cocked her head and looked at me.

"Do you remember that?"

I shook my head.

"I thought you would," she said, shrugging with a twitch of her eyebrows. "It was your life."

CHAPTER 14

Through the Garden

An explosion of peonies. White. Pink. Ruffled red. Ecstasy: a delicate scent. Heavy heads hanging from stems. Others unfolding under the relentless pace, ants across tight marble round buds. I press petals to my face and inhale pink. My face open, receiving. I am a child leading my mother through a garden. I take her hand and we wind through the twists and turns of blazing daffodil clusters, breathy pink clumps of asters, snapdragons, the two-lipped purple lobelia, narcissi, jonquils, their orange coronas protruding from faces of pale petals.

I pause and peer down into a long-stemmed poppy, blood-red petals forming an upturned bell, fluted edges overlapping thickly and plunging into the center where the clapper is a round black button resting soundlessly in a bed of black pollen.

A jeweled hummingbird dips and whirs, whirs and dips. My mother and I stare in amazement. Then I turn toward her. She is as young as I have ever known her. The sun catches the mane of her auburn hair. Her face tilts down, her features lost in the shadows. I take her hand and in a child's voice whisper to her as I point out the flowers: creeping pinks; primroses, flat red and yellow jewels nestled in dusty leaves; forget-me-nots; yellow purple white croci bursting forth with saffron tongues. I repeat back to my mother the names she has taught me: shasta daisies, pink foxgloves, fairy slippers with their yellow tassels, and next to the green cupped edges of the lady's mantle, lilies of the valley, tiny pale pink and white bells barely visible under the dahlia blossoms and myrtle branches. My mother remembers each plant, each blossom, the young shoots she has tended as if they were an extension of herself.

We walk farther down the path, along the borders of violets in cloaks of deep purple, past the pansies, petunias, the begonias' translucent petals. The air is redolent: the scent of lavender intermingles with the sudden breath of hyacinths. Hollyhocks wave in the breeze as we walk under trellises of climbing roses: the pink French rose, the China and Cathay rose, the spicy yellow tea rose, the Joseph's coat of many colors, pinks, reds, yellows.

Lilies, orange russet day lilies, torch and madonna, the red fleur-de-lis, amaryllis bend into irises. Fluted blossoms spill into rainbows: purple lavender, amethyst blue, pink orange, yellow gold. They unfold to reveal the golden crested centers: mythical wings attached to the tunic of the young maiden awakening. I peer into the magical chamber. My mother takes the fluted petals lightly in her fingertips, holds them up and examines the fine cross-hatched lines as if looking at her own needlework. I lean forward and inhale. The irises are all that exist: the velvet scent, the molecular dance of time. Everything is in season at once and at once moving toward death.

I am growing, keeping pace with the dogwood saplings that stretch white and pink blossoms toward the sun. I am the same height as my mother, then taller as we reach the stone wall at the end of the garden. Around us, the petals have become creased and wilted, brown at the edges, falling away, leaving empty stalks. I bend down to touch the wispy paper-thin end of an iris stalk. My mother walks in front of me. Her hair is short and gray, the strands brittle. She turns back, looking into my face and then at the irises. Their green spears quiver even as the life drains from the petals. With her head tilted downward and her shaggy hair falling around her face, she resembles a peony about to shed itself.

She steps over the low stone wall of the garden into a golden meadow. Stalks of yellow wheat jut into blue sky. I follow. In the distance: a gradual incline of hill. A line of women stands on the slope, single file up to the horizon. The long full skirts of their dresses billow against the sun, sails of a great ship waiting to cross the sea. The women stand with arms outstretched to us, beckoning. My mother turns away and walks toward them. I call her back, pointing out the sparse flowers in the field, the names she has taught me: the dusty blue chicory flowers, the yellow mullen stalk, the jagged leaves of the stinging nettle. She still walks toward the horizon, but nods to her left and right, pointing out the few remaining flowers: blue hyssop with its leafy spikes, St.-John's-wort, shepherd's purse, calendula, shaggy red heads of bee balm, purple spears of loose strife. As she walks ahead of me, she speaks each flower's name. Some plants she mentions are new to me. I call her back, telling her she still has things to teach me.

"Ask the earth," she says stubbornly. "Mother Earth, the best mother you will ever have." She continues her walk to the horizon. Anything I say is pointless. She has to go back. I walk in her footsteps. Stalks of tall grass bend down under her feet and spring back up, razor sharp blades of grass nicking my legs. The grass grows dry until the ground looks scorched. I look ahead as my mother cries out: "Mama." My grandmother is the first woman standing closest to us on the hill. She looks just as I remember but different: her gray hair swept back into a bun, a few wisps curling at her ears, her eyes a flashing hazel emerald, the sun glinting off the silver frames of her bifocals. Skirt billowing behind her, she leans forward to embrace my mother. Her cheeks are full, not drawn and pinched as I remembered them. Her lips, which once formed a creased fold in the center of her face, have deepened into fullness.

She turns toward me, casting her radiant smile around me. I step into her embrace. A heaviness lifts. My grandmother, even after her death, inhabited my mind with fireflies and sunbeams, moonlight and dreams. When I laugh, I am reminded of her love of life as it erupts from my throat. My grandmother, mother and I stand in the circle of our arms, tears streaming down our faces. Laughing and crying at once. I look into my mother's face and see that the frustration she has carried all her life has melted away. She is old, but young too, the lines smoothed from her face, her shoulders relaxed, head thrown back, laughter shaping her features into gleeful ripples.

I look beyond my mother and grandmother to the other women standing higher on the hill. Their arms outstretched, faces beatific. I turn around and lay back in my grandmother's arms. A warm breeze rustles through the grass, bending the long stalks into a green wave. My knees relax as I go limp. I am weightless in the air, held securely in the crook of my grandmother's arms. I feel the firm grip of her hands. The broad fingers, that in her life were calloused and cracked, now cradle me with gentle strength. She speaks to me without words, telling me I am going back...back...to a place where I have come from but have never been...

As she passes me back to the woman standing behind her, I look up into a face I have seen only in old faded photographs. My own features mirrored back to me: the same square chin and full cheeks chiseled from the triangular lines. A flash of recognition passes between us, filial. Her features have changed from the few old photos I have seen. Fear has fallen from her face like a mask. Her strong hands cradle me, the resilience of a woman who knelt and scrubbed and, when she could do no more, kept on kneeling and scrubbing. The features of her face that were once tense and drawn have softened into wrinkles that fold easily in on themselves. Her face is lined with immeasurable wisdom. Dissolved in the cadences of time, transmuted between life and death, is the contempt she felt for her only daughter: my grandmother, abandoned by her husband, who raised two children on her own and was destined to live out the same fate as her mother. Staring into her blue gray eyes, I feel the tension in my shoulders dissolve. Tensions that I have never acknowledged, passed down to me from my mother, and to her by her mother, back to my great-grandmother and beyond.

More than a century of forgiving and forgiveness passes between us. I am safe, secure in her arms, feeling waves of compassion flow over me as she passes me back...

The next woman, the next and the next, are women I have never seen before. My life has been bereft of even their names. I see my future imprinted in the lines of their faces: the crow's feet, the shaggy eyebrows, the broad peasant cheeks, even in the bottom row of small distinct teeth that are the same as mine. These women, flesh of my flesh, speak to me silently with their eyes, green-gold triangles of light, one inside the other, reflecting a thousand times back into darkened chambers where they lived the lives of women who never flinched, who always flinched, women who jumped when they were spoken to, women who defied the whip. Their lives come pulsing through the long broad fingers of the hands that cradle me back...back...

When I reach the crest of the hill, I stare up into the eyes of someone I have met in my dreams: a young woman who was not able to live out her years. Her eyes are oceans. Turbulent eddies whirl behind the delicate lines of her lashes. I rise and fall on the waves of her life, feeling her strength surging in the hands that hold me, firm yet ethereal, callused but soft. Her life burns with an intensity that ignites the ridges in my back, the muscles in my shoulders and arms. I am an ember infused with her flames: the flames she cast on her master's bed, devouring the walls of her prison, his body, his house, the same flames that later consumed her as she met the fate of a servant who murdered her master: burned at the stake. I smolder in her arms, the flames burning away the part of me that fears myself and lives imprisoned in self-doubt. There is a long raw moment between us as the flames sputter. Then they rise unfathomably, consuming the air, before they die down again. Our faces are left unsheathed.

She passes me back to her mother, back to her grandmother and great-grandmother, back before that. I go back before the rise of feudalism resting on its foundations built by the greed-driven church fathers, back to the green pastures lush with fruits of plenty growing next to clean waters. I think of my mother reciting the Twenty-Third Psalm and suddenly understand her tears:

Yes, there was a time when we feared no evil.

I am cradled in arms that now pass me forward. The faces that stare down at me blur into one woman, one eternity that disappears as I find myself in the meadow. Alone. My mother has stayed behind the horizon. I am the last of my line to go back. Sitting in the green grass, I feel its long blades tickle my arms and legs. I am sad that I have been left alone, but strangely comforted. A gust of wind blows along the ground. Tiny white stars-of-Bethlehem have sprung from nowhere. They are growing around me in a circle, bowing their tiny star-shaped flowers at me. At once they are nodding, dancing, standing still. They pull me into the undertow of sleep. Before closing my eyes under the night sky, I see hundreds of thousands of stars, Milky Way galaxies spiraling down into my darkness.

The tape recorder clicked to a stop. The meditation was over. I blinked my eyes open in the late afternoon sun of my mother's small bedroom. Her eyes were pinpoints of light. "I brought something back," she said, holding her closed hand in front of her. "At first I thought I was being greedy. I wanted something to hold in my hot little hand, a pretty rock or gem, a diamond or ruby. But then I found something else..."

She stretched her arm out to me in an abbreviated reach as far as she could without hurting her shoulder, and opened her hand—the same hand I would hold as she slipped into death when she took her slow rattling last breath, before I held the white cardboard box that contained her ashes, heavier than life itself, and scattered them in the park, before spring would come and the tiny white stars-of-Bethlehem would grow up from her bones, before the long howling silence that would be her absence—she reached out to me with her open hand to share what she found:

"Here it is," she said, "Esteem."

I stared into her outstretched hand. Its emptiness was lucid like the water just poured into a teacup. Deep under the surface in the cup of her hand, I saw the fallen petals of the garden we just walked through. The colors were swirling down more deeply and darkly into the depths. In their descent they became less like petals and more like twigs, sticks, fragments, brackish brown tea leaves.

Suddenly, without thought or words, I could read the hearts and rings, the clouds and crosses, the good omens and bad. As the rest of my life came rushing toward me with clarity and purpose, I saw that I was my own mother and my own daughter. I was my own grandmother and great-grandmother, years before my hair turned gray. I was all the women of my line from all times and I was myself in a precise pinpoint of time.

I saw that it did not make any difference that I did not have a daughter. There was a tiny but fierce bright light shining from deep inside of me. Planets—indeed entire constellations—come to an end. But their light can be seen for years afterward. Light years. The women of my line reached out to me, shaping and reshaping the circles of my destiny, unending.

SOLILOQUY

Five years later, tears still came to my eyes when I thought about my mother's death. I could not replace my final memories of her with a previous, healthy image until at least a year after she had died. During this time, I asked myself over and over why I waited until the last possible moment to tell her what a good mother she was. Even though I did finally tell her, I don't know if she heard me. She had slipped into a coma early one morning, and my father and I took turns sitting at her side until the nurse came.

I told my father to talk to her. I had read once that a person who is in a coma could actually hear and understand when someone speaks to them. I left the room as my father held her hand and spoke to her and when I came back he said she was trying to tell him that she loved him. I did see her jaw moving back and forth, so perhaps she did hear him and was trying to answer. When the nurse came, I asked her how long my mother would be in the coma. As the nurse spoke, she turned to my mother, bent down, and as she put her hands along the sides of my mother's face, she died.

Her breaths—which had become slower and farther apart—simply stopped.

Later, I thought it was no coincidence that my mother died at this moment. She took final control over her destiny, ceasing to breathe when I asked how long her coma would last. She may have felt safe in the nurse's competent hands. Perhaps she sensed the panic of my father and me, our utter ineptness at the prospect of her dying at home, in our hands alone.

I took my mother's death extremely hard. All the strength that I had when I was taking care of her drained out of me. In the first months, and even through the first year, I became ill frequently and was often so tired I had to take a nap in the afternoons. I dreaded talking to casual acquaintances because when they asked what was new I would have to tell them.

When I went through my mother's things, it was evident that she had indeed thrown out her sketches and drawings. But in the very back of her portfolio, hidden in a small brown envelope that I hadn't seen before, I found a certificate. My mother had completed the course requirements for Commercial Art in the Adult Educational Program of the Bucks County Technical School. The certificate lists the dates she attended as 1974 to 1975. These were my hell on wheels high school years that blurred together so badly that I could barely remember my own life. I certainly had no memory of my mother attending a commercial arts program. My father didn't remember anything about my mother taking this course either.

There must be a reason why my mother never mentioned this. Modesty perhaps, or humility. Then again, perhaps it wasn't either of these things. Maybe obtaining this certificate was simply something she wanted to do for herself.

Regardless, the artwork she must have produced to obtain the certificate was nowhere to be found. The absences in my mother's life continued after her death.

Next to her bed, she left a small spiral-bound notebook with a few pages filled in. I opened this notebook, after her death, with great anticipation. It felt as if my mother had come back to talk to me. A few pages were filled in with her handwriting that grew shakier by the page. The last entry, written in pencil, was entitled, "A letter to my unexpected daughter-in-law, Barbara."

In the last month of her life, my mother told me that she was writing this letter. When I encouraged my mother to show it to her, she said, "I don't want it to go to her head." Every year on my birthday and on Mother's Day, Barbara thanked my mother for giving birth to me. "You always make it sound like I had her just for you," my mother would retort. In the beginning of the letter to Barbara she wrote, "Many times you thanked me for giving you Janet. Now it is my turn to thank you for lending her back to me these past months of my illness."

Upstairs, in the room that was my mother's bedroom before she became too weak to climb the stairs, I found another notebook. It was titled *A Woman's Book*, and its pages—which have a quotation from a woman writer at the top of each page—were mostly blank. But several of them were filled with her handwriting—the letters are strong and the ink dark, her usual handwriting before she became ill. On the opening page, dated 1984, roughly ten years before she died, she writes, "I am proud of my daughter...because she is herself—honest, loving, and is kind to her parents—"penciled in after this, she wrote—"and other poor slobs."

Between her brief thoughts on anonymity, solitude, the constraints of society, there were interesting asides such as, "I like to embroider or crochet, but doing macramé drives me knots." There is a quote from George Sand, written in a letter to her mother in 1831: "Oh God! What is this frantic desire to torment each other, which possesses human beings? This frantic desire to reprove each other's faults bitterly, to condemn pitilessly, everyone who is not cut upon our own pattern." My mother was the daughter of a mother and the mother of a daughter. She knew, better than I, that the conflict between mothers and daughters is timeless.

In the last entry in her journal, she mused on the fact that she had always hoped to die peacefully in her sleep: "Who am I to think that I should escape the pains of life—the degradation of disablement, the humility of dependency, the fear of worse to come. Who am I? I guess I've just joined the human race."

Earlier in this two-page entry, she wrote: "I hope only to be remembered as someone who was kind to those who survive me. I was not always as human and loving as I could perhaps have learned to be... Now I look back on my own life and see that I did not take care of myself as well as I should have; therefore I could have cared for others in a greater degree than I did..."

She ended this piece by writing, "If one loves oneself, one loves others, as Shakespeare says: 'This above all: to thine own self be true, and it must follow as night the day, thou canst not then be false to any [hu] man.'"

Six months after my mother died, my father found a letter she wrote to me in a notebook that my mother kept for detailing my parents' financial assets. She had written the letter more than a decade prior to this—to tell me what I should do in the event that my parents would both die together. I was reading aloud, as my father requested, and at the end of the letter my mother wrote, "I, in my little dust pile, love you. You are one good worthwhile person and I'm proud of being your mother."

I broke down into sobs. My father put his hand tentatively on my shoulder. "She knew," he said through his own tears. "Even then she knew she would end up a pile of ashes…"

In her clear-eyed foreseeing of the inevitable, my mother became a prophet to my father and me, a seer into the certainty that we never thought possible.

There is much that I did have to go through in the process of my mother's death. Since my father was still living, I did not have to sell the house and its contents. Because my mother died when she was seventy-four, I did not have to witness a prolonged old age for her, the possible dropping away of her faculties, her sight, her ability to care for herself over a long period of time or—God forbid—the erosion of her mental capacities.

My mother's keen mental perception was the most important thing to her and she was lucky to have it, despite the intense physical pain she suffered, right up until she slipped into a coma in the early morning and died several hours later. I knew she was near the end, and I was hovering around her the night before, fixing her blankets, reading to her, asking if there was anything she wanted. Finally she made her last statement to me: "Janet, stop bugging me and go do your work." Then she said "Good Night," precisely and sternly, with a firm grasp on her last shred of dignity.

I was grateful that I did not have to put my mother into a long-term care facility or nursing home. She wanted to die at home and my father and I were able to give her that last gift. Still, I wish she had been able to live into her eighties or nineties like I had expected her to. I saw middle-aged women with elderly, barely able to walk mothers and I envied them. I wished I had known what my mother looked like as she grew older. Sometimes when I saw old women who slightly resembled her I searched their faces for clues. A year after my mother's death, the hardest part was still ahead of me. To simply do what was expected—to go on living without my mother—was no small feat.

In the course of these five years, there came a time when my mother's death no longer defined me. I don't remember exactly when, maybe several years after her death, perhaps sooner or later than that. When I saw people I had not seen in years, it was not the first thing I told them about. My grief had ceased to consume me.

Writing this memoir enabled me to continue my conversation with my mother. At the time of my mother's death, I still had not reached the age my mother was when she had given birth to me. Those years—between thirty-five and forty—were a kind of limbo for me. The life I had constructed so carefully was intact around me, including my close circle of friends who had always helped me keep it together. Despite all this, I felt dreadfully adrift. The writing, and the contemplation of those lives that led to mine—my grandmother's and my mother's—gave me an understanding of myself that transcended my lifetime. The writing became my anchor.

With the completion of this work, my conversation with my mother ended abruptly. I was tossed into a new kind of limbo. Barbara and I were drifting apart. Both Barbara and then my mother, when she was dying, had been the center of my universe. Now with my mother gone and Barbara increasingly distant, I felt as if I had woken up one morning and didn't know whose life I was in. That which I valued most seemed dangerously close to disintegrating.

One of the most difficult challenges for me was returning to the place where I had grown up. I finally did, to find that every transgression of my youth—committed by me and against me and, perhaps worst of all, the acts of self-hatred committed against myself—rubbed my nerve endings beyond raw as I drove down a highway that threatened to consume me.

When my mother was alive and after her death while I was still writing about her, she was the buffer that stood between me and eternity. I had heard stories of adult women and men, usually lesbians or gay men who had taken on the caretaker role, who had left their chosen adult homes to go back and take care of aging parents, and after their parents had died they could not return to their former lives. They felt they had lost their place in the world.

Barbara was my place in the world. She was still the love of my life and still home to me. I told myself this over and over but I still felt torn in the winds. I wanted to be with her but I felt adrift.

My father continued to live in the house he had shared with my mother. He was getting older, his eyesight diminishing. Eventually, he totaled his car and gave up his license. He needed me, and I began visiting more frequently, though I still wasn't spending as much time there as I had during my mother's illness.

At first I felt split. I was with Barbara but dreaming about being somewhere else, in other lives that weren't my own. I managed to keep the details of my everyday life intact, but on some basic level I no longer knew who I was. When I went back to Levittown to visit my father, I felt physically ill and I was not proud of this fact. Cloudy days—the sky pressing down on me like a curtain of lead—were the worst.

"I smell the plant," I said to my father outside the diner where we had been having lunch. It was a cloudy, humid day. The scent of the plant hung thickly in the air. My father declared that he didn't smell anything. "I see the plant," I said, pointing to a smokestack jutting up behind a warehouse on the opposite side of the highway.

My father looked, but didn't say anything. What he did point out, repeatedly, was that the nurse wrote down my mother's cause of death as cardiac arrest. Her heart did stop beating at the end as everyone's does in the end. But it wasn't her heart that killed her; it was the cancer. The nurse was most likely following protocol in filling out the death certificate. I told my father there must be more cancer around than anyone admitted to. He said nothing. But our conversations were full of revelations. The wife of one of his closest friends from the plant died from cancer. The man who lived next door to my parents for more than thirty years died from cancer. His wife had been in and out of the hospital. All she would say was that she was being treated for "female problems." The wife of another co-worker of my father's from the plant also died from cancer. Like my mother, this woman's cancer had spread to almost every organ of her body. This man's son, a man my age, died a year ago from cancer. This man, who I knew as a childhood acquaintance, was the first in his family to graduate from college and afterward he went back to the plant where he worked as a foreman. At forty years old, he died from stomach cancer. When I asked if the man smoked, my father shook his head. This man's name was Rusty. Shortly after he died his mother died, the same way that mine had, and then his father died. Rusty was not married and had no children. His family was extinguished like a star that had run out of hydrogen.

The plant was no longer feeding nearly as many families as it used to. Many of its operations had been transferred overseas. The line of men and the few women punching in and out had dwindled. It was fast becoming a shell, a phantom from the past.

I didn't know if the runoff from the chemical plant contributed to my mother's death. It may have. There were several chemical plants in the area in addition to the one where my father worked. And there were always rumors of illegal dumping.

The numbers were not high enough to make this a Love Canal. But there were local stories about other women my mother's age, physically fit and active, who just like her woke up with a crushing pain and found out they had cancer that had metastasized. The man my father met while having coffee at McDonald's around the corner from his house said that his wife died during the biopsy. "You must have the wrong person," this man said when the hospital called. "My wife can't be dead. She's never been sick a day in her life."

Maybe this woman was a gardener, too? Maybe not.

I didn't know if toxic chemicals in the air, soil and water seeped into my mother's bones. Any more than I knew if it was the food she ate, the electric range she cooked at for thirty-plus years, or the resentment she carried all her life toward the father who physically abused and then abandoned her. More than likely it was a combination of all of these factors.

The plant was only part of my internal landscape, the geography from the present that hooked into my past, leaving me feeling as if I were suffering from jet lag by the time I made the forty-five minute drive back to my home in the city.

Somehow my feelings about where I had come from became mixed up with my feelings for Barbara. When I look back on events, it makes sense in a way. Barbara was my home as well. I came to the conclusion that if I didn't make peace with where I came from, its ghosts would haunt me forever. Gradually, as I began to make notes of the voices that entwined and conflicted from the past and present, my feelings about where I grew up started to shift. Barbara and I started to become closer again—but still I felt adrift.

Then there was my father. I needed him as much as he needed me, perhaps more. In the neighborhood where I grew up, where I had lost contact with everyone I ever knew, he was my only link to the past. My father reminded me of who I was. So many of my strengths came from my mother, but they came from my father too—from his steadfastness, his humbleness and simplicity, his quiet sense of humor. Still there was this wide sad gulf between us: the absence of my mother, his wife.

Despite making amends with my past, I was restless. I had a need for an alternative landscape inside of me. Not to replace the one I grew up in—now built up more than ever with suburban strip mall consumerism—but rather to place beside it. I had always been fascinated with Greece so I began to plan a trip. I intended to go alone to make a pilgrimage, just as my mother had traveled to England alone after her mother's death. The time was right. I was forty. My mother's death, and the taking care of her, was behind me. My father, at age eighty-one, was still able to get around. He walked four miles every day. His friends drove him places. He could survive for a month without me.

I also needed to go away by myself for a while without Barbara, to sort things out. Barbara, who still hated change, was initially opposed to the idea. "Greece is too far away," she said at first. "You can't go."

I told her I had already arranged to take the time off my freelance business, and I had already bought the ticket. I don't know if the latter part was true, but it was what I told her. Eventually, as the date of my trip came closer, I was the one who relented and asked if she wanted to come with me.

She shook her head resolutely. "I can't get off," she said. "Besides, isn't the point that you want to go by yourself?"

I nodded, but already I had the feeling that I was going to miss her, profoundly miss her.

And I did. I was walking along a sea wall in Crete next to the brilliant blue Aegean sea when I experienced what the Greeks call Pothos, the divine power of longing. I was in Crete toward the end of my journey, and I knew with all my senses that I missed Barbara and our life together.

This trip, even in the planning of it, had brought me closer to myself and also to my mother, allowing me to pick up the conversation with her from where we left off. A friend told me that in the neighborhood called the Plaka, in Athens, there are tavernas where for the price of a meal you can break your dishes against the wall afterward. My mother was the one who broke dishes, and eventually me, but it was my father who found the idea of the tavernas amusing, saying, "Think of all the money they save on dishwashers."

One day, visiting my father, I picked up a book of poetry I'd given my mother years ago, *A Book of Women Poets from Antiquity to Now*, edited by Aliki Barnstone and Willis Barnstone. My mother had read the book so often that it split down the center. She taped the spine back together with gray electrical tape. I opened to the table of contents and saw that my mother had checked off her favorite poets. There were pencil check marks beside the names of all the female Greek lyric poets. These were the poets who had so vividly captured my imagination: Sappho from the sixth century B.C., and the female lyric poets who wrote in the centuries after her, particularly Praxilla and Korinna.

When I went through the letters my mother had written to me, I found a quote from Korinna in my mother's handwriting:

I Korinna am here to sing the courage
Of heroes and heroines in old myths.
To Tanagra's daughters in their white robes
I sing. And all the city is delighted
with the clean water of my plaintive voice.

In the same group of letters, I found a scrap of paper where my mother joined my name with Korinna.

Janet-Korinna.

My mother often told me that she wished she had given me two names. Perhaps this was her way of doing it, leaving a message for me to find after her death. In doing so, perhaps she was pointing me in the direction of my own destination.

This is where the conversation began again.

I was the same age as my mother when she gave birth to me.

We would have many new things to talk about.

We could begin with Sappho who had a mother and a daughter, both named Cleis. The three of them contained a certain universe. My mother was the first woman in my life, and as her only daughter, I was the last woman in her life.

Barbara stood solidly in the center of all of this. She had stood next to me when I scattered my mother's ashes with my father and a small circle of friends. Years later, I would be by her side, when her mother was buried.

In between our mothers' deaths, we had the same twists and turns in the road that most people in long-term relationships encounter. But through it all there was no denying that each of us was the love of the other's life.

We encircled eternity.